& TRANSLATION TABOO

DOUGLAS ROBINSON

NORTHERN

ILLINOIS

UNIVERSITY

PRESS

Published by the Northern Illinois University Press,
DeKalb, Illinois 60115

Design by Julia Fauci

Material used with permission:

"Translation, Mystery, and the Transformation of the Reader" *Modern Poetry in Translation* 5 (1994): 162–70;

"The Ascetic Foundations of Western Translatology: Jerome and Augustine" *Translation and Literature* 1 (1992): 3–25.

Library of Congress Cataloging-in-Publication Data

Robinson, Douglas.

Translation and taboo / Douglas Robinson.

p. cm.

Includes bibliographical references and index.

ISBN 0-87580-209-5. — ISBN 0-87580-571-X

1. Translating and interpreting—Social aspects. 2. Taboo, Linguistic. 3. Language and culture. 4. Language and languages—Religious aspects. I. Title.

P306.2.R6 1995

418'.02—dc20 95-39478

CIP

for HELJÄ past all taboos

"When the lights go out and it's just the three of us
You, me, and all that stuff we're so scared of"

—Bruce Springsteen,
"Tunnel of Love"

CONTENTS

PREFACE

Picture this: a conference friend of mine who teaches modern languages and translation at a state university, a man with a Ph.D. and several published book-length literary translations to his name, comes up to me at the American Translators Association meeting in Philadelphia after a session on Larry Venuti's concepts of foreignizing and domesticating and asks whether I've read any of Larry's translations. I haven't, and admit as much, then ask him why he asks.

"Well," he says, "I find them a little disturbing."

"How so?"

"He doesn't always use good English."

"Really?"

"Yeah. Sometimes he gets prepositions mixed up and uses English words strangely, so you can't really tell what the original is trying to say."

"Well," I say a little dubiously, "that *is* what's involved in foreignizing, giving the translation the feel of the foreign original."

"But the public doesn't *want* books that sound foreign," he protests; "I've done six translations into good English, and every one's been published."

And I'm so busy registering the repressed assumptions coursing through his claims that I can't even begin to respond: (1) that acquisitions editors' decisions accurately reflect "the public"; (2) that the public's desires as reflected by what gets published are monolithic and determinable; (3) that these monolithic desires truly do mandate translations that sound as if they had originally been written in the target language; (4) that this public disdain for translationese is "natural" rather than ideological, "human" rather than socially constructed; (5) that a "good" translator is (restrictively) someone who strives to satisfy these "natural" "human" desires as channeled by acquisitions editors; (6) that a translator who fails or refuses to translate into "good" or "ordinary" English (or other target language) is therefore simply a bad translator, not, say, someone addressing a different audience (because, remember, the audience is monolithic) or trying to address the same audience in a different way (because that would be unnatural, hence perverse).

The person I'm talking to is intelligent and well-read. He is not only a recognized translator; he is extremely active in ATA and ALTA and attends both conferences nearly every year. He has been exposed to contemporary translation theory and has even written some himself—largely antitheory theory, the kind that says translators don't need theory. But still.

And the telling thing about this story—lest you think I'm singling out some poor benighted soul who is not representative of the profession—is that the repressed assumptions that my friend brings to his thinking about translation are largely unquestioned in theoretical writing about translation as well. It is not until fairly recently, in fact, not until the seventies, that sociologically minded translation theorists around the world have begun to challenge these assumptions and the repressions that keep them sounding "natural": polysystems people such as Evan-Zohar and Gideon Toury, who analyze the source- and target-cultural systems that control what will be translated and how; *skopos* people such as Katharina Reiß and Hans Vermeer, who insist that the variable target-cultural purpose of a translation regulates the translation process and its results far more than does a static ideal of equivalence; *Handlung* people like Justa Holz-Mänttäri, who study the social network of translators and their actions within that network; foreignists and postcolonialists like Antoine Berman, Lawrence Venuti, and Tejaswini Niranjana, who brand ideals of "fluency" in translation as a complicity in assimilative capitalist/colonialist ideologies and call for a dissident neoliteralism.

But the old dualisms and dogmatisms still dog this new work. Hot new issues are broached, issues that were formerly nonquestions—the impact of translation on a target culture for the polysystems and *skopos* people, the impact of translation on a colonized source culture for the postcolonial foreignizers—are now raised and discussed in serious and pressing ways, but the same old exclusions still lock into place when someone deviates from established theoretical norms and must be branded either a heretic and booted out or dismissed contemptuously as a misguided novice, a dilettante, a surface skimmer trying pathetically to rise above her or his station by renaming all the masters' central concepts. Polysystems theory in particular (uneasily including what Edwin Gentzler calls "translation studies") has gained a quite impressive power base in several European countries and Israel, even though (or perhaps precisely because) its thinking about translation has stagnated—been bureaucratized—since the early eighties. Foreignism is currently generating excitement in the United States among the critical theorists who are flocking to translation studies in ever-increasing numbers, and while the relative paucity of translation studies programs on this side of the Atlantic has prevented the foreignists from engaging in the kind of institutional empire-building occurring on the Continent and in the United Kingdom, there are signs that foreignists' postromantic approach to translation is becoming a kind of elitist academic orthodoxy as well. Nonetheless, translation theorists on the peripheries of these camps must either conform to group standards or suffer various kinds of exclusion, ostracism, shunning.

The striking thing is that repression runs rampant in every camp. Perhaps that's what makes them "camps"—that they repress in their theoretical articulations the exclusionary drives that constitute them as coherent schools of thought: this, but not that. Social *systems*, but not the experiences of translators and readers as social beings. Rigorous empiricism, no confused anecdotalism. Careful scrutiny of the matter at hand, translation as narrowly defined by the accepted paradigm, but no self-awareness, no self-scrutiny, no reflection on your own complicity in the things you attack, no testing of your theories against your own experience (do I really translate this way? do I really feel this way when I translate?). Certainly no willingness to entertain notions that stray from the fold, even in passing, even heuristically.

Thus Tejaswini Niranjana can do brilliant political readings of Benjamin, de Man, and Derrida—she can deconstruct and demystify the imperialist subtexts of ethnographic translation theory—and can still perceive the translator's choices in tidy dualistic terms, as a simple binary between assimilative sense-for-sense translation, which she associates with colonial discourse, and radical literalism, which she associates with transformative postcolonial discourse. Venuti, a left-leaning materialist thinker who brilliantly analyzes the upper-middle-class cultural politics that drive (and are repressed in) Schleiermacher's call for foreignism, twists and turns his argument until insisting upon foreignism seems materialist (Schleiermacher's elitist attack on "commercialism," as Anthony Pym has pointed out, becomes in Venuti's hands a protomarxist attack on capitalism). In the midst of the exciting, groundbreaking work these thinkers are doing on translation, in the midst of all their restless iconoclastic impatience with the received wisdom about translation, they continue to dualize the field in traditional ways: a translation for them, as for two millennia of Western thinkers in the field, is either source- or target-oriented, foreignized or domesticated, visible or invisible, good or bad. They too rely heavily on that old staple of dualistic thinking, the *non distributio medii:* if you don't translate as I do, or as I know you ought to, you're a bad translator.

Distributing this *non distributio medii*, exploding the excluded middle, was one of my focal concerns in *The Translator's Turn*. My discussion of six tropes of translation and seven or eight kinds of version was an attempt to open translation theory up to something approaching the full complexity of the choices available to translators. But at some point my explanatory models from *The Translator's Turn* stopped satisfying me. They were all right as far as they went, but they didn't go far enough. For as long as I had been trying to write about translation I had been puzzled and fascinated and frustrated by a certain powerful blockage, or maybe hundreds of them, that I felt permeating the whole field. I struggled with those blockages in *The Translator's Turn*, fought them, wrestled with them, and, I thought, pinned them to the mat two falls out of three—especially with my notion of ideosomatics, the programming of collective norms into our bodily knowing, the neural loops that control our autonomic behavior. We think about translation in narrow, restrictive, conceptually confusing, and contradictory ways and find it difficult to break out of these ways and think about translation differently because we have been *programmed* to think about it through them; and our bodies resist any move beyond our programming and indicate their displeasure with our "deviant" or "rebellious" behavior with somatic anxiety signals, a tightness in the throat or chest, a racing pulse, etc. So effective is this programming that we don't even notice it and are inclined to laugh (un)easily at claims that we have been programmed, or that our behavior is controlled somatically through anxiety or other somatic signals.

But it wasn't long before this explanation was no longer enough. *Why* were we programmed this way? Why did a stabilized abstract semantic equivalence become the only acceptable criterion for translational success? What motivated the orthodox position on absolute translatability, the notion, still the most widely accepted truism about translation today, that anything that can be said in one language can be said in another? It is easy enough to cite the dogmatic pressures of systematic theology, and I did a good deal of that in *The Translator's Turn;* but this explanation seems to imply that Christian theology was first systematized and then everything else, including translation, was fit into the system. Such was not the case. The debate on translation was integral to the very formation of an exoteric church, a church open to all and sundry, a doctrine understandable to the masses, a sacred text translatable into all tongues. The ideosomatic pressure toward a single acceptable translation model existed from the start, may even have *conditioned* the unificatory dogmas of the church. Why?

Even more troubling for the "easy" explanation that mainstream translation theory is simply somatized theology was the fact—which I could only bring myself to address obliquely in *The Translator's Turn*—that the literalist model gradually displaced between 500 and 1500 years ago by the exoteric church survived that displacement and has not only remained just as strong and attractive (in some circles) today as it ever was, but its twentieth-century adherents seem even more dogmatic than their mainstream counterparts. The intensity with which, say, Walter Benjamin, Martin Heidegger, Antoine Berman, and Lawrence Venuti defend various literalisms or foreignisms is exceeded only by the indignant condemnation they hurl at the sense-for-sense or domesticating mainstream. The exoteric church has never set literal translation up as the end-all and be-all of theological correctness. Literalism preceded the orthodox Christianity of Jerome and Augustine by a good half millennium, and since those two church fathers wrote, literalism has been its major foe, its negative exemplar, its nightmarish Other. And yet translators and non-translators throughout the Christian era have clung to literalism fervidly, nervously, needily—like addicts to their drug of choice—and have accused orthodox translators and translation theorists from Jerome through Luther to Nida of heresy. Why? What holds them to literalism?

Remembering George Steiner's writings in *After Babel* of the ban on translation in the ancient mystery religions, I wondered whether that could be it. Could some ancient mystical interdiction have been internalized by all of ancient civilization, or by enough of it that it survived into the Christian era—indeed, that it was unconsciously transformed into a foundation for Christian dogmas about translation that were specifically designed to overthrow ancient mystical practices and beliefs? This theory seemed plausible enough, so I began to research it—but found precious little to go on. Steiner had primarily addressed not the ancient mystery religions that preceded and partially conditioned Christianity but rather medieval Jewish mysticism; and even then he mostly skirted the issue of an overt *ban* on translation:

> In medieval Hasidism, it is the word rather than the alphabetic sign whose hidden sense and unaltered preservation are of extreme importance. To mutilate a single word in the Torah, to set it in the wrong order, might be to imperil the tenuous links between fallen man and the Divine presence. Already the Talmud had said: 'the omission or the addition of one letter might mean the destruction of the whole world.' Certain *illuminati* went so far as to suppose that it was some error of transcription, however minute, made by the scribe to whom God had dictated holy writ, that brought on the darkness and turbulence of the world. . . . In brief: God's actual speech, the idiom of immediacy known to Adam and common to men until Babel, can still be decoded, partially at least, in the inner layers of Hebrew and, perhaps, in other languages of the original scattering. (61)

These ideas struck many significant chords with my reading in the history of translation theory; all through the Middle Ages orthodox translators adhered to and defended similar translation models and had similar deep-seated fears about divine wrath or cosmic dissolution if they altered so much as a single letter or syllable in the texts they were translating. But Steiner's remarks remained frustratingly vague. Where were the mystical texts, texts uncovered in the Roman and later Christian assaults on the temples and translated into modern languages, that warned mystai (initiates) against translating the mysteries for the profane? Nowhere. Either nobody made such a warning, or needed to, for it was simply *understood;* or priests made the warning, but it was never written down; or else there never was such a ban. Or a rich pagan sacred literature was systematically destroyed by intolerant Christian conquerors—a theory popular among scholars of the mystery religions around the turn of the century but since largely discredited (see Burkert 69). The closest we have to a ban on translation is the ban on *divulging* the mysteries to the profane, which is well documented: many mystai who wrote about their experiences stopped just short of full disclosure and said that it was not permitted to say more; the writers of apocalypses in the Hellenistic Judaism of the intertestamental period (from the canonical books of Daniel and Revelation to the noncanonical Book of Enoch) all relate their instructions from an angel to write down what they saw and then to seal it up.

I have found only two ancient texts that reflect or articulate some deep-seated anxiety about the translation of sacred writings. The first is the famous "Letter of Aristeas," probably written in the latter half of the second century B.C.E. The pseudonymous author recounts the creation of the Septuagint a century and a half before, pretending to be Aristeas, an actual participant in that momentous event; and then, when the glorious translation has been read to the assembled multitudes at Alexandria and everyone has declared the translation so perfect that not a jot should ever be altered, King Ptolemy asks his courtier Demetrius why more poets have not sung of this book, the Hebrew Scriptures (which the author, here for the first time in recorded history, refers to in Greek as the Biblia or Book or Bible). Demetrius replies:

> "Because the Law is holy and has come into being through God; some of those to whom the thought did occur were smitten by God and desisted from the attempt." Indeed, he said, he had heard Theopompus say that when he was on the point of introducing into his history certain matter which had previously been translated from the Law, too rashly, he suffered a derangement of the mind for more than thirty days; upon the abatement of the disorder he implored God that the cause of what had befallen be made plain to him, and when it was signified to him in a dream that it was his meddlesome desire to disclose divine matters to common men, he desisted, and was thereupon restored to health. "And of Theodectes also, the tragic poet, I have heard," he added, "that when he was on the point of introducing into one of his plays something recorded in the Book, his vision was afflicted with a cataract. Conceiving the suspicion that this was the reason for his calamity, he implored God and after many days recovered." (223–25; ll. 313–16)

The second is an anonymous text in the Oxyrhynchus Papyri from the second century C.E. that reflects a deep-seated fear of translating an Egyptian description of the miracle of Imhotep or Imouthes (called Asklepios in Greek), an Egyptian physician of the Third Dynasty who was worshipped as a god after his death:

> Having often begun the translation of the said book in the Greek tongue, I learned at length how to proclaim it; but while I was in the full tide of composition my ardor was restrained by the greatness of the story, because I was about to make it public; for to gods alone—not to mortals—is it permitted to describe the mighty deeds of the gods. For if I failed, not only was I ashamed before men, but also hindered by the reproaches [?] that I should incur if the god were vexed and by the poverty of my description, in course of completion, of his undying virtue [?]. But if I did the god a service, my life would be happy and my fame undying; for the god is disposed to confer benefits, since even those whose pious ardor is only for the moment are repeatedly preserved by him after the healing art has failed against diseases which have overtaken them. (Grant 125)

A serious illness finally ends his vacillation: he reads the illness as a sign from Imhotep that he has dawdled too long and his healing as a sign that he will be rewarded for completing the translation, so he does. Striking in his account is the claim that "to gods alone—not to mortals—is it permitted to describe the mighty deeds of the gods," since the text he proposes to translate already exists in Egyptian and thus has presumably already been proclaimed to mortals. The implication, buried in his concerns, is that the "mortals" to whom it is not permitted to "proclaim" or translate the sacred text are Greeks, pagans who do not know Imhotep as god. We might, therefore, paraphrase his dictum as implying that "for initiates alone—not to the profane—is it permitted to translate the mighty deeds of the gods."

Still, this is a speculative and debatable reading of the passage. The anonymous author is still not saying "Thou shalt not translate"—though he may be coming closer to saying it than anyone else. And the anecdotal evidence put in the mouth of Demetrius that the Hebrew God frowns on the translation of his Holy Writ and will punish anyone who transgresses seems no less equivocal; it appears, after all, in the context of a Greek translation of that same Holy Writ that has just received official blessing.

Was there a ban on translation, or wasn't there? If there was, how do these writers even come to consider the possibility of translating the Egyptian or Hebrew sacred text into Greek? If there wasn't, where did their fear of punishment come from?

My breakthrough in this research came with a rereading of Apuleius' book from the same period as the anonymous reflection on whether to translate, the second century C.E., the *Metamorphoses* or *Transformations of Lucius,* usually known in English (following Augustine's derogation of the book in *The City of God*—"*Asinus aureus,*" 18.18) as *The Golden Ass.* At the end of this work, in Book 11, during the preparations for his initiation into the mysteries of the goddess Isis, Lucius is read to *in Greek* from an original Egyptian text of the Book of the Dead by the priest Mithras—in other words, the priest *translates* the mysteries into Greek—and then, in a manner of speaking, Lucius declines to pass the translation on to his Roman readers, for it is forbidden:

> Thereupon the old man took me by the hand and led me towards the spacious temple; and after he had duly performed the rituals of opening the doors and of making the morning-sacrifice, he produced from the secret recesses of the shrine certain books written in unknown characters. The meaning of these characters was concealed, at times by the concentrated expression of hieroglyphically painted animals, at times by wreathed and twisted letters with tails that twirled like wheels or spiralled together like vine-tendrils—so that it was altogether impossible for any peeping profane to comprehend. From these books the high priest interpreted to me the matters necessary for my mystic preparations. . . . Then, after the uninitiated had withdrawn to a distance and I had donned a new linen gown, the priest grasped my hand and conducted me into the Holy of Holies.
>
> Perhaps, curious reader, you are keen to know what was said and done. I would tell you if it were permitted to tell. But both the ears that heard such things and the tongue that told them would reap a heavy penalty for such rashness. (Lindsay 248–49)

This passage, and the events surrounding it (both in *The Golden Ass* and in the world in which it was written), will be my concern throughout chapter 1. To anticipate only slightly, let me note here that the passage remains patently problematic as evidence of a general ban on translation in the ancient mystery religions. For one thing, translating from the Egyptian Book of the Dead is still not overtly banned, although it is clearly something that is only done by the priest within the ritual space; what Lucius is explicitly prohibited from divulging to the profane is the mystical experience itself. Implicitly the ban extends to everything concerning the initiation, including the instructions translated from Egyptian to Greek by the priest—but only implicitly. In addition, this is a single event in a fictional narrative (albeit a highly autobiographical one); even if we take this event as evidence that translation was banned in the Isis cult, how are we to extrapolate from this evidence, already shaky, to the mystery religions in general? Let alone, of course, from this evidence to some surviving remnant of that ban in the theory and practice of translation today, which will be my concern in chapter 2.

There may never have been an actual *ban* on translation. Nevertheless, I believe that Lucius' initiation does hold some kind of key to Western thinking about translation, some deep ideosomatic nexus that runs all through the history of translation theory. My title, *Translation and Taboo*, reflects my conviction that this nexus is nothing so overt and legalistic as a ban, but rather a taboo, a collectivized anxiety about sacred texts that has survived massive demystificatory assaults and has generated through the centuries an astonishing variety of avoidance behaviors that can best be explained, it seems to me, through the notion of taboo. The Biblical and Classical words for "sacred" or "holy"—Hebrew *k-d-sh* or *qadosh*, Greek *hagios*, Latin *sacer*—are all very close in meaning to the Polynesian word *tabu*, which was first appropriated for European use by Captain Cook and his crew: separated off, untouchable, uneatable, undoable except by people with enough clout to withstand or channel the thing's destructive "mana" or power.

And while we don't normally think of sacred texts as taboo any more, it should be clear that the deep ideosomatic alignments of taboo still survive: ask any Christian, or just about any atheist who was raised a Christian, or just about anyone raised in a Christian society, to throw a copy of the Bible on the floor and jump on it, or rip out its pages, or spit inside it, or urinate on it. Everybody knows, these days, that it's just a book, a physical object, an infinitely reproducible commodity, and in any case "only" a translation of the original. The dogmatic pressure away from veneration of the actual physical book toward a transcendentalized worship of the abstract spiritual truth contained in or above or beyond its words is at least as old as the church itself. But ask someone to trash a Bible and see whether what "everyone knows" truly corresponds to what "everyone does" or what "everyone feels."

This example illustrates the importance of staying in touch with the anecdote, the casually remembered and related personal experience, which remembers what the theory all too often forgets: the peripheral confusions, the emotional charges and connotations and associations, the half-conscious situatedness and directedness of an idea or a plan, the inchoate or semichoate feeling that all this matters for some specific reason (if only I could put my finger on what it is!). Despite a good deal of academic irritation with this "unscholarly" aspect of *The Translator's Turn*, I'm sticking with the anecdotal, the experiential, the excursional, the centrifugal here as well. I hope you'll read this book in more or less the same spirit as I wrote it, in process, without a clear sense beforehand of where I'll be taking you, and above all without an exclusionary ethos that precludes certain assumptions or questions in advance. My argumentation throughout the book is more exploratory and digressive than syllogistic; the "payoff," if there is one, lies in the heuristics on every page, not in some stunning revelation at the end. The book was difficult to write, because I kept butting up against a disconcerting and almost ubiquitous resistance or blockage, as if what I was trying to articulate didn't want to be written about. I hope it is not as difficult to read, indeed, that it might even be exciting to read; but I can imagine that it will take a certain kind of patience, a willingness to wrestle with one thing at a time and not to keep flipping ahead for the triumphant conclusion (sorry, but there isn't one), not to hurl the book aside in frustration. Everything in the book is speculation, a poking and a prodding and a probing into this and that seemingly tangential topic in quest of a way through the blockages to *truth;* if I never quite reach that august goal, I do turn up some interesting things along the way, and I'm hoping readers will not only be satisfied with these incidentals but will find them productive for their own thinking about translation and culture.

But where was I? Oh yes, trashing a Bible. Ancient taboos on harming sacred texts have spread far beyond the Christian Bible, throughout Christian civilization. The book-burning scenes in *Fahrenheit 451* or *Indiana Jones and the Last Crusade* or other movies about tyranny stir deep anxieties in us. In an era of mass-production capitalism we know that it is virtually impossible to burn every single copy of a book; no matter how many copies the tyrants burn, some are likely to survive. And yet we cringe as the books go into the fire. Surely one of the reasons why the radical academic voices raised against the despotism of the (implicitly white male) "classic"—its overshadowing of equally interesting and provocative works by white women and men and women of color—provoke so much ire in cultural conservatives is that the great canon debate awakens echoes of book burning, which touches the taboo on sacred texts. I have raised my voice against classics, too, and have called for the scrapping of the canon; and yet, iconoclastic as I am, I would find it extremely difficult to pull some literary classic off my shelf and throw it on the fire.

I say radical heretical things about the Bible, too, but I probably couldn't bring myself to destroy one. I hasten to reassure myself that this is because I have so much respect for books period, not just the Bible (could I really be so possessed by ancient taboos?). But I would find it much easier to destroy a

Harlequin Romance than a Bible—and in fact if I had to destroy a Bible, I'd rather sacrifice a Living Bible than a King James.

In chapter 1, as I say, I propose to look closely at *The Golden Ass*, teasing out of it insights into translation as it may or may not have murkily been conceived before translation theory as we know it today began to be written. A lingering look at this critical literary moment in the history of the mysteries seems worthwhile to me, because no one has ever read *The Golden Ass* or any other mystery text in terms of the light it can shed on translation, and there is a surprising amount of that light—even if it comes to us only as a series of flickers in the long initiatory night. My pace in chapters 2 and 3 is fairly leisurely as well, but there at least I will be focused on the history of translation theory from the beginning of the Christian era to the present—in chapter 2 on the aggressively "tolerant" demystifications of mystery attempted by the mainstream exoteric church, and in chapter 3 on the survival of ancient taboos in the displaced but still powerful strands of literalism in romantic and postromantic theory, especially in terms of magic and ghostly doubles.

My leisurely and meandering course through this history may be problematic for some readers, especially my digressions into seemingly unrelated things like the double bind and addictions (chapter 1), the schizoid personality (chapter 2), and "going doubled like a ghost," Friedrich Schleiermacher's horrified analogue for writing originally in a foreign language in his 1813 lecture on the different methods of translating (chapter 3). This is not a narrative history; it is certainly not a comprehensive one. There are holes in it that you could drive a Mack truck through. But the book does loosely use the chronology of the last two and a half millennia in the Near East and Europe to "organize" (if that is the word for such a perambulatory tour) my speculations about translation and culture in terms of taboo. I hope you will agree that the many side trips are worthwhile—that they add complexity and theoretical richness to the bare bones of the history around which I weave them. I am, in any case, more a theorist than a historian; my primary interest throughout lies in what all this tells us about our attitudes about translation today. The history is mainly a means to that end.

If ever there was a book whose author took full responsibility for the ideas expressed therein, this is it; half the time even I didn't know where this stuff was coming from, but it came through my fingers, so I guess it's mine.

But I also had help. Bill Kaul and Robin Bodkin read bits and pieces of the book as it emerged. I tried out early versions of these thoughts on Fred Will, by mail and by fax and by phone, and later at a miniconference Fred organized on translation at the University of Iowa; he also gave me detailed comments on chapter 3. Carol Maier read and responded to a dozen pages of notes I jotted down at some point, long before I started writing; it turned out she had been thinking along similar lines and was able to complicate my thinking in useful ways. In the spring of 1993 I wrote and distributed to a half-dozen friends a paper called "Why Don't We Talk About Translation?," broaching there several of my more off-the-wall suggestions about translation and taboo, and then organized a session by that name at the ALTA meeting in Atlanta the next fall, with wonderful responses to my questions by Mike Doyle, Bill Park, and John Biguenet. Peter Bush later published parts of our session in his journal *In Other Words*.

Two segments of the book as it stands here also appeared elsewhere, in quite different form: the end of chapter 1 in *Modern Poetry in Translation* and the discussion of Jerome and Augustine in chapter 2 in *Translation and Literature*. My thanks to the respective editors, Danny Weissbort and Stuart Gillespie, for their helpful suggestions. The parts of chapter 2 dealing with Tejaswini Niranjana have been accepted for publication in substantially revised form by *The Economic and Political Weekly of India*, under the title "O Kannada: Tejaswini Niranjana and the Problem of Retranslation." Niranjana read these pages herself and made valuable suggestions and corrections; thanks also to Shantha and Sucheta Murthy, who helped me do a detailed analysis of the Kannada text. Dan Coran and Mary Lincoln at Northern Illinois University Press made helpful suggestions that forced me to think a little more closely about what I was trying to do and why and how. Marilyn Gaddis Rose and Samuel Weber read the manuscript for the press and read it in very different but equally provocative ways; it is a privilege to be read by two such critical and yet sympathetic people (especially when publication depends on their reading!). Working with a press's designer has never been as exciting for me as it was with this book; Julia Fauci's ideas for the cover, front matter, and facing pages grew out of a deeply perceptive and imaginative reading of the book, took shape in long phone conversations with me, and ultimately exceeded my wildest hope.

Without Heljä, to whom I dedicate this book, I would never have had the courage to push past taboos in our life together, let alone in print; it seems to me that the usual "without whom none of this would have been possible" accolades to spouses and partners are more appropriate in this book than in any I've ever written. Our relationship has proven to us that taboos *can* be worked through and set aside, though not without enormous pain and anxiety; and that life is better on the other side of at least some of taboo's massive psychic walls.

TRANSLATION & TABOO

The Translations of Lucius

CHAPTER 1

Lucius Apuleius was born in 125 of the Christian era in Madaura (or Madauros, modern Mdaurusch in northern Algeria) to a prominent citizen, a mayor and councillor, and thus a member of the *Ordo,* or ruling class, in the town. Apuleius may have spoken Punic natively, but would have grown up speaking Greek and a provincial dialect of Latin; he was educated in Carthage, Athens, and Rome, and he later related the difficulties he had in exchanging his early provincial trilingualism for the metropolitan dialects of Greek in Athens and of Latin in Rome. Well educated in Platonic philosophy and the author of the treatise *On the God of Socrates*—one of Augustine's major secondary sources for his critique of Platonic doctrine in *The City of God* (see Haight)—Apuleius was well-known in his day as a brilliant and erudite speaker and writer, as a lawyer, and as a priest of Isis and Osiris.

His *Metamorphoses* or *Transformations of Lucius* is one, and certainly one of the best known, of a group of prose narratives written in classical antiquity that are episodic and picaresque in narrative structure, satiric in style and tone, encyclopedic in social description, and most commonly engrossed in the vicissitudes of sex and love (see Reardon, Tatum). Typically these narratives revolve around the misadventures of a pair of beautiful lovers who are separated by bandits or pirates before their love is consummated, often because their beauty awakens the jealousy of the gods; their chastity is frequently threatened, as are their lives (and the heroine often seems to have been killed, but then reappears, only to suffer further setbacks), but finally, again often through the merciful intervention of a god or goddess, they are reunited and live happily every after. (Movies like *Honeymoon in Vegas* and *Indecent Proposal* are striking modern renditions of the genre.)

The Greeks invented this genre but had no special name for it; the terms *plasma* "fiction" and *genomena* "happenings, events" were usually sufficient to designate these narratives. Lucian of Samosata, born five years before Apuleius in 120 C.E. and probably author of the Greek tale that is *The Golden Ass*'s most obvious predecessor (and in some sense source text), *Lucius or the Ass,* called his blend of Platonic dialogue and humorous narrative Menippean satire after the Greek author Menippus, whose works do not survive.

Apuleius himself, however, called *The Golden Ass* a Milesian tale *(sermone isto Milesio)* after Aristides of Miletus, who wrote in that style in the second century B.C.E. The most famous Latin collection of Milesian tales was the *Satyricon* of Petronius Arbiter from the mid–first century C.E., and many later readers have associated the two, the *Satyricon* and *The Golden Ass*, as sexy satirical picaresque narratives and as the two greatest extended prose narratives—novels or romances—of ancient Rome.

But as recent scholars of Apuleius have noted, this is a misleading comparison. Where Petronius is brash, slangy, lewd, modern, irreverent, Apuleius is pious and devout, tells his sexy stories as cautionary tales (stay away from black magic and the wrong kind of people or you'll be transformed into an ass and repeatedly humiliated), and writes in an elaborately ornate rhetorical style that recalls earlier and loftier stylistic models. As James Tatum remarks in his book on *The Golden Ass*, the Milesian tale was an odd genre for a Platonic philosopher and devout priest of Isis like Apuleius to be working in: "reading or writing Milesian tales was the mark of a depraved character—suitable material, in fact, for political invective" (98). Tatum continues:

> From even this brief survey of the evidence, it is difficult to avoid the conclusion that Apuleius described his novel in such a way as virtually to guarantee its being taken for a piece of triviality; for trivial the Milesian tale would surely seem when compared to such respectable works as orations or philosophical treatises. But . . . *The Golden Ass* also expresses in Book 11 an evidently sincere and powerful evangelism; the "entertainment" of the Milesian narrative tends with ever clearer irony toward a philosophy of life that turns away from the enticements that abound in the first ten books; and there is reasonably good evidence that Apuleius took pains to arrange the entire novel in a coherent way, so that it would be possible for him simultaneously to entertain and to edify his audience by his complex story. (101–2)

I want to discuss the tricky or deceptive structure of the book later in this chapter and begin my reading elsewhere, with a close look at the devout ending in Book 11. For most modern readers this is the least problematic (and least interesting) part of the book; but it is also one of the fullest depictions we have of a conversion ritual in the ancient mystery religions, and as I showed in the preface, it deals in passing with translation.

As Book 11 begins, Lucius (the ass) finds himself alone and free on the beach at Cenchreae; after ritual purification in the ocean—"I immersed my head seven times because (according to the divine Pythagoras) that number is specially suited to all ritual acts" (Lindsay 235)—he prays to Isis to free him from his beastly prison. Falling asleep, he sees Isis herself rising from the waves; despite his asinine appearance (the ass was anathema to Isis), she speaks to him, telling him she has had pity on his situation and will deliver him from it the very next day during a procession in her honor. He is to approach the high priest, who will have been instructed by Isis to hold a bouquet of roses (the antidote to the potion that transformed Lucius) and to expect an ass to approach, eat the flowers, and be transformed back into a man. In return, Lucius must promise to devote the rest of his life to her service.

Lucius obeys and is transformed. News of his miraculous fate spreads across the region to his hometown—which was Corinth in the beginning but now, through a telling Freudian slip that I will return to later, is Madaura, Apuleius' own hometown. His slaves and relatives had thought him dead and now rush to his side bringing clothes and money, which he will need for his initiation into the Isiac priesthood, an exorbitantly expensive process that effectively screened out the lower orders. He waits for a signal from Isis to be initiated into her mysteries, for initiation without such a signal can be fatal:

> Not indeed that there was a single man among them who was so lost to common sense or so foolhardy that he would dare in rank blasphemy to undertake the ministries of the Goddess, which without her consent would be an invocation of destruction. For the gates of shadow as well as the bulwarks of life were under the Goddess's control; and the act of initiation had been compared to a voluntary death with a slight chance of redemption. Therefore the divine will of the Goddess was wont to choose men who had lived their life to the full, who were coming near to the limits of waning light, and who yet could be safely trusted with the mighty secrets of her religion. These men by her divine providence she regenerated and restored to strength sufficient for their new career. (Lindsay 247)

One night the call comes in the form of a dream: Isis appears and instructs Lucius to appear the following day before the priest Mithras, who will conduct him through the rites. The next day Lucius goes to the temple to tell Mithras his vision, but Mithras has had one too and knows exactly what is to be done. He takes Lucius into the sanctuary, performs the morning sacrifice, and takes out the scrolls of the Egyptian Book of the Dead in demotic Egyptian script, translating the relevant passages from them into Greek for Lucius so that the novice will know what must be done. Having arranged for the purchase of all necessary items, Lucius is taken to the public baths where he bathes and then is publicly instructed to fast for ten days; at the end of that period he is led into the inner sanctum and initiated into the mysteries, which he refuses to describe for his inquisitive readers, lest they and he be punished severely for their impiety. Following the solemn rites, which last all night and involve some sort of ecstatic enactment or experience of death and rebirth, he emerges from the temple robed in twelve stoles and holding a lighted torch in his hand; the curtains are drawn back and he is revealed to the multitudes—"as when a statue is unveiled, dressed like the sun" (Graves 280). He spends the day in celebration with friends and undergoes further rites (which he does not recount) in the following days; under orders from the goddess he then travels to Rome, where he is initiated into the mysteries of Osiris, and then once again—bringing the number of his initiations to the magical three—into the Roman Isiac mysteries. And so ends his story.

Translation and Initiation

In order to explore the significance of all this for later Western thinking about translation, we need to place the high priest's ritual act of translating from the Egyptian in the context of Lucius' entire conversion and initiation. How did the ancients feel about translating sacred texts? Which—if any—of those feelings survived in subarticulate, somatized form in and through Christianity into our own day?

The process Lucius describes is structurally repeated several times, once in his transformation from an ass to a man, once again in his initiation into the Corinthian mysteries of Isis, then twice more in his initiation into the Roman mysteries of Isis and Osiris. We are told little about the last two initiations, but the first two sequences pass roughly through the same six steps of surrender of will, supplication, instruction, purification, transformation, and dramatization (in the sense of the ritual display of changed status)—albeit in slightly different order in the two transformative events. In the first sequence the surrender of will is most striking, and this step reappears in the second sequence as little more than constant devoted openness to the goddess's call. In the second sequence Lucius purifies himself only after he has been instructed, and his instruction comes in two stages, the first from Isis herself, the second from the priest Mithras (or, one might say, the first from Isis in person, the second from Isis speaking through the Egyptian Book of the Dead as translated by the priest).

Here is the first sequence:

1. *Surrender.* On the beach at Cenchreae Lucius surrenders all control of his fate to Isis.

2. *Purification.* He purifies himself by dipping his head seven times in the ocean.

3. *Supplication.* He begs Isis for her mercy, asking her either to restore him to human form or to grant him the gift of death.

4. *Instruction.* Isis appears to him in a vision and promises to deliver him; she tells him what to do the following day and what the cost of this salvation will be (devoting the rest of his life to her service).

5. *Transformation.* On her orders he enters the ritual procession of Isis, eats the roses proffered him by the high priest, and regains human form.

6. *Dramatization.* The priest displays the transformed Lucius to the populace as dramatic evidence of the great power and mercy of the goddess.

And here is the second:

1. *Waiting.* Lucius spends several days, perhaps weeks, devoting every moment of his time to service of the goddess, receiving visions from her every day that bid him to be initiated (but that do not yet say when).

2. *Supplication.* He repeatedly begs the high priest to initiate him, but the high priest declines, citing the grave dangers of haste.

3a. *Instruction-as-vision.* Isis appears in a dream to call him to initiation and tells him when and where it will happen and who will perform the ceremony.

3b. *Instruction-as-translation.* After morning sacrifices, the high priest

Mithras translates passages from the Egyptian Book of the Dead, telling Lucius how to prepare for his initiation.

4. *Purification.* He prepares for initiation by bathing, fasting, and abstaining from sex.

5. *Initiation.* He is inducted into the nocturnal trance experience in which he experiences death and rebirth and is transformed.

6. *Dramatization.* The following morning he is revealed to the assembled populace garbed like the sun.

There is a shuttle rhythm to both of these sequences, moving from words to wordless experience and back again—between what we might call the ineffable and the effable, or between what the Greeks called *ta arrheta* "the unspeakable" and *logos* "speech." Lucius collapses on the beach at Cenchreae in inarticulate despair, utterly bereft of either the strength to seek out the roses that will restore him to human form or the words to describe his surrender. This giving over of will, of control, becomes sleep, an anticipation of his later mystical initiation into death and rebirth, and he awakens to a nocturnal visionary landscape: "Not long afterwards I awoke in sudden terror. A dazzling full moon was rising from the sea. It is at this secret hour that the Moon-goddess, sole sovereign of mankind, is possessed of her greatest power and majesty" (Graves 261). Then, still wordless, he purifies himself in the ocean, and finally finds his voice—actually, since in his asinine body voiced praying would have been braying, his internal speech—and prays to Isis for deliverance. Then the goddess appears and speaks to him, giving him verbal instructions; his obedience is once again wordless, as is the transformation that it precipitates; and the priest dramatizes his miraculous transformation once again in words. The sequence alternates: the experience of surrender, the verbal exchange with the goddess, the experience of transformation, the verbal dramatization of his experience.

This same rhythm flows through Lucius' actual initiation: his verbal supplications are finally answered in Isis' verbal instructions, both in the vision of the night and in the translation provided him by the high priest; he is purified, transformed, and revealed in silence. This second sequence is patently divided into two distinct phases, that of instruction (words) and transformation (no words): in the instructional phase Lucius walks around talking to people about what is about to happen, Isis keeps appearing in visions of the night and giving him pep talks, the high priest himself appears to him in a dream and tells him things, and finally he receives verbal instruction from the goddess herself, in a vision and then in a translation. What then follows is a sequence of symbolic events that he experiences wordlessly: ritual purification, ecstatic death and rebirth, public appearance in full priestly garb.

The <u>Arrheta</u> and the <u>Aporrheta</u>

The question that interests me here is, What part or parts of all this must he not divulge? He says explicitly that he must not divulge the mysteries and seems to mean only his ecstatic experience in the temple and the mystical trance that takes him through death to rebirth; but he tells us as much about that experience as he does about any other part of the initiation process and says that, without the actual experience, we cannot understand it. There is a viscerality to lived experience that often defies verbalization. Language describing an experience yields meaning only to the knowing looks of those who have had the experience themselves; and this is surely a large part of what Lucius means in predicting that we will not understand. In *Ancient Mystery Cults*, one of the best (if problematic) books available on the subject, Walter Burkert writes:

> It could be held that the quest for mystery texts is essentially futile for more basic reasons: no Nag Hammadi library of mysteries will ever be discovered because it never existed, and there was not even a shipwreck as imagined by Cumont. Is it not true that the mysteries were "unspeakable," *arrheta*, not just in the sense of artificial secrecy utilized to arouse curiosity, but in the sense that what was central and decisive was not accessible to verbalization? There is an "unspeakable *sympatheia*" of the souls with the rituals, Proclus states, and much older is the well-known pronouncement of Aristotle that those undergoing mysteries *(teloumenoi)* should not "learn" *(mathein)* but should "be affected," "suffer," or "experience" *(pathein)*. (69)

Throughout his book Burkert uses his considerable expertise on the mystery religions to debunk them, especially to debunk the notion that they might have survived the ban on pagan gods of 391/92 C.E. and might have had any continuing impact on Western thought whatsoever. It will obviously be important for me to address this claim closely, since my argument hinges on the survival, in some ideosomatic form, of the ancient mysteries or the taboos that they channeled right into our own day. Let me simply say for now that in jumping from the perception that there was no real need for secrecy (since the "secrets" could not be communicated anyway) to the assumption that the only possible reason for insisting on secrecy was for advertising purposes, Burkert willfully ignores the emotional impact of taboo, of collectivized fear and anxiety and resulting avoidance behaviors. He takes pains throughout his book to portray the mysteries as just something a few rich people did—as nothing that could have influenced even them very profoundly, let alone anyone after the fourth century C.E.

The important thing to consider at this point, though, is the implication that the bans on divulging the mysteries to the profane never really existed, or if they did, they were secondary and not very important, late developments that did not truly characterize the ancient mysteries per se. This is a thesis first advanced by Karl Kerényi in 1944, in an article called "The Mysteries of the Kabeiroi":

> In Greek religion this secrecy is not positive and intentional but rather negative and involuntary. There is no serious intention of maintaining the secrecy

> of the secret. The study of the religions of nature shows that in the secret cults it is a question of the same thing found, according to Goethe, in nature itself: a sacred open secret. What was concealed in the Greek cult must certainly have been known to all those who lived in the vicinity of the cult sites, but it was unutterable. It possessed this character—the character of the *arreton* (ἄρρητον)—independently of the will of those who participated in the cult. For in the profoundest sense it was ineffable: a true mystery. Only subsequently did express prohibitions make the arreton into an *aporreton* (ἀπόρρητον) ["forbidden thing"]. (37)

And Kerényi goes on to argue that the "closedness" etymologically associated with the *mysteria* through their Greek root, *mueo* "to close the eyes or the mouth," had less to do with closed mouths (not telling) than with closed eyes (not seeing):

> what we should imagine here is not a silence (closing the mouth) in the presence of the arreton but a ceremony of closing the eyes. Herakles is seated with his head totally covered: the Mysteria begin for the mystes when, as sufferer of the event (μυούμενος), he closes his eyes, falls back as it were into his own darkness, enters into that darkness. The Romans use the term "going-into," "*in-itia*" (in the plural), not only for this initiating action, the act of closing the eyes, the *myesis*, which is exactly rendered as *initiatio*, but for the Mysteria themselves. A festival of entering into the darkness, regardless of what issue and ascent this initiation may lead to: that is what the Mysteria were, in the original sense of the word. (38–39)

Does this mean, then, that we have to choose between interpretations? Either the mysteries are ineffable and need no enforced secrecy to guard against the prying of the profane (the closed-eyes reading), or else they are knowledge that must be fenced in lest outsiders gain access to it (the closed-mouth reading)? I don't believe so. Kerényi notes that express prohibitions "subsequently" banned the speaking of the unspeakable—at the very least we're talking about cultural evolution here, the gradual shift from a more primitive form of the mysteries in the nature religions, where no ban was needed, to a more sophisticated and institutionally regimented form, where mystai were systematically warned against divulging what they had experienced—and in any case this "evolution" took place fairly early on. As early as the fifth century B.C.E., in fact, we find Herodotus obeying these "express prohibitions" and refusing to reveal the mysteries—whether out of fear of divine reprisal or, more likely, out of tolerant respect for the wishes of the cults he describes.

It seems more reasonable to suggest that in the ancient mysteries proper, from about the sixth century B.C.E. to the fourth century C.E., the overt prohibitions on divulging the mysteries to the profane did exist, but that they existed in a complex dialectical relationship with the difficulty of divulging them, the problem of ineffability that Kerényi and Burkert address. If mystical mouths are forcibly closed near the beginning of the age of mystery religions, and if Kerényi's vivid description of the mystical experience as a closing of the eyes and entering into the dark remains just as valid seven and eight centuries later, it will not suffice to say that the closing of mouths is the product of a long evolutionary process. We don't yet have enough conceptual apparatus on the table to determine what explanation might suffice, however, so I want to put this issue too on hold for a few more pages, until after I've delved into the problem of taboo.

For now, note that Lucius tells us more about his supposedly ineffable *(arrheta)* ecstatic experience than he does about the priest's Greek translation from the Egyptian Book of the Dead. Of the former we learn that it involved a passage through death to rebirth; of the latter we learn nothing. Is this significant? If the secrecy of the mysteries extended only to the experience of death and rebirth in nocturnal trance—whether because that experience was ineffable or because it was the mystical experience proper, that which was forbidden to tell—why didn't he tell us what the high priest "interpreted" to him out of the Egyptian script? Was it because, as he seems to imply, it was just insignificant stuff about what clothes to wear? If so, why does he tell us that the hieroglyphics were partly "ordinary letters protected against profane prying by having their tops and tails wreathed in knots or rounded like wheels or tangled together in spirals like vine tendrils" (Graves 278–79)? If the original Egyptian text of the sacred writings protects them against "profane prying," presumably there is something to be protected, some divine utterance that is to be divulged only to the initiates—who, because they are not taught Egyptian, require a translation into Greek.

Was the Egyptian book originally written to conceal the mysteries from the profane? Probably not—though who knows. This parallels, of course, the debate that raged over vernacular Bibles in the fourteenth, fifteenth, and sixteenth centuries: whether the Latin Bible was written in Latin to conceal it from the profane or to make it accessible to the common folk who couldn't read the original Hebrew and Greek. I'll be returning to this quagmire in chapter 2.

In any case, an ethnocentric impulse in the Isis cult militated against or, at the very least, problematized translation. "Because the clergy always stressed the relationship with Egypt and the necessity 'to worship the gods of the fathers with the rites from home,'" as Burkert writes, "'the Egyptian' had to be present to perform the sacrifice 'with expertise'; therefore at least some of the priests would normally have been Egyptians" (39). This restriction points to an implicit prejudice against translation and translatability: Isiac mystagogues clearly thought of their cult as a local Egyptian rather than as a potentially universal one and went to great lengths to ensure that the mysteries remained grounded in the original language of their god and goddess. Burkert tells us that the Isiac mysteries, open to select members of the general public—like Lucius, a Berber—were a Greek invention, or rather, perhaps, an adaptation of the original Egyptian rites to prevailing

Greek assumptions about the *mysteria;* in Egypt the Isis cult initiated only Egyptian priests (40). As it spread outside Egypt, the Isis cult adapted to local conditions, but did so grudgingly, controlling non-Egyptian access to the mysteries by insisting, for example, on a direct call from the goddess herself before initiation could be extended to a new candidate. Initiations must, in fact, have been fairly rare. The Egyptian priests could have restricted access to the Isiac mysteries further by insisting that all new candidates first learn Egyptian, so as to hear the original words of the god and goddess; but they didn't. This is a course of action that would be recommended by prominent later antitranslation theorists, such as Roger Bacon in the thirteenth century and Arthur Schopenhauer in the nineteenth—don't translate, learn the original languages—and it remains an implicit or explicit ideal in many departments of classics, modern languages, and comparative literature even today. Two of the world's major religions, too, Judaism and Islam, prefer to teach their children and converts the language of their sacred text, Hebrew and Arabic, rather than assuming that they can safely rely on vernacular translations. The Isiac priests in Apuleius' book translate the Book of the Dead into Greek, but only within the ritual space, orally, to carefully selected candidates for initiation.

For it was considered essential that initiates be verbally prepared for their ecstatic experience:

> In fact, there are quite a few testimonies about the preparatory "learning" and "transmission" *(paradosis)* that took place in mysteries, as well as about the "complete" or exact "knowledge" that was to be acquired. Speech, *logos,* had an important role to play, and the injunction "not to tell" the uninitiated was taken so seriously because verbalization was central to the proceedings. Mysteries were presumed to possess a "sacred tale," *hieros logos,* and this could well have been contained in a book. (Burkert 69–70)

In the Isis cult this "book" would have been primarily the Egyptian Book of the Dead, but also various other hieratic texts, such as hymns to Isis, Osiris, Amon-Ra, or the Nile. In the case of Lucius's initiation, however, the *hieros logos*—the verbalization that Burkert rightly identifies as "central to the proceedings"—is not limited to instructions translated from the Book of the Dead. It also comes from Isis herself, directly, in nocturnal visitations, and from the high priest, who gives Lucius private instruction in the proper performance of the secret rites. But of these three types of verbalization—the visionary speech of Isis, the translation of the Book of the Dead, and the instructions from the priest—only the latter two are kept secret. In every one of her visitations to him, Lucius gives us the words of the goddess verbatim. If the words of the Book of the Dead and of the high priest are guarded against the profane, shouldn't these words be as well? "He gave me certain orders too holy to be spoken above a whisper, and then commanded me in everyone's hearing to abstain from all but the plainest food for the ten succeeding days, to eat no meat and drink no wine" (Graves 279). The priest's orders are too holy to speak above a whisper—and, presumably, too holy to be written in Lucius's book, which will be read by the profane—but the goddess's are common coin? One would think that priestly translations and instructions were further removed from divine speech, and therefore less important to keep secret than the words of the goddess; but Lucius quotes Isis in full and blacks out the other.

For that matter, in what language did the goddess address Lucius? Since he had no Egyptian, presumably it would have had to be one of the languages he understood, but was it his native Punic dialect, or Greek, or Latin? Later, when he begins practicing law in Rome, he complains about having to plead his briefs in Latin; apparently he felt more comfortable in Greek, the language of the Corinthian society in which these events are taking place, the language into which Mithras translated the passages from the Book of the Dead. Would an Egyptian goddess, worshipped by priests who jealously guarded the original Egyptianity of their cult, speak to an ass in Greek?

It may well be that all the verbal preparations—the visitations of the goddess, the translations of the sacred text, the holy whispered orders—are cumulatively essential for the mystical experience, specifically for prestructuring it, so that the imagistic progression past the gates of death to the perception of the sun and the gods will take on the specific form of the mysteries of Isis. As I. M. Lewis says in *Ecstatic Religion*, the trance experience, however induced—whether through "alcoholic spirits, hypnotic suggestion, rapid over-breathing, the inhalation of smoke and vapours, music, and dancing," or "the ingestion of such drugs as mescaline or lysergic acid and other psychotropic alkaloids" (39)—is universally human, but is *conditioned* in specific ways in specific social contexts, and therefore actually experienced differently around the world. Steven T. Katz seconds this notion more strenuously still in an article devoted to the thesis that there is no "neutral" or "uninterpreted" mystical experience:

> Mystical experience(s) are the *result* of traversing the mystical way(s), whatever specific *way* one happens to follow, e.g., the Jewish, Sufi, or Buddhist. What one reads, learns, knows, intends, and experiences along the path creates to some degree (let us leave this somewhat vaguely stated as yet) the *anticipated* experience made manifest. That is to say, there is an intimate even necessary connection between the mystical and religious texts studied and assimilated, the mystical experience had, and the mystical experience reported. (6)

Could it be that the preparatory words, because they give the Isiac mysteries their characteristic shape and flavor, because they *preshape* the ecstatic trance somatically, are the secret part of the whole process, that which must be most carefully guarded against prying eyes? "Behold," Lucius says, "I have told my experience, and yet what you hear can mean nothing to you" (Lindsay 249)—because the mere sequence of visual images can mean nothing without the preparatory words? Or because the verbal description of the experience means nothing without its visceral impact? In any case, Apuleius makes sure that his readers lack the *combination* of verbal preparation and visceral experience that might make the mystical experience available to the profane. Even if he had been able to give us a sensory experience equivalent to his mystical trance, the missing connection with the words of the translation would render it still mysterious.

Also, of course, now that we have translations of these texts, we think we understand the mysteries, but without the connection to the visceral experience of Isiac trance the translations remain words on the page, and again mysterious—so maybe translation wasn't as dangerous as the mystagogues thought?

The Book of the Dead and the Alien Word

After all this it is odd to read the Book of the Dead in English translation. I pick up the *Egyptian Literature* volume of *The World's Greatest Literature*, containing (in English translation) the Book of the Dead, Egyptian tales, the Tell Amarna tablets, cuneiform inscriptions, and hieratic papyri, and as I read part of me wonders whether this is what all the fuss was about—but another part is hooked, the mystery has me too, and I keep looking over my shoulder to see whether anyone is watching me read this forbidden text. The Book of the Dead, rendered here into English by E. A. Wallis Budge, consists of individual chapters intended as litanies for the living to memorize and the deceased to recite for their journey to the underworld to protect them there from harm. The chapters are generally given in three parts, an announcement of the chapter and its speaker, the first-person litany, and instructions for use. For example, the Chapter of Knowledge:

> THE CHAPTER OF KNOWING THE "CHAPTERS OF COMING FORTH BY DAY" IN A SINGLE CHAPTER. The overseer of the palace, the chancellor-in-chief, Osiris Nu, triumphant, begotten of the overseer of the palace, Amen-hetep, triumphant, saith:
>
> "I am Yesterday and To-morrow; and I have the power to be born a second time. [I am] the divine hidden Soul, who createth the gods, and who giveth sepulchral meals to the divine hidden beings [in the Tuat (underworld)], in Amenti, and in heaven. [I am] the rudder of the east, the possessor of two divine faces wherein his beams are seen. I am the lord of those who are raised up, [the lord] who cometh forth from out of the darkness. . . . I am the god of the Inundation *(Bāh)*, and 'Qem-ur-she' is my name. My forms are the forms of the god Khepera, the hair of the earth of Tem, the hair of the earth of Tem. I have entered in as a man of no understanding, and I shall come forth in the form of a strong *Khu*, and I shall look upon my form which shall be that of men and women forever and forever."
>
> I. [IF THIS CHAPTER BE KNOWN] BY A MAN HE SHALL COME FORTH BY DAY, AND HE SHALL NOT BE REPULSED AT ANY GATE OF THE TUAT (UNDERWORLD),

> EITHER IN GOING IN OR IN COMING OUT. HE SHALL PERFORM [ALL] THE TRANSFORMATIONS WHICH HIS HEART SHALL DESIRE FOR HIM AND HE SHALL NOT DIE; BEHOLD, THE SOUL OF [THIS] MAN SHALL FLOURISH. AND MOREOVER, IF [HE] KNOW THIS CHAPTER HE SHALL BE VICTORIOUS UPON EARTH AND IN THE UNDERWORLD, AND HE SHALL PERFORM EVERY ACT OF A LIVING HUMAN BEING. NOW IT IS A GREAT PROTECTION WHICH [HATH BEEN GIVEN] BY THE GOD. THIS CHAPTER WAS FOUND IN THE FOUNDATIONS OF THE SHRINE OF HENNU BY THE CHIEF MASON DURING THE REIGN OF HIS MAJESTY THE KING OF THE NORTH AND OF THE SOUTH, HESEPTI, TRIUMPHANT, WHO CARRIED [IT] AWAY AS A MYSTERIOUS OBJECT WHICH HAD NEVER [BEFORE] BEEN SEEN OR LOOKED UPON. THIS CHAPTER SHALL BE RECITED BY A MAN WHO IS CEREMONIALLY CLEAN AND PURE, WHO HATH NOT EATEN THE FLESH OF ANIMALS OR FISH, AND WHO HATH NOT HAD INTERCOURSE WITH WOMEN. (46–48)

This next passage is from a different papyrus containing the same chapter but different instructions, these directed at the deceased but containing largely the same promises:

> II. IF THIS CHAPTER BE KNOWN [BY THE DECEASED] HE SHALL BE VICTORIOUS BOTH UPON EARTH AND IN THE UNDERWORLD, AND HE SHALL PERFORM EVERY ACT OF A LIVING HUMAN BEING. NOW IT IS A GREAT PROTECTION WHICH [HATH BEEN GIVEN] BY THE GOD.
>
> THIS CHAPTER WAS FOUND IN THE CITY OF KHEMENNU, UPON A BLOCK OF IRON OF THE SOUTH, WHICH HAD BEEN INLAID [WITH LETTERS] OF REAL LAPIS-LAZULI, UNDER THE FEET OF THE GOD DURING THE REIGN OF HIS MAJESTY, THE KING OF THE NORTH AND OF THE SOUTH, MEN-KAU-RA (MYCERINUS) TRIUMPHANT, BY THE ROYAL SON HERU-TA-TA-F, TRIUMPHANT; HE FOUND IT WHEN HE WAS JOURNEYING ABOUT TO MAKE AN INSPECTION OF THE TEMPLES. ONE NEKHT(?) WAS WITH HIM WHO WAS DILIGENT IN MAKING HIM TO UNDERSTAND(?) IT, AND HE BROUGHT IT TO THE KING AS A WONDERFUL OBJECT WHEN HE SAW THAT IT WAS A THING OF GREAT MYSTERY, WHICH HAD NEVER [BEFORE] BEEN SEEN OR LOOKED UPON.
>
> THIS CHAPTER SHALL BE RECITED BY A MAN WHO IS CEREMONIALLY CLEAN AND PURE, WHO HATH NOT EATEN THE FLESH OF ANIMALS OR FISH, AND WHO HATH NOT HAD INTERCOURSE WITH WOMEN. AND BEHOLD, THOU SHALT MAKE A SCARAB OF GREEN STONE, WITH A RIM PLATED(?) WITH GOLD, WHICH SHALL BE PLACED IN THE HEART OF A MAN, AND IT SHALL PERFORM FOR HIM THE "OPENING OF THE MOUTH." AND THOU SHALT ANOINT IT WITH *ANTI* UNGUENT, AND THOU SHALT RECITE OVER IT [THESE] ENCHANTMENTS. (48)

Note several things about these instructions. First, the ceremonial purifications they describe—bathing, fasting, sexual abstinence—are prescribed for and undergone by Lucius as well. When he says that the priest interpreted for him out of the books what must be done, this may be what he meant. Since his initiation was a visionary enactment of death and the journey to the underworld, and since the Book of the Dead was designed precisely to prepare the traveler (dead or alive) for that trip, the idea would also have been for Lucius to *learn* the chapters, to *know* them, so as to be able to recite them when he died, primarily, and secondarily when he underwent initiation. Since Lucius doesn't read Egyptian, and Mithras only reads them to him once, he can hardly *learn* them; all he can do is sit passively and listen while they are *recited* to him by his ritual translator—as if he were already dead and at his own funeral. This is one of the prices paid in importing a foreign religion. The sacred litanies that must be spoken to gain power over the guardians of the afterlife become accessible only through one or another more or less inadequate compromise: (a) training for all initiates in the original language, such as Bacon and Schopenhauer and more recent professors of these original languages have called for, and as is common practice within Judaism and Islam; or (b) further mystification of the mysteries through concealment in a foreign language, with a gain in solemnity and a loss in understanding (cf. the Latin Mass until Vatican II); or (c) demystification of the mysteries through the universalization and simplification of their semantic content and the propagation of absolute translatability. Psychologically speaking, of course, the important thing for Lucius' initiation is that he be prepared mentally and emotionally by Mithras' translation to experience the mystical experience along the desired lines.

Second, the two papyri give instructions to, respectively, the living and the dead, and the instructions and promises are almost identical, with the exception that a living person recites the litany her/himself while a dead person has it recited over his corpse by a ceremonially purified person (a priest, probably), after this person had placed a scarab in it and anointed it. Still, both the living and the dead are promised victory on earth and in the underworld.

Third, both papyri speak of the chapter as a transcription of a "mysterious object which had never [before] been seen or looked upon," or "a thing of great mystery, which had never [before] been seen or looked upon." Does mystery mean secrecy here? Almost certainly not. The term seems, in fact, almost synonymous with "wonder," as "mysterious object" in the first papyrus is equivalent to both "wonderful object" and "thing of mystery" in the second—something that awakened the wonder or awe of the beholder. It is a found object that is picked up by a humble workman or the royal son and taken to the king. It is covered with strange writing, perhaps difficult to understand (hence mysterious?), but someone understands it and recognizes its sacred power. It is almost certainly a taboo object.

Fourth, at no point is secrecy required of those who read the text—only ritual purification, which merely indicates that the chapter is of such mighty sacred power that an unclean person could be destroyed by it. No one is told to place a seal on the chapter, as would later be the case with Greek and Latin mystical writings (including, in the Judeo-Christian tradition, apocalypses). There are no warnings against translating or otherwise revealing the chapter to the profane. In fact, in a later "Coming Forth By Day" chapter, instructions are given either to recite the litany over the deceased or to inscribe it on his coffin (57)—in other words, the sacred text is made public, read aloud at a funeral and/or written on the coffin that is borne ceremonially through the streets, accompanied by the singing of hymns, the "burden" of which, as Epiphanius Wilson writes in his introduction to the volume, was always "To the West!" (v). Earlier, during the procession in which he is transformed from an ass back into a man, Lucius sees a ship "consecrated and dedicated to the Goddess . . . with Egyptian hieroglyphics painted over the entire hull" (Graves 273); the sail too is covered with "the prayer for the Goddess's protection of shipping during the new sailing season" (Graves 273–74)—in what language the prayer is written, and how he knows what it is about if it is in Egyptian, Lucius doesn't tell us.

These points suggest that the Book of the Dead became off-limits to the profane, and therefore was not to be translated except within the ritual space, only when the Isiac cult moved to Greece and Rome. This supposition in turn would imply the religious use of what V. N. Voloshinov calls the "alien word" to heighten and mystify priestly authority over the laity:

> The first philologists and the first linguists were everywhere priests. History knows no nation whose sacred writings or oral tradition were not to some degree in a language foreign and incomprehensible to the profane. To decipher the mystery of sacred words was the task meant to be carried out by the priest-philologist.
>
> It was on these grounds that ancient philosophy of language was engendered; the Vedic teaching about the word, the Logos of the ancient Greek thinkers, and the biblical philosophy of the word.
>
> To understand these philosophemes properly, one must not forget for one instant that they were *philosophemes of the alien word.* If some nation had known only its own native tongue; if, for that nation, word had always coincided with native word of that nation's life; if no mysterious, alien word, no word from a foreign tongue, had ever entered its purview, then such a nation would never have created anything resembling these philosophemes. . . .
>
> One is sensible of one's native word in a completely different way or, to be more precise, one is ordinarily not sensible of one's native word as a word crammed with all those categories that it has generated in linguistic thought and that it generated in the philosophical-religious thought of the ancients. Native word is one's "kith and kin"; we feel about it as we feel about our habitual attire or, even better, about the atmosphere in which we habitually live and breathe. It contains no mystery; it can become a mystery only in the mouth of others, provided they are hierarchically alien to us—in the mouth of the chief, in the mouth of the priests. But in that case, it has already become a word of a different kind, externally changed and removed from the routine of life (taboo for usage in ordinary life, or an archaism of speech); that is, if it had not already been from the start a foreign word in the mouth of a conqueror-chief. Only at this point is the "Word" born, and only at this point—*incipit philosophia, incipit philologia.* (74–75)

Mystery, in this reading, is a by-product of the alienation of language from ordinary everyday use, so that, whether Lucius is required to learn Egyptian or to listen to the priest reading from the Book of the Dead in

Egyptian or is given semantic access to the litanies through ritual translation, the somatic effect on him is very much the same: to envelop what he hears in mystery, in anxiety and fear, in an aura of deep and awesome solemnity—in taboo.

Of Doves and Oak Trees

In *The Poetics of Translation* Willis Barnstone advances an intriguing theory that parallels mine in some suggestive ways: "Translation," he says bluntly, referring specifically to the translation of sacred texts, "denies itself. Since it popularly signifies unoriginality it is taboo for religious authors—and even more so for gods. Any authentic self-esteeming god or goddess must deny being born of translation. What powers would remain were it known that a century earlier a divinity was working for another civilization?" (144). Thus, for example, the Canaanite word for "gods," Elohim (plural of *el* "god"), is "translated" into Hebrew by a writer whom Bible scholars call the Elohist as the name of a single god, the only god, whom another writer, the Jahwist, calls YHWH or Yahweh. The plural form of the foreign word is retained but employed in Hebrew with singular forms of the verb: *Gods is,* which the translators for King James render "the LORD is." "Among its many tricks and faces," as Barnstone comments, "*translation is divine reincarnation,* a way of reincarnating into biblical figures the deities of the Canaanites, and even of the Sumerians and Babylonians who gave their gods, under changing alibis, to the peoples of the Near East, including the Jews and the Greeks" (142). And aphoristically, "*translation is frequently a historical process for creating originals*" (141).

But not always. Barnstone's own discussion makes it amply clear that, despite his bold statement to the contrary, translation even of sacred texts doesn't always deny itself. In Mesopotamia, he shows, "translation of religious scriptures was common" (146)—and, apparently, unabashed, judging from texts like "the seventh-century B.C. bilingual Akkadian/Sumerian hymn to the moon god Sin" (146). Could it be that more primitive religions actually translated *more,* and more freely, than the mystery religions of the classical era? This freedom of translation would make sense in terms of the general consensus that the ban on divulging the mysteries was a late development in the mystery cults: that no secrecy was involved in the more primitive forms of vegetation worship and that the mysteries only began to be protected against the profane as the religions became increasingly institutionalized (and, as we'll see in a moment, increasingly rationalist).

There's an interesting parallel with this (possible) development in the genesis of a story of translation as it is passed from the Egyptians through Herodotus to Plato's Socrates. Herodotus makes no bones about it: the Greeks borrowed their religion (and just about everything else of value) from the Egyptians through a process of cultural translation. In book two of his *Histories,* the section devoted to Egypt, he documents at length the borrowings or translations of Egyptian gods and goddesses into Greek and the later and rather pathetic attempts Greeks made to explain the many similarities between their own deities and the more ancient ones of Egypt (Herakles, for example, traveled to Egypt and was captured by the Egyptians—"one of the silliest," Herodotus says, "of many [Greek] stories with no basis in fact" [147]). For the translation scholar the most interesting tale he tells of cultural translation from Egypt to Greece is this one:

> About the oracles—that of Dodona in Greece and of Ammon in Libya—the Egyptians have the following legend: according to the priests of the Theban Zeus, two women connected with the service of the temple were carried off by the Phoenicians and sold, one in Libya and the other in Greece, and it was these women who founded the oracles in the two countries. I asked the priests at Thebes what grounds they had for being so sure about this, and they told me that careful search had been made for the women at the time, and that though it was unsuccessful, they had afterwards learned that the facts were just as they had reported them. At Dodona, however, the priestesses who deliver the oracles have a different version of the story: two black doves, they say, flew away from Thebes in Egypt, and one of them alighted at Dodona, the other in Libya. The former, perched on an oak, and speaking with a human voice, told them that there, on that very spot, there should be an oracle of Zeus. Those who heard her understood the words to be a command from heaven, and at once obeyed. Similarly the dove which flew to Libya told the Libyans to found the oracle of Ammon—which is also an oracle of Zeus. The people who gave me this information were the three priestesses at Dodona—Promeneia the eldest, Timarete the next, and Nicandra the youngest—and their account is confirmed by the other Dodonaeans connected with the temple. Personally, however, I would suggest that if the Phoenicians really carried off the women from the temple and sold them respectively in Libya and Greece, the one who was brought to Greece (or Pelasgia as it was then called) must have been sold to the Thesprotians; and later, while she was working as a slave in that part of the country, she built, under an oak that happened to be growing there, a shrine to Zeus; for she would naturally remember in her exile the god whom she had served in her native Thebes. Subsequently, when she had learned to speak Greek, she established an oracle there, and mentioned, in addition, that the same Phoenicians who had sold her, also sold her sister in Libya. The story which the people of Dodona tell about the doves came, I should say, from the fact that the women were foreigners, whose language sounded to them like the twittering of birds; later on the dove spoke with a human voice, because by that time the woman had stopped twittering and learned to talk intelligibly. That, at least, is how I should explain the obvious impossibility of a dove using the language of men. As to the bird being black, they merely signify by this that the woman was an Egyptian. It is certainly true that the oracles at Thebes and Dodona are similar in character. (151–52)

The two legendary priestesses, captured and sold into slavery in what would later become Libya and Greece, are translators by necessity: finding themselves in lands where no one understands their Egyptian speech, they learn the local language and translate their worship of Amon-Ra into local cults, the priestess at Dodona into a Greek cult of Zeus.

But note now what happens when that great "rationalist" Socrates, Herodotus' younger contemporary, picks up this story and retells it in Plato's *Phaedrus*. Socrates has been telling the story of the invention of all "learning"—"number and calculation, geometry and astronomy, not to speak of draughts and dice, and above all writing" (274d)—by the Egyptian god Theuth (or Thoth): Theuth/Thoth and Theban king Thamus discuss the value of the various branches of learning, and Thamus accepts all the gifts but writing, saying that "If men learn this, it will implant forgetfulness in their souls; they will cease to exercise memory because they rely on that which is written, calling things to remembrance no longer from within themselves, but by means of external marks" (275a). Writing is an externalization of memory that alienates the knower from what he or she knows. Phaedrus calls this story Socrates' fabrication, and Socrates snaps back with a story he remembers out of Herodotus, which he may have heard Herodotus himself declaim at a festival gathering (internal evidence in the *Histories* suggests that Herodotus lived for a time in Athens and knew Sophocles personally):

> Oh, but the authorities of the temple of Zeus at Dodona, my friend, said that the first prophetic utterances came from an oak tree. In fact the people of those days, lacking the wisdom of you young people, were content in their simplicity to listen to trees or rocks, provided these told the truth. For you apparently it makes a difference who the speaker is, and what country he comes from; you don't merely ask whether what he says is true or false. (275bc)

Gone here is the Egyptian source of the bird, and of the bird's voice, and of the story itself, which Herodotus specifically tells us he first heard, in a rather less mythological form, from the Egyptian priests at Thebes. Gone indeed is the bird-speaker, as Socrates seems to be saying that the oak tree itself, or a divinity through the oak tree, utters the prophecy: a tree is patently more "Greek," more geographically stable, and thus more indigenously "divine," than birds that fly across cultural boundaries. In Socrates' telling, the story has lost all traces of translation from Egyptian to Greek; in citing his sources for Phaedrus ("the authorities of the temple of Zeus at Dodona"), Socrates has "forgotten" or repressed not only the Egyptian priests and abducted Egyptian women, but Herodotus as well, the Greek source who "remembers" too much about Greek indebtedness to Egypt—remembers too much, in fact, about translation. The mystagogic imagination of Socrates invents a mythic "fall" of sorts from the people of an earlier day who heard unmediated mystical truth and obeyed regardless of the source, to the young people of his own day who ask "who the speaker is, and what country he comes from"—never mentioning, of course, that *his* source, Herodotus, was himself a skeptical and modern "person of an earlier day" (fifteen or twenty years older than Socrates) who asked "who the speaker is, and what country he comes from." And while Socrates nostalgically refuses to "fall" with Phaedrus, clinging instead to the mystical *spoken* voice of truth, clearly this rationalist "fall" is the trend of ancient civilization, aided and abetted by Plato himself—as by Herodotus before him.

But in fact the situation is more complex than that. I want to develop the complexity slowly in the rest of this chapter and throughout the next; but it seems plausible to me to suggest tentatively that Socrates' denial or repression of translation is at least as strongly conditioned by his emergent rationalism as it is by his continuing attachment to mystery (the divine voice out of the oak tree). The "modern" temper that asks "who the speaker is, and what country he comes from" is embodied not only in Phaedrus, the young Greek skeptic, but in Socrates himself, in the very anxiety that makes him feel defensive about Phaedrus' skepticism and compelled to ridicule it. Socrates taboos and represses the cultural fact of translation partly out of a continuing reverence for divinity, but partly also out of a need to control knowledge, to impose rational constraints on who knows what and how. His is a transitional, early-rationalist stance exactly parallel to the mystery religions' intensifying need to maintain strict boundaries between initiates and the profane. Paradoxically, Herodotus seems at once more calmly rational than Plato's Socrates, more willing to explore the historical roots of Greek religion, and more calmly mystical, more pious in his respect for the arcane mysteries. "I have already mentioned the festival of Isis at Busiris," he writes; "it is here that everybody—tens of thousands of men and women—when the sacrifice is over, beat their breasts; in whose honour, however, I do not feel it is proper for me to say" (153). Socrates is violently invested in his beliefs, mystical and rational alike, and rebounds in Plato's dialogues from tendentious humor to dogmatic insistence—an eerily modern model for rationalist thought that I'll be exploring at length in the next chapter. Herodotus, whose charming, easy-going inquiries into the nature and origins of various cultural events and phenomena seem by contrast far more "rational"—in the idealized sense, meaning calm, unobsessed, undriven by deep-seated emotional conflicts and needs—may actually be not only the older but the more primitive man.

Death and Taboo

Compare this conflicted "drivenness" of the ur-rationalist Socrates now with Walter Burkert's description of Apuleius at the end of *The Golden Ass:*

> The so-called conversion to Isis [of Lucius] does not result in withdrawal from the world and worldly interests; on the contrary, the runaway student who had been roaming wildly through the Greco-Roman world now finally becomes integrated into respectable society. He starts his career as a lawyer in Rome

> and proves to be quite successful. This is felt to be a result of the favor of Isis and Osiris: they are givers of riches, *ploutodotai*, quite deservedly in this case because the repeated initiations had literally cost a fortune and deprived the man from Madaura of all his father's inheritance. Indeed, the man's success is so remarkable that it arouses envy; this brings on a new nervous crisis with anxiety, sleep disturbances, and noctural visions. The initiation therefore must be repeated once again; the god then personally assures the ambitious man that he should pursue his glorious career without qualms, and himself elects him to a respected and unassailable position in the collegium of the *pastophori* of the Egyptian gods. Professional stress is alleviated by a religious hobby, with the mystery god taking the position of psychiatrist. Whatever the autobiographical content of this story may be, the therapy is seen to make sense. (17)

Burkert calls this a "so-called conversion to Isis" because he wants to polarize the mystical experience and conversion. Regarding the oath of secrecy sworn by Isiac mystai at the initiation ceremony, "by the gods I revere," Burkert writes: "This, of course, is the absolute opposite of 'conversion,' of the injunction to 'burn what you have adored.' There is no unsettling or destroying of personality in mystery initiations of this kind, but rather a deepening or extending of preexisting piety through a new intimacy with the divine in both familiar and novel shapes" (50). As usual, here Burkert is eager to drive absolute wedges between the mysteries and Christianity: whereas conversion requires the destruction of personality, the burning of what you adored, the mysteries didn't require this, so they had nothing to do with conversion. But of course Christian conversion can also be "a deepening or extending of preexisting piety"; and Lucius does undergo quite a remarkable conversion in the course of the book, a conversion that comes to a dramatic crisis on the beach at Cenchreae and is merely affirmed in the initiation ceremony.

Burkert's key observation here for my purposes is that Lucius experiences "a new nervous crisis with anxiety, sleep disturbances, and noctural visions," necessitating a new initiation, which sounds very much like the process of habituation or tolerance familiar to us from addictions: Lucius needs a new fix. Burkert wants to attribute Lucius's anxiety response to envy, a reading for which there is only problematic textual evidence: the only reference to envy in Lucius's narrative comes *after* his third initiation, after the event that supposedly alleviated his envy-caused stress, when Osiris appears to him in a dream and tells him "that I should not fear the slanders of the malevolent who naturally disliked me on account of the learning I had studiously acquired" (Lindsay 254). It is not that worldly success provokes envy, which leads to stress, which is alleviated by what Burkert rather disparagingly calls his "religious hobby"; the envy Osiris warns him against will itself *be provoked by* his devotion to Isis and Osiris. This "hobby," clearly, is a far more mixed bag for Lucius than Burkert will admit.

In fact it's probably a more mixed bag than even Lucius will admit. The promise of "spiteful slanders" is the only sour note he strikes in these concluding pages of his narrative—the only hint of unpleasantness in the narrative, in fact, since his transformation back into human form. And this hint comes from the god Osiris, who is not only warning him against but in an important sense also delivering him up to these "spiteful slanders," putting him at odds with himself and his society—in the same breath as he is promising to carry him through the hard times and to throw good jobs in his way (which may earn him some of the envy Burkert mentions). There is, of course, a significant difference between telling someone not to be afraid and actually assuaging that fear—especially when the promised frightening experience is still in the future. It seems to me that Lucius's initiations make him feel both better and worse—a strange somatic complex that will need some unpacking as we proceed.

The "therapeutic" or analgesic impact of Lucius's initiations that Burkert points to is obviously there, undeniably part of the equation—but only part. Burkert claims that the "most precious gift of Isis, the gift of life . . . evidently means life in this world of ours. It must be a 'new life,' since the old one has worn down and is about to break" (18). I take it he hasn't read the Egyptian Book of the Dead, which explicitly and repeatedly promises power over both this life and the next. "This, then, must have been the immediate experience of successful mysteries: 'feeling better now'" (19). Well, yes—but maybe there's more to it than that? More to the immediate experience, and more to the experience than its immediate aspect? Surely a part of even the immediate experience would have been a belief that this "feeling better now" would, at the very least, guarantee bliss after death? There must have been an eschatological component to this therapeutic transformation, but we rational moderns feel uneasy about that stuff (we know, don't we, that such "supernatural etiologies" are sheer fictions anyway, so why pay attention to them?), and so Burkert downplays the transformation, psychologizes it in order to dismiss it: "Thus mysteries were meeting practical needs even in their promises for an afterlife. It remains for us to wonder what really constituted the intrinsic unity of these two dimensions of mysteries—realistic cures and immunizations, on the one hand, and imaginary guarantees of bliss after death, on the other" (23).

Because Burkert fancies himself modern enough and rational enough to be immune to "imaginary guarantees of bliss after death," he believes that the "practical needs" those guarantees met were purely analgesic—designed to diminish the initiate's fear of death and make him "feel better now." But one of the things that reading the Egyptian Book of the Dead even in English does for me is to impress on me the potential terror of any direct or indirect mystical experience of the events it describes—events that are, after all, as the book's title itself proclaims, experienced by the *dead*. The book is a manual for dead people, or for people who will one day be dead, outlining just what is going to happen to them when they die and what they have to do to survive the dangers of the underworld—what ritual (largely verbal) protection they must have in order not to die the second death that lasts forever, in order to have eternal life and to perform in death "EVERY ACT OF A

LIVING HUMAN BEING." Wouldn't this have raised the hairs on the back of Lucius's neck? Our civilization has collectively devoted more than a few centuries to the demystification of death, usually through its remystification along less terrifying lines: the Christian talk of walking through the gates of paradise (it's always the other guy who's going to hell); the funeral-home rhetoric of eternal rest; the pharmaceutical dulling of death at the end of an IV drip or the quick plunge of a hypodermic needle; the hiding of death behind closed nursing home and hospital doors.

How much more terrifying, then, is a text about death that is not written in my language—a sacred document that makes no sense to me but is treated with reverent care by foreign priests before whom I stand in awe, carefully stored in the temple and retrieved only after ritual purification, its pages festooned with what look like mystical characters and figures? It is a book about death, written in the language of the true goddess and god, Isis and Osiris, possibly by their very hands, at least from their dictation, and translated into Greek by Egyptian priests only within the ritual space. This would, unquestionably, be a book of great power, or what the Polynesians and Melanesians called mana, an overwhelmingly powerful energy that would kill or maim anyone not specially suited or trained to withstand it.

Much has been written on mana and taboo in this century, most of it tending to discredit the most famous Victorian theorist of taboo, James Frazer, whose work (relying heavily on his theologian predecessor Robertson Smith) tended to associate taboo with "primitive" religions and thus tacitly (and sometimes not so tacitly) to dignify major world religions like Christianity as "beyond" such ancient superstitions. All of the significant work on taboo in the twentieth century—by Sigmund Freud, Franz Steiner, Mary Douglas, and others—has confirmed that taboo is, if not intrinsically human, then at least incredibly tenacious, able to survive generation after generation of "modern" enlightenment, rationalism, demystification, and certainly as much with us today as it ever was.

Freud's *Totem and Taboo*, a title I am obviously playing on in my own, has passed the test of time surprisingly well—except for his speculative tracing of all totem and taboo back to a single cannibalistic act of patricide—especially considering that he wrote it not too many years after Frazer wrote and relied heavily on Frazer's books in his research. Freud defines taboo fairly traditionally, at first: "The meaning of 'taboo', as we see it, diverges in two contrary directions. To us it means, on the one hand, 'sacred', 'consecrated', and on the other 'uncanny', 'dangerous', 'forbidden', 'unclean'. The converse of 'taboo' in Polynesian is '*noa*', which means 'common' or 'generally accessible'. Thus 'taboo' has about it a sense of something unapproachable, and it is principally expressed in prohibitions and restrictions" (18)—except often not overt prohibitions. Taboo is often something one tacitly understands, something one picks up from other people's behavior, something that is not spelled out and doesn't need to be. Taboo restrictions, Freud notes, "have no grounds and are of unknown origin"; they seem to come from nowhere or "to impose themselves on their own account" (18).

"The source of taboo," Freud writes, summarizing an ethnographic account of taboo by Northcote W. Thomas, "is attributed to a peculiar magical power which is inherent in persons and spirits and can be conveyed by them through the medium of inanimate objects" (20)—including pieces of writing, which thereby become "holy writ," sacred (i.e., taboo) texts. Certainly the Egyptian Book of the Dead was a taboo object in the priest's room, to be touched only by the priest, to be picked up only by him, to be read out of and translated from only by him. "As in the case of taboo," Freud notes of obsessional behavior, "the principal prohibition, the nucleus of the neurosis, is against touching" (27), and in important ways translation is an extension of touching: first you touch the sacred text with your hands, then you touch it with another language. In the Hebrew Bible the Philistines capture the Ark of the Covenant and are beset with seven months of plagues, so they give it back; in subsequent battle against the Philistines the Ark is kept near the front on a cart, and when it suddenly tilts Uzzah steadies it with his hand and is struck dead on the spot (2 Samuel 6:6–7). The Hebrew Bible has been translated many times, but it remains sacred for Jews in the Hebrew original and is touched by Torah scholars only with the *yad*, a symbolic hand, never with any actual part of the body. Devout Muslim readers of the Koran are similarly taught to touch the physical book only with "clean hands," after washing up. And the Christian Bible, as I mentioned earlier, remains taboo to us enlightened moderns in much the same "ancient" or "primitive" or "superstitious" way: no matter how many theological treatises have been written to demystify the actual physical object, it remains just as difficult to destroy or even damage a Bible today as it ever was. Illiterate Christians in the Middle Ages see the veneration with which the Bible is treated in church and learn not to go near it, not to touch it, not to try to read it, let alone translate it, even if they later go to school and learn Latin—and their fear is still with us today. Taboos do not die easily. They are passed on from generation to generation at deep unconscious levels of our behavior, through the contagion of somatic response.

The same fear would have pervaded the mystery religions as well, where many outsiders participated in the festivities but learned to taboo the mystical relics (including texts) and even the initiates—witness Lucius' splendor before the worshipping crowds after his initiation. Lucius, too, though he is an initiate and even a priest, realizes that the sacred text is not something for him to touch; there's a *reason* for his inability to read it, which is, I presume, that the mysteries are hidden from him in it. Certainly it seems as if the important thing in all this isn't any overt *ban* on translation but an all-pervasive air of taboo surrounding the mysteries and their reliquary, including the texts. You just *know*—you feel it in your whole body, the overwhelmingly contagious awe or domesticated terror or dread with which the priests approach the sacred texts, and then only after ritual purification, because the taboo is ideosomatic and moves from body to body with incredible speed and ease—that you're not supposed to go near the texts. And if through a series of ritual precautions the priests above you convince you that there are ways of handling the texts without being destroyed, you gradually overcome your terror, or perhaps only domesticate it as awe, intense respect, and worship, and learn to handle them—but you certainly don't go around handing them out to just anyone, because you know that "just anyone" would be destroyed, and in fact they know it too, from your body language: your whole body tells them that they should stand back, stay away, not come near.

A useful parallel might be made with the handling of extremely dangerous materials today: you know when you watch a television bomb squad dismantle some terrible explosive device that you would *never* go near it. The actors communicate the danger with their bodies—hands trembling, forehead sweating, nervous glances—and your body nods confirmation. You don't *need* an overt prohibition. Because parents and other adults have drummed into you an ideosomatic dread of certain kinds of their own anxieties—they had to teach you to stay away from electrical outlets and the like when you were small, or their bedroom (especially when the door was closed), or your own genitals—all you have to do (and in fact your body does it for you) is transfer that ideosomatic avoidance behavior to new taboos whenever some authority figure's body language signals that a similar danger exists.

How do we learn, as children, that the Bible or another sacred text is not to be treated like any other book? That it possesses some sacred power that is not to be toyed with? How do we learn, for that matter, that mommy's and daddy's books are to be treated differently from our own? If parents venerate books, their children sense that veneration and very quickly internalize it themselves; the ideosomatics of taboo are intensely contagious. My children scribbled in a few of my books when they were small, between one year and two years old, but the intensity of my horrified anger must have scared them quickly, for they soon stopped—even though they watched *me* marking the margins of the books I read with a pencil. Two or three years later, having internalized the taboo against writing in books but having also learned to analyze and articulate their analyses in language, they asked me why I could write in books and they couldn't. I felt a bit hypocritical and struggled to come up with a plausible justification for my behavior; but my hypocrisy didn't undo my kids' taboo on writing in books. Apparently, in Thomas's terms, my mana was strong enough that I could violate the taboo with impunity—and without diminishing its power in my children's eyes (and bodies).

Taboo, Obsession, Addiction

Freud psychologizes taboo in terms of obsessional behavior: "The most obvious and striking point of agreement between the obsessional prohibitions of neurotics and taboos," he writes, "is that these prohibitions are equally lacking in motive and equally puzzling in their origin. Having made their appearance at some unspecified moment, they are forcibly maintained by an irresistable fear. No external threat of punishment is required, for there is an internal certainty, a moral conviction, that any violation will lead to intolerable disaster" (26–27).

This association is initially attractive: the cult initiate as obsessive personality, sucked into an irrational system of irresistable fear maintained not by external threats but by internal certainties. For that matter, the association can be extended: the foreignizing or domesticating translator as obsessive personality, irrationally afraid of excess "freedom" in every word or phrase choice he or she makes, the foreignizer angry at translators who disregard expressive textures in the source language, the domesticator angry at translators who disregard expressive norms and interpretive needs in the target language. Certainly Freud's analysis of taboo as an obsessional neurosis fits my observation from the introduction, translators and translation theorists freezing up with "prohibitions [that] are equally lacking in motive and equally puzzling in their origin," that "are forcibly maintained by an irresistable fear." We're not yet ready to trace the history of the sacred-book taboo from ancient times to the present, but it seems clear that some sort of powerful taboo is at work in much contemporary translation and translation theory as well. These translators and theorists are too angry at people whose work deviates from their own not to be deeply afraid.

Another and, as I began to suggest above, perhaps a better psychological analogue or modern name for taboo might be addiction, especially in the broad sense of that term, including addiction not only to substances but to behaviors and thought and speech patterns as well—to a wide range of things that may vary in harmfulness but that all progressively enslave the addict. Specifically, taboo is what Gerald G. May calls an "aversive addiction," a slavish attachment to an aversion or an avoidance—examples of which might include phobias, which taboo objects or actions, anorexia nervosa, which taboos food, and bigotries, which taboo groups of people.

Thus we might portray Lucius at the end of *The Golden Ass* as addicted to Isis and Osiris or to the mysteries: just as heroin is terrifying to the nonaddict but gradually becomes heaven on earth to the junkie, so is Lucius gradually habituated to the mysteries, ritually inducted into the "junk" of the Isis cult: the baths, the prayers, the nocturnal visitations, the vestments, the reliquaries, the sacred Egyptian texts, and finally the "trip" itself, the mystical experience, which may or may not have involved the ingestion of hallucinogenic drugs. Having experienced the initiative process once, he can't get enough: as Walter Burkert says, he is soon troubled once more by anxiety, sleeplessness, and nocturnal visions, all of which drive him to be initiated again, and yet again. Apuleius only tells us of three initiations, but there is no reason to assume Lucius stopped there; it was not uncommon in antiquity for mystery junkies to be initiated dozens of times, and not always to the same god: *collecting* initiations and mysteries and deities, as the phenomenon has been seen till now—or, as the addiction analogy would suggest, building *tolerance* to initiation.

And as I will be showing in greater depth in the next chapter, the translator too might be seen as an addict, addicted not only to his or her craft but to a certain phobic or aversive conception or practice of that craft: anxiously shunning or avoiding certain translation approaches or tasks or texts and carefully repressing all traces of that anxiety, letting it surface only indirectly, in the displaced form of hurt anger or dogmatic indignation, whenever anyone questions his or her integrity as a translator (negative critiques from in-house readers, external evaluators, translation reviewers) or when another translator or translation theorist publicly embraces the approach she or he shuns (foreignism for the domesticator, domestication for the foreignizer; pretheoretical anecdotalism for the systems theorist, blandly repressive empiricism for me).

It might be interesting to trace the translator-junkie's progress from repression through denial to rationalization, a three-step motion that might be thought of as the primal scene of translation theory, the process that transforms a translator into a theorist. When repression no longer works, when external assaults on your addiction grow too powerful to ignore, you shift into denial ("What do you mean, addicted, I'm no addict, I'm a translator, it's a perfectly respectable profession"), and when that no longer works, you rationalize your addiction and become a theorist—"Look, the important thing is conveying the textures of the original text to the reader, giving the target reader a feel for the source text, which she or he can't read in the original *(and I'm not phobic about excess freedom!)*," or "If the source text is to *live* in the target-cultural context it is to be written in a vibrant target-language idiom, the target reader has to feel comfortable with it as a work of art in the target culture *(and I'm not phobic about the worship of foreign classics!)*."

Taboo and Ideology

But I remain unconvinced that the taboo-related behavior Freud describes is restricted to a few obsessional neurotics or addicts. Freud's descriptions of "the obsessional prohibitions of neurotics" sound to me far less localized and specialized than he suggests—sound, in fact, very much like somatized ideological norms, the collectively instilled but individually felt injunctions and prohibitions that we call "values," the pricks of "conscience," and so on. And from William Burroughs to Gerald G. May, students of addiction are increasingly convinced that we are all addicts, that addiction is not only humanly normal but ideologically normative—that (though this may just be me pushing it further than most people would want to go) addiction is simply the physiological form that conformity to ideological norms always takes.

Which is not to say, of course, that addiction is always ideologically normal. Addiction to controlled substances like heroin or cocaine is ideologically deviant, addiction to Prozac or Valium is ideologically normal—but this difference, as Deleuze and Guattari would say, is only a cut that the ideological authorities make in the flows of addiction. Addictions to child abuse and date and spouse rape have been ideologically normal for millennia, supported by all our sacred documents and legal institutions; now they are under serious assault from all sides, and in a hundred years may become ideologically deviant. To say that addiction is the normative form of ideological conformity is not to say that all addictions are normative; the isolation of certain addictions as socially deviant is a critical step in the repressive definition of addiction *as* deviant, and thus of ideological conformity as no addiction at all. As William Burroughs would say, calling a heroin addict a junkie is a way of *not* calling law-and-order addicts junkies.

In this expanded sense, then, taboo as obsession or addiction would be the ideosomatic fabric that holds a society together, the shared bodily feel for right and wrong that causes us to shudder at (and feel powerfully and fearfully attracted to) socially deviant behavior:

> Taboo is a primaeval prohibition forcibly imposed (by some authority) from outside, and directed against the most powerful longings to which human beings are subject. The desire to violate it persists in their unconscious; those who obey the taboo have an ambivalent attitude to what the taboo prohibits. The magical power that is attributed to taboo is based on the capacity for arousing temptation; and it acts like a contagion because examples are contagious and because the prohibited desire in the unconscious shifts from one thing to another. The fact that the violation of a taboo can be atoned for by a renunciation shows that renunciation lies at the basis of obedience to taboo. (Freud 34–35)

We are all, in this light, obsessional neurotics and addicts who cling to our "values" or "norms" or "rules" in a desperate bid not so much for social stability, though our clinging does usually have that effect, but for emotional security—an emotional security that, as Freud illustrates at length, is illusory at best, since it rests on the uneasy repression of our own ambivalent desires, our wish to both observe and violate the taboo, to both punish and become the transgressor.

We could thus imagine the rival translation norms that run all through Western history—faithful and free, word-for-word and sense-for-sense, foreignizing and domesticating, source- and target-oriented—as ideosomatic norms powered by taboo. Both sides of the ongoing debate, despite their conflicts, despite the uneasy history of accommodations between them ("as faithful as you can, as free as you must"), are taboo-driven and normative. Both *feel* right; and that "right feel" is enforced socially by somatic anxiety signals whenever a translator wanders too far from either. There is a taboo on translating too freely and another on translating too closely: thus the translator is boxed in by his or her own inwardly conflicted ideosomatic response, the bodily representative of thousands of years of sociopolitical authority, or what Nietzsche called the internalization of mastery.

Translation and the Other

Let me now expand this discussion to fine-tune the conception of "ideology" that I've been invoking rather loosely so far. Just what is ideology, how does it work, where does it get its authority and how does it channel it? Recent Marxist theorists have attempted to refine Marx's conception of ideology by associating it with institutional power, as in Louis Althusser's phrase "ideological state apparatuses," or with the ruling class, as in Antonio Gramsci's term "hegemony," or with the repressed psychic forces that govern us without our knowledge, as in Fredric Jameson's term "the political unconscious." In *The Translator's Turn* I reconceived ideology as ideosomatics, drawing on Jameson's political unconscious but arguing that neomarxist usages remain unspecific about how hegemonic or ideological or political-unconscious norms are transmitted to and enforced in the individual and thus also about how they are handed down from generation to generation. My theory of ideosomatics was an attempt to trace the inscribing of collective ideology or hegemony onto individual subject bodies and then into the enforcement of hegemonic norms in those individuals' behavior through somatic response.

Here, however, I want to move beyond that *Translator's Turn* terminology to a conceptual framework that I developed in *Ring Lardner and the Other;* there I still spoke of ideosomatics, but I particularized this term further by conflating Michel Foucault's concept of "discourses of power" with Jacques Lacan's concept of the unconscious as the "discourse of the Other" and speaking of the Other in a succession of overtly politicized (but also always psychological) forms: the Other-as-parent and the Other-as-child, the Other-as-father and the (m)Other-as-child, the Other-as-majority and the Other-as-minority, the Other-as-culture and the Other-as-anarchy. This proliferation of Other-speakers enabled me to explore what Bakhtin might call an authoritarian heteroglossia, the multitude of "voices" or forces (verbal or otherwise) that come from outside us through our interactions with authority in society but are felt inside us as inward somatic pressures to act, feel, speak, and believe in certain ways and to avoid acting, feeling, speaking, and believing in certain other ways. In his introduction to Lacan appended to his translation of Lacan's *Speech and Language in Psychoanalysis,* Anthony Wilden provides a useful nondefinition of the Other, a definition by association:

> It is not possible, for instance, to define the Other in any definite way, since for Lacan it has a functional value, representing both the "significant other" to whom the neurotic's demands are addressed (the appeal of the Other), as well as the internalization of this Other (we desire what the Other desires) and the unconscious subject himself [or herself] (the unconscious is the discourse of—or from—the Other). In another context, it will simply mean the category of "Otherness," a translation Lacan has himself employed. Sometimes "the Other refers to the parents: to the mother as the "real Other" (in the dual relationship of mother and child), to the father as the "Symbolic Other," yet it is never a *person.* Very often the term seems to refer simply to the unconscious

itself, although the unconscious is most often described as "the locus of the Other." (263–64)

In the terms I used in *Lardner*, the Other is "an internalized Voice that, in Lacan's psychologization of Heidegger's language mysticism, *speaks us*" (42); my project there was to politicize what Lacan psychologized, to explore the speaking of various social power-voices inside our heads, as well as certain childish, rebellious, minoritarian voices that help us resist absolute assimilation to power norms. In the transition from *The Translator's Turn* to *Ring Lardner and the Other*, ideosomatics (and Bakhtin's authoritative word) became the internalized power-voices, the Other-as-parent, the Other-as-majority, the Other-as-culture, and idiosomatics (and Bakhtin's internally persuasive word) became the internalized voices of rebellion, resistance, refusal, or of childish playfulness, the Other-as-child, the Other-as-minority, the Other-as-anarchy. I plug Bakhtin into those transitional dualisms now because, in the course of discussing his distinction in the "Dialogue Contra Instrumentalism" section of *The Translator's Turn* (114), I discovered that idiosomatics is never purely individual, never strictly speaking idio-anything; and if the voices or somatic forces that enable us to fight back against ideosomatic programming come from outside, too, if we somatize them out of our ongoing dialogues with other people, then the Other can be deviant, antirepressive, antiauthoritarian as well.

Myriam Díaz-Diocaretz has a similar notion in *Translating Poetic Discourse*, where she speaks of the "translator-function," a construct that she adapts from Foucault's "author-function." This adaptation has immediate appeal: it would suggest that the idealized roles that society assigns actual translators, the way societal Others "speak" us as translators, guide our transfers from source to target cultures in socially acceptable ways. The "self" or "persona" who translates appropriately, correctly, acceptably is thus no holistic person, steeped in a wealth of specific experiences and driven by emotional and intellectual motives, needs, intentions, but rather a collectivized actant, a social function, a "translator-function" that is wielded by society's need to regulate translation ideologically.

But this is not how Díaz-Diocaretz uses the term. In her book it becomes a kind of idealized (abstracted) form of the translator-as-active-subject—she repeatedly refers to what *her* translator-function did, as if she controlled it, as if it were her slave, her robot, the minion of her desires. In Lacan's psychology this is the role of the Subject, that mask that comes to seem like your whole personality but is really only an idealized self, the persona you project outward into the world in order to *conceal* your conflicted motives, your (failed) attempts to model yourself on other people (your father, your mother, your lover), your utter susceptibility to the whispering of a million collective Others. The translator-function in Díaz-Diocaretz's sense is the translator's public mask, designed, constructed, and maintained in order to control readers' approach to the target text. The translator-function in Foucault's sense would be *society's* ideal or abstraction or robotic role, instilled "in" the translator but (in Lacan's terms) "behind" the translator's Subject, wielding or "speaking" that Subject through an Other-voice in deep cover.

Or rather, it would *be* that Other-voice, those Other-voices, all the ways that society uses the translator to ferry vetted messages from robotized authors to robotized readers (and also, of course, the ways in which various rebellious Others thwart and subvert those messages or their transmission). The construction of the translatorial Other-as-culture or hegemonic "translator-function" is one of the great achievements of the Christian Middle Ages, that which made it possible to stop protecting the lay public from the Bible and to translate the Bible into the vernacular. Until that Other was constructed and rendered fully operational in every translator's and reader's head, translation of the Bible had to be banned.

Mystery and Reason

The two Other-voices that I want to adapt to my discussion of translation and taboo are the Other-as-culture and the Other-as-anarchy, though the connotations of "anarchy" may in this case be slightly misleading. I want to posit two consecutive but overlapping Others-as-culture: an Other-as-mystery that ruled over ancient civilization and was, from about the fifth century B.C.E. to about the fifteenth century C.E., in what was during the same period coming to be called the "West," only very gradually overthrown and superseded (but never quite banished) by an Other-as-reason, which rules over or "speaks" us today. The Other-as-mystery would have been the force that once, in "prerational" civilization, tabooed consciousness—or rather, that instituted a bodily knowing-without-knowing, a knowing-without-being-able-to-tell, an inarticulate understanding that could never prove that it understands because that would entail articulation. The only proper or possible response to the speaking of the Other-as-mystery is an experience of light, of sight, an inarticulate "hey, wow, now I see"—the opening of the eyes in the mystical experience, while the lips remain sealed. For the Other-as-mystery, there is no proof. There is no verification or duplication. There is understanding and not-understanding.

Because the Other-as-mystery imposes a restriction on conscious or articulate knowing, however, on understanding and telling, it creates within itself, through repression or negation, its own rebellious or "anarchistic" counterpart, the Other-as-reason, which is a kind of Other-as-child, the Other that says at the emperor's parade, "But Daddy, he isn't wearing any clothes!" The tailors in the story of the emperor's new clothes are spoken by the Other-as-mystery: they mystify the emperor and the townspeople about the very act or state of wearing clothes, of being dressed, so that people, including the emperor himself, become able to "see" (or at least not-not-see) clothes that aren't there.

Spoken as powerfully as we are by the Other-as-reason, this part of the story seems odd to us; how is it possible for the townspeople to not-see the emperor's nakedness? But of course we not-see the emptiness of advertisers' images, politicians' promises, and normative scholarly assumptions all the time. Clothes seem so much more tangible than promises that we think it would take a crazy or strung-out person, a schizophrenic, a junkie, to see clothes on a naked man. But there was a time in the history of the "West"—the territory controlled militarily by the Roman church by about the tenth century C.E.—when the Other-as-mystery spoke much more powerfully than it does today and the Other-as-reason's voice was weak; also, and in many ways more importantly, the relative strength of the Other-as-reason's voice in our society today has the effect of blinding us to the continuing strength of the Other-as-mystery in our everyday lives. We too are mystified by thousands of perfectly ordinary lies every day. Sexism, racism, ageism, homophobia, xenophobia of all sorts would be impossible without the speaking of the Other-as-mystery. Politics and economics would be impossible without the speaking of the Other-as-mystery. For that matter, science and logic, the Other-as-reason's domain, would be impossible without the speaking of the Other-as-mystery: who would believe generalizations from statistics or argumentation, predictions based on probabilities or plausible premises, if the Other-as-mystery weren't whispering in our ears?

The child who "notices" the emperor's nakedness at the parade, then, is the becoming-articulate that the Other-as-mystery had repressed. As rebellious forces in ancient society are increasingly spoken by this childish Other-as-reason and insist more and more on blurting out what they know to all and sundry, the Other-as-reason begins to accrue power, patriarchal power wielded socially by a male despot and his rationalist advisors, later by the advisors (Parliament in parliamentary monarchy, later the legislative, executive, and judicial branches of representative democracy), and finally (or ideally) by the principle of rational advisor or advice internalized by every member of the society. But just as the despot could only replace the mystagogic advisor (shaman, wise wo/man, astrologer or sorcerer/ess, priest/ess) with rationalist advisors by internalizing the mystery and fear and awe that drove the mystagogue, so too does the Other-as-reason seize power from the Other-as-mystery only by becoming mystagogic. The ruler who rules through the speaking of the Other-as-reason must mystify the source of his power through three channels:

1. *Political:* The Divine Right of kings and the concept of majority vote both derive justification for rule from mystery, whether from a personalized god whose will can only be heard, understood, and interpreted by a priestly caste, or from a bureaucratized god whose will lies in the statistical proportions of numbers (votes, opinion polls) taken to represent a mystified abstraction called "the will of the people."

2. *Epistemological:* Because the Other-as-reason claims to know everything and to be able to explain everything, it must mystify everything it doesn't know or can't explain as either not worth knowing or nonexistent.

3. *Psychological:* Because the Other-as-reason rules through rational, which is to say conscious, choice, it must mystify its own unconscious power over rationalist rulers.

Communicability, Translatability

And this raises an interesting point. The unconscious as theorized by Freud is a survival of mystery, a knowing-without-knowing, a knowing-without-being-able-to-tell, and reason is the censor that forces mystery to distort its messages (through dreams, jokes, parapraxes, etc.). Psychoanalysis is part of reason's assault on mystery, an attempt to map out the unconscious, to reveal mystery's secrets; Lacan says, in effect, that mystery is structured like *la langue*—a rationalist sign system. This notion suggests that the mystery religions too may have had their impulse to communicate, which was blocked by some mystagogic censor—and that both the impulse and the censor were reason germinant. Reason wants mystery both to talk and not to talk, to translate and not to translate; reason wants at once to prevent and to undertake the translating of mystery, and in important ways those two projects are the same.

In this sense *The Golden Ass* is Apuleius' becoming-rationalist attempt to have it both ways, to talk and not to talk, to reveal and not to reveal, to translate and not to translate: he translates everything about his experience of becoming an initiate of Isis *except* the actual words from the Egyptian Book of the Dead that the priest translated for him; he translates around the tabooed content and thus beats the censor by distorting his message (using the dream-image of the ass). The priest who translates from the Egyptian thus not only serves as censor blocking dissemination of the mysteries but provides Apuleius with his disseminatory model—which he must employ in displaced ways. Apuleius writes a devout narrative in a depraved form, celebrates the celibate mysteries of Isis in a Milesian narrative about the sexual misadventures of an ass. He solves this dilemma by dropping hints along the way that his ludicrous picaresque narrative is an allegory of profane humans' "bestiality" before their initiatory transformation into the image of their deities; but this stratagem only raises a new problem. As a priest of Isis he is not supposed to divulge the mysteries to us, the profane, and he tells us as much, explicitly, immediately before telling us exactly what happened in his initiation. He taunts us with our lack of understanding, saying his disclosure will divulge nothing because without the experience of the initiation itself we cannot comprehend it; but his allegory, to which his conversion and initiation provide the climax, is set up precisely to give us the kind of experience that will enable us to understand the mysteries. He wants us, to put it as succinctly as possible, to understand and not to understand; he wants both to translate the mysteries from Greek into Latin (hence his book) and *not* to translate them, to preserve their mystery inviolate.

If we read *The Golden Ass* as the criss-crossing speaking of both the still-dominant Other-as-mystery and the emergent Other-as-reason, these internal conflicts may make more sense. As a priest of Isis, Apuleius wants to know without knowing, certainly to know without telling; but as a Platonic philosopher, author of *The God of Socrates,* he wants to understand and make others understand. Two of the strongest strands of his personality are in conflict. What does he do? He writes a dream-narrative that distorts and displaces the mysteries, and thus, he hopes, beats the censor. He can't translate the mysteries for his readers directly from Egyptian to Greek (he has no Egyptian) or, for that matter, from Greek to Latin (it is not permitted), so he "translates" them in a dream-like narrative form, the dream of an ass becoming fully human as a dream-like "translation" of the mystery of a human being being possessed by the goddess. Note that the goddess appears to Lucius in a dream to tell him that the day of his initiation has come—"there was no darkness in the visions that admonished the darkness of my sleep. She appeared and told me that the day of my desire had arrived, the day which would fulfil my dearest wishes" (Lindsay 248)—and that the priest's translation from the Egyptian Book of the Dead is followed by an induced narcosis or dream-like state in which Lucius experiences firsthand what the translation merely described: "I approached the confines of death. I trod the threshold of Proserpine; and borne through the elements I returned. At midnight I saw the Sun shining in all his glory. I approached the gods below and the gods above, and I stood beside them, and I worshipped them" (Lindsay 249). But throughout the narrative, dreams (and dream-like realities) are treacherous things. "The dreams that come in daylight," the bandits' old woman tells Charite, "are not to be trusted, everyone knows that, and even night-dreams often go by contraries" (Graves 95). Before he is transformed into an ass, Lucius comes home drunk and surprises three bandits trying to break into his host's house; killing all three, he is arrested for murder the next day, convicted, then informed that it was all a joke: the three "bandits" were inflated wineskins. That same night bandits do break into his host's house and escape by riding Lucius, who is now an ass. What is "real" when wineskins become bandits and then wineskins again and their convicted and acquitted murderer becomes the butt of the townspeople's joke *and* the ass on which the bandits ride out of town? At one point Lucius is owned by devotees of the Syrian goddess, whom he contrasts unfavorably with Isis; but their mystical experiences are as radical as his own, and his attack on their ecstasy has the unintended effect of undermining his own: "A strange notion, this, that divine immanency, instead of doing men good, enfeebles or disorders their senses" (Graves 190).

"Here, then," as Freud writes in *Totem and Taboo*, "we have an exact counterpart of the obsessional act in the neurosis, in which the suppressed impulse and the impulse that suppresses it find simultaneous and common satisfaction. The obsessional act is *ostensibly* a protection against the prohibited act; but *actually*, in our view, it is a repetition of it" (50). Writing *The Golden Ass* is a devotional act designed simultaneously to justify and to conceal the mysteries of Isis, to give the reader a becoming-rationalist understanding of the mysteries without actually translating them; this act is obviously a repetition of the prohibited one, a translating-without-translating, but in a rather more complex way than Freud suggests. Certainly a narrative about the mysteries of Isis that leaves only the words from the Egyptian Book of the Dead untranslated comes so close to breaking the taboo, while yet making all the gestures of obedience to it—refusing to translate, calling Mithras's instructions too holy to voice—as to transform it, to simultaneously expand and suspend it.

And here is another complication. Reason is the dream of total freedom from the unconscious, from mystery; but the Other that dreams this dream is ("in") the unconscious, where it retreated from the uneasy rages of the rationalist Subject that would build its life on the conscious cogito, the *spoken* I-think. The Self that says "I think" creates a world of rationalist control by that saying but can only say it insofar as it is spoken by the Other-as-reason, which lies beyond its control.

Taboo, clearly, is spoken by the Other-as-mystery; hence the importance for Robertson Smith and James Frazer at the end of the nineteenth century of clearing Christianity of any possible charges of primitive taboo-driven spirituality. The Other-as-mystery spoke taboo; the Other-as-reason speaks ethics. Christianity, an ethical religion, is a "modern" and thus far better religion than the mystery cults of antiquity. Invidious as this distinction is, it is clear that a shift of some sort has taken place from ancient to modern religion, a shift from what I am calling mystery to reason; but it should be equally clear that the shift is far from absolute. What is invidious about the distinction is the implication that "primitives" never thought and that "we"—modern rationalists—never succumb to ancient irrational fears, anxieties, dark whisperings, taboos.

In *Totem and Taboo* Freud ascribes the speaking of what I'm calling the Other-as-mystery to "primitives"—but it doesn't take much introspection to discover in our own lives the same elements of confusion and lack of control Freud calls primitive:

> Every sort of thing is forbidden; but they have no idea why, and it does not occur to them to raise the question. On the contrary, they submit to the prohibitions as though they were a matter of course and feel convinced that any violation of them will be automatically met by the direst punishment. We have trustworthy stories of how any unwitting violation of one of these prohibitions is in fact automatically punished. An innocent wrong-doer, who may, for instance, have eaten a forbidden animal, falls into a deep depression, anticipates death and then dies in bitter earnest. (21)

What we do in a rationalist regime, of course, what the Other-as-reason coaches us to do, is to rationalize our fears, our obsessions, our addictions, to find some good (but *ex post facto*) reason for acting as we do, even if our actions are first driven by fear or other emotional compulsions and only then rationalized. For example, when a text gives us the willies, when it feels too potent to translate, we call it too *difficult* to translate, and leave it alone. We say that we are worried about how a reader in the target culture might misunderstand our translation, and leave it alone. Or we overcome our misgivings, telling ourselves it's just words on a page, and translate it anyway. It's important for us not to believe, not even to suspect, that we are afraid of some atavistic threat of punishment, some punitive power that dwells in the text itself.

This is not to identify the speaking of the Other-as-mystery with repression. The taboo on consciousness is similar to repression, but different in significant ways. The primal scene for both repression and taboo is some sort of punishment, or perhaps guilt that projects a punishment, but the freezing or locking of somatic response in the two is divergent: repression shuts down awareness of unacceptable behavior (including thoughts and desires), whereas taboo *blocks* forbidden behavior. The somatic response is similar: numbing or paralyzing anxiety signals in the face of unacceptable behavior. But the blocked or paralyzed behavior in repression is awareness, whereas in taboo it is an external action like incest or communication.

Of course, if we assume that the taboo on communication in the mystery religions included communication to oneself, then taboo is very close to repression: the taboo on communication is repressive insofar as it keeps revelatory articulation unconscious. But this is a retrospective conception of repression. The Other-as-reason denigrates mystical experience with nasty names like irrational, hysterical, drug-induced, schizophrenic—and one of these names might well be repressive—but that is a projection of its own repressive regime back onto that which it would displace. The Other-as-reason represses mystery, represses powerful and transformative emotional experience, represses celebratory feelings of belonging or being one with others, represses knowing-without-knowing (it fosters just plain *knowing*); but because the most important thing that it must repress is the fact that repression is the key to its success, it projects its own repressions onto the mystery religions, claiming that they repress reason, that they repress people's natural desire to know things, understand things, explain things, work out the connections between things.

Also, of course, as people become more rational, they become more and more ashamed of their mystical past, and then they do increasingly repress it. I *never was* inclined to mystify things, to have irrational experiences; I *always was* in complete rational control of my experience.

Thus one of the things the Other-as-reason has to repress as it gradually takes over from the Other-as-mystery is the taboo on communication. The Other-as-reason fosters belief in absolute communicability: there is nothing that cannot be known, and nothing that can be known cannot be spoken. The Other-as-reason fosters an ideal of the absolute knowability and communicability of everything, from God's will to the lives of demons in hell, from subatomic waves/particles to the origin of the universe—the TOE, theory of everything. Hence we have the rationalist notion of absolute translatability, the belief that anything that can be said in one language can be said in another. Related is the reductive method for achieving this absolute translatability: reducing a text to a stabilized semantic object, a decontextualized and detexturalized "message," stripping the text of its sensual or carnal aspects, the sound and feel of it, none of which ever translates. The Other-as-mystery prefers the feel of a text, the intuitive, preverbal experience—and you can't translate a feel or an experience. The Other-as-reason prefers the sense of a text, and the sense is all you can translate with reliable equivalence.

Mystery and the Receptor

So am I saying that the Other-as-mystery doesn't want texts translated because the "feel" doesn't translate? If so, maybe this belief reflects an emergent concern for equivalence as well. But no. The Other-as-mystery did foster and channel belief in the mysteries, which were experiential truths, powerfully experienced messages about life and death and the afterlife. But the reason the translation of sacred texts was tabooed and later—in the medieval church—banned altogether was *not* that equivalent renderings of these truths were impossible in other languages. It was banned because, as we'll see in the next chapter, the uninitiated weren't *ready* for them.

The Other-as-mystery didn't institute translation theory, even to taboo or control it; the careful conscious articulation of its regime was alien to its purposes. But it's interesting to note that the "atmospheric semiotic" of mystical (anti)translation (to borrow a term from Deleuze and Guattari that I'll be exploring in the next chapter) is already receptor-oriented and that as the Other-as-reason gradually insinuates itself into a position of hegemonic control, it articulates this receptor-orientation only transitionally, en route to the stable semantic objectifications required for a focus on equivalence—which is to say, only in order to silence and displace it.

In *The Golden Ass*, for example, the mysteries had to be translated by a priest, a mystagogue, someone who knew *how* to translate them, and *when*, and *to whom*—someone who could control the total context of translation, including, as far as possible, the target-language hearer's frame of mind. The mysteries also had to be interpreted orally, which further regulated the dissemination of the sacred text: a written translation might fall into the wrong hands. This remained a focal concern among good Catholics through the end of the sixteenth century, that a vernacular Bible might fall into the wrong hands; oral "translation" or paraphrase of the Bible, or singing (Caedmon) or teaching or preaching about it, allowed a greater degree of control of the message and its reception. The physical presence of the authority figure would also have gone a long way toward calming the initiate's fears; the priest took the initiate through a series of ritual steps to create the ritual space in the initiate's body, to prepare him or her somatically for the controlled breaking of taboo.

Receptor-oriented translation theory has been written, of course, during the Christian era; we will see some of it in the next chapter, from Aelfric in the tenth century to Thomas More's *Dialogue Concerning Heresies* in the early sixteenth century. It deals primarily with concerns about vernacular speakers' readiness for a vernacular Bible, whether people who haven't learned Latin or studied theology can read the Bible without misunderstanding its many "mysteries"—very much the same mystical-becoming-rationalist concerns that begin to emerge, even if only allusively, in *The Golden Ass*.

In the rationalist equivalence-oriented tradition that has displaced this mystical receptor-orientation, however, these passing moments of concern for readers' readiness are typically ignored, forgotten, even repressed. Indeed, they have been so effectively peripheralized in the rationalist history of translation theory that they are not even *thought* of as translation theory. Thomas More doesn't discuss how to translate, how best to achieve equivalence—he only discusses whether we ought to translate the Bible and for whom—so he doesn't theorize translation. More on More in chapter 2.

What would a mystical receptor-oriented theory of translation look like without the intervention of the repressive Other-as-reason? That is an impossible question to answer, of course, since these days we are always already spoken by the Other-as-reason. But I want to begin to conclude this chapter by essaying an answer anyway, in a roundabout way: by tackling an actual translation problem from *The Golden Ass* and exploring through it the *practical* consequences of the theoretical issues I've been unraveling throughout the chapter.

The key to a mystical receptor-oriented theory of translation, it seems clear, would have to be felt experience (somatic response) rather than abstract structural equivalence; but this hypothesis still leaves enormous scope for speculation. Whose experience? The author's? The translator's? Each individual reader's? Obviously not the author's, in a receptor-oriented model; but then should one reader's felt experience (say, the translator's) take precedence over another's (say, an individual target reader's)? If so, doesn't receptor-orientation somehow get transformed at some point in that process into sender-orientation? The translator, after all, may start out as a reader, but for the reader in the target language the translator has become an author. If on the other hand the target reader's experience is to be made primary, how is this goal to be achieved, exactly?

The passage from *The Golden Ass* that I want to look at fits my taboo theme: it is a warning to Lucius not to divulge the mysteries he hopes to learn by spying on Pamphile, his sorceress landlady. The words are spoken by Fotis, Pamphile's serving girl, who is sleeping with Lucius and has promised to sneak him in to watch her mistress at work: "quaecumque itaque commisero huius religiosi pectoris tui penetralibus, semper haec inter conseptum clausa custodias, oro, et simplicitatem relationis meae tenacitate taciturnitatis tuae remunerare" (quoted by Tatum, 147).

As James Tatum says in his book on *The Golden Ass*, this passage is typical of Apuleius's archaic and rather stilted rhetoric: the regular, almost metrical rhythms, the rich overlapping of sounds in assonance, consonance, and alliteration *(pectoris . . . penetralibus, conceptum clausa custodias, tenacitate taciturnitatis tuae)*, the flowery figurative language. What is a translator to do with these aspects of a text? They are, of course, precisely the aspects that translate least well into another language, and thus precisely what domesticators have insisted translators sacrifice to easy access and what foreignizers have insisted they retain. Might a mystical receptor-oriented approach point us beyond this impasse?

Tatum notes that "to imitate the sound of Fotis' warning is risky business: a 'simplicity of my relations held with the tenacity of your taciturnity'" (146); but if I'm going to break new ground here I have to be willing to take some risks. Tatum tries his hand at the passage, seeking a working compromise between "risky" imitations of sounds and total assimilation to contemporary American English—striving for alliterative effect while still conveying sense: "Whatever I entrust then to the sanctuary of your religious breast I beg you to keep always closely concealed there. Reward by the strict seals of silence the honesty of my story" (147).

But this rendering doesn't quite make it, does it: breast/beg, keep/closely/concealed, and strict/seals/silence are a start, but Tatum has just been telling us about Apuleius's fluency, his rich, easy punning, and his tensile rhythms, and there's a startling discrepancy between my expectations as a reader of Tatum's descriptions and my experience as a reader of Tatum's translation. (Tatum's is also suspiciously close to Jack Lindsay's rendering from 1932, which runs: "Whatever then I entrust to the sanctuary of your godfearing breast I beg you to keep closely concealed there. Reward by the strictest seals of silence the frankness of my story" [79]. Unconscious plagiarism?)

This translatorial "failure" is, of course, nothing new. It is the primal scene of Western translation, grounded in the Other-as-reason's co-optation of ancient taboos on sacred texts: a source text that possesses mystical power, that speaks in the ancient tongue of the deity, or, one step further toward a secularized modernity, that attains an unsurpassably brilliant fusion of sense and sensation, semantics and somatics, meaning and feeling, but *only* in the original; and a target-language reader who can't read the source language, and wants to know not only what it says but how it feels, wants to experience its full brilliance firsthand. There is an original text, an original secret, an original mystery, which is taboo, sacred, not to be approached, touched, transformed: thus speaks the Other-as-mystery, and even today the Other-as-reason is unable to root out that ancient belief. The impulse to go ahead and translate anyway is the Other-as-reason's demystificatory response, which seeks both to clarify the mysterious and to (re)mystify the clarity it achieves: the target text "is" the secret, and it isn't; it "contains" the mystery, and there isn't one. By striving for equivalence with the original the target text kills the original, saps its force, and says with a shrug, *you can't make an omelet without breaking eggs*. For the Other-as-reason this loss is at once a limitation on translation and translation's most significant function: sorry, folks, something's always lost in translation, and what's lost is, oops, the reader's mystical experience, precisely that which the Other-as-reason is most concerned to eradicate. Hence the Other-as-reason's address to the translator in terms of equivalence, which (as Louis Althusser would say) speaks or hails (and thus creates) him or her *as* translator: respect the original text enough to transfer as much of it as you can into the target language, knowing full well that you'll never get it all and that you'll lose the most important part (which we'll eventually train you to think of as *least* important, mere dross); inure yourself to failure, buck up, keep trying, but never expect full unqualified success.

The implication of all this for translation of Apuleius' narrative from Latin would appear to be, therefore, that Apuleius heeds Fotis' warning by writing untranslatably, seeking in every line what Tatum calls an effect that "is difficult to capture in English—at least in English that means anything" (147). If *The Golden Ass* is written virtually in verse, full of golden assonance and silvery consonance and almost always alliteratively, then translations will never reveal the mysteries that he translates without translating, tells without telling. A translation into English will be like his description of the visionary experience, complete without transmitting true knowledge of what went on. No matter how the translator tackles the passage, whether loosely or closely, some essential ingredient will slip out of the target text and leave the reader just short of true knowledge.

But this explanation doesn't begin to address the problematic of receptor-orientation. By grouping receptors as initiates and noninitiates, those in the know and those for whom everything will have to be explained (and even then they won't get it), this approach simply makes actual readers into ideal extensions of the mysteries themselves and thus collapses back into equivalence-orientation. The original mystery (or text) enforces its own accessibility by making it impossible for those who don't understand *to* understand; actual receptors have no power to transform the terms of their reception, let alone to be transformed by it, because they are mere inert ciphers in a drama whose only real actor is the mystery of the original text.

Transformative Translation

But what is really at stake here, it seems to me, is a transformative *experience:* watching Pamphile transform herself into an owl gets Lucius transformed into an ass; praying to Isis on the beach at Cenchreae gets him transformed back into a man. The "mystery" of Apuleius' narrative is not a stable semantic content, easily abstractable and articulable in a new language, but an experiential dynamic, a (shape-)shifting that the reader feels in her or his gut.

Actually, what is at stake is not a single transformative experience but a whole series of them: metamorphoses, as the book's Greek-becoming-Latin title tells us. And transformation is always to something new: not the one true and universal experience, but change. Lucius's goal throughout the book is to get back to what he was before, a student in human form, and in the end he achieves this goal, in a sense: Isis transforms him back. But she also adds something to the equation: she requires him to change his whole life for her, and so he ends not with more of the same but with something totally different—not, in translational terms, with equivalence but with transformed experience.

This idea of transformation as difference works on higher levels as well. Lucian's Greek prose romance *Lucius or the Ass* is transformed into a Latin prose romance called *The Metamorphoses of Lucius*—and it becomes something new, a narrative experience very different from Lucian's rather terse and uninteresting tale. Even the genre Apuleius works in transforms his story: a sexy Milesian narrative is transformed into a devout conversion narrative; the devout conversion narrative Apuleius sets out to write is transformed into a story about a man transformed into an ass. Forbidden to communicate the mysteries, Apuleius communicates more about them than does any other ancient author and gives us a displaced *feel* for the transformative moment at their core. Forbidden to translate the mysteries, he translates the stories of Lucian and Miletus into allegorical narratives about the mysteries, which then *become* the mysteries—or rather, become the occasion for the reader experiencing something like what Lucius experienced in his mystical initiation (but transformed!).

Similarly, Lucius Apuleius of Madaura writes through the narrative persona of Lucius of Corinth, but in the eleventh book, after his initiation into the mysteries of Isis *at* Corinth, he refers to his narrator as Lucius of Madaura—another translation/transformation, this time from an ass of a narrative persona into the writer himself. Apuleius undermines even this transformation early on in his novel, when Lucius goes to a Chaldean astrologer and is told that his quest "would make me very famous and that I should write a long book about it which nobody, however, would take seriously" (Graves 34)—whereupon the astrologer, Diophanes, is immediately discredited, and by the end of the novel, when Lucius has become the author, Lucius of Madaura, he describes his future without a single mention of writing a book about his experiences—though Lucius of Madaura did in fact write a book about his quest, which was designed to be taken both seriously and unseriously (and has been).

The narrator's transformation into the writer himself is analogous to—constitutes the same kind of ontological quantum leap as—the transformation of an ass into a human, or for that matter the transformation of a human into a quasidivine being, of an ordinary North African scholar into a priest who holds power over the underworld and is worshipped for his power by the populace. Actually, Lucius's transformation from narrator to author is like a transformation into Isis herself because she, like the writer (each within the sphere of her or his influence, the world and the book), has the power to control human metamorphoses. Indeed many chapters of the Egyptian Book of the Dead cover the performing of transformations—into a hawk, a bennu bird, a heron, a swallow, the serpent Sata, a crocodile, a lotus, a governor, a living soul, and finally into the god Osiris himself. An actual initiation similar to Lucius' fictional one would have been a symbolic becoming-Isis, a becoming-Osiris, a death and rebirth as the deity; and it is fit that Lucius should emerge from such experience no longer the hapless Lucius of Corinth who is kicked about the Mediterranean as an ass but the authorial Lucius of Madaura.

Applying this principle to the translation into English of Apuleius (or of anyone else), we might argue that a mystical receptor-oriented theory of translation strives not to convey stable information, nor to replicate a normative experience, but to *change* the reader—to change him or her in, perhaps, unpredictable ways. Thus when Robert Graves gives us "But remember what I told you: you must promise to keep the most faithful silence about all this" (66) for the ornate Latin sentence I quoted a few pages ago, the equivalence-oriented observation would be that he elides both the translator and the original writer in order to give us "pure" "sense," which is to say, denatured equivalence—a good thing or a bad thing, depending on whether your equivalence-orientation is, respectively, "metempsychotic" (see chapter 2) or "magical" (see chapter 3). The receptor-oriented observation would be that he elides, or perhaps merely bureaucratizes, in any case fails to transform, the reader: by avoiding "marking" his translation as either ancient or modern, as aggressively Latinate or slangily English, by keeping his English as plain and unmarked as possible, Graves creates a gray little industrial office space for the reader to read in, an experiential environment that is as much like the presumed or ideal reader's status quo as possible and therefore unlikely to be *noticeably* experienced. (You can't eliminate experience; but it is possible to *numb* experience, to thwart awareness of experience, and thus to have the same impact on a person's life as if she or he had been rendered incapable of experiencing at all.) Having repressed the verbal assault the Latin makes on his life, his body, his sense of who he is and what he lives for, Graves coaches the target reader to do the same.

But then, the literal translator who gives us something like this, "Whatever therefore I commiserate to the penetrations of this your religious breast, always these closed within an enclosure custodiate, I pray, and the simplicity of my relations with the tenacity of your taciturnity remunerate," thus exfoliating the "risky business" Tatum starts, doesn't give us much to go on either. In some ways this translation is more transformative than Graves' rendition: as the foreignizers are quick to note, there is an unsettling movement to a passage like this, a disorientation, an almost vertiginous experience, when you go from "commiserate" to "to," when you have to figure out what kind of breast penetrations we're talking about, when easy understanding is blocked by alien collocations and word orders ("always these closed").

And this disorientation is potentially transformative. The problem is that a literal translation of this sort shows so few signs of having itself been transformed or of having emerged out of the translator's transformation. Some grammatical and lexical transformation is required to make English words work even remotely like Latin words—in *huius religiosi pectoris tui penetralibus*, for example, every word except *penetralibus* (a dative) is inflected as genetive, and that's pretty hard to do in English. "This's religious's breast's yours to-inner-sanctum"? "To this religious breast of yours' interior"? But even here the Latin is leading, and the translator (ego, me), rather than *himself* being transformed along with his words, is merely following.

Closer to the transformative experience might be a phonetic translation like the Zukovskys' rendition of Catullus:

Why kook-way he talk-way? Come is a row: who use religious pectorals to

> penny trolley-bus, some pair hike in their conception-clause custodian. Oreo ate simply key, taught 'em relation's meow; ten hockey taught me talkie-tourney toddies' two-eye remand a rarity.

But again, despite the increased scope a translation like this leaves for the transformative Englishing of nonsense syllables, the translator of this passage is still following slavishly rather than surrendering to a holistic transformative experience.

Maybe we've lived in a rationalist regime too long to imagine an alternative to this translation process. The Other-as-reason, which would submit *everything* to the regime of reason, of a plan, of conscious control, had been gaining strength for several centuries when Apuleius wrote, and it shows in his book, which as I've been arguing is dedicated as much to the explication of the mysteries as it is to protecting them from the profane. The mystery cults by Apuleius's day had seen a massive influx of reason, specifically in the form of heightened control over the nature of, and access to, the mystical experience; five or six centuries earlier they had been folk festivals celebrating sexual and natural fertility in a shifting variety of forms. By the beginning of the Christian era they had hardened into institutionalized religions. Almost two millennia later the Other-as-reason has won with spectacular success almost all the remaining territory of the Other-as-mystery. How then can we imagine a blind irrational surrender to transformative experience—to the very experience that our rationalist civilization has worked hardest to (teach us to) repress?

The rationalist version of the mysteries, whose translational counterpart I've been calling equivalence-orientation, is predicated on the existence of a single stable form of mystical experience—or at least a single stable form of *each* mystical experience, so that, say, the *Odyssey* and *The Golden Ass* (and the Eleusinian and Isiac mysteries) will give their respective initiates four different experiences, but each one will give *all* its initiates always the *same* experience. No individual variety. No historical or geographical fluidity. No shifting or sliding interpretive horizons, as Hans-Georg Gadamer would say. No experiential nomadism. There is a single experience, and it is infinitely worth having; to have it, you must put by the distortive lenses of personal bias and assimilate yourself to the idiom of the mystical experience itself, let yourself be possessed by it. Then, by the grace of the god, you will have the one true and universal experience of the mysteries.

To the extent that the Other-as-reason tolerates talk of transformation at all, of course, it calls for a transformation that leaves the source text exactly the same, or as exactly as possible. *Plus ça change, plus ça reste la même chose.* Identity in difference. This is the rationalist ideal for translation—familiar to everyone because the Other-as-reason keeps whispering it in our ears. This, it never stops reminding us, is what translation *is*, identity in difference, equivalence across the language barrier.

There must be a regime, says the Other-as-reason; there must be a plan, an order, a command, a rationale. Nothing that is worth doing, nothing that is even doable, can be done without first being subordinated to reason. An action that is not prestructured by reason is no action at all. It's a whim, an impulse—hence an accident.

The problem is, however, that the Other-as-mystery lives on within the Other-as-reason's regime and screws things up in a million little ways, throws wrenches into every rationalist works—so that, for example, it remains impossible to translate without idiosyncratic interpretations (and wouldn't the Other-as-reason like to iron out *that* particular bug!); so that even the most scientific and objective evaluations of translation success or quality or adequacy remain subject to the idiosyncratic interpretations of the evaluators; so that nothing subjected to rationalist control ever *stays* controlled or stable, everything changes, and even if five objective evaluators reached a consensus on the success of a particular translation, by tomorrow two would have changed their minds, a third would be wracked by serious doubts, and a fourth would be sick in bed with a killer fever and beyond all systematic thought. The Other-as-mystery and the Other-as-child and the other rebellious voices in our heads will not be silenced, and that makes individual experience *always* potentially deviant.

Ultimately, to invoke the worst-case scenario in a rationalist regime, anything does go, even if only in the gaps and seams of largely successful rationalist control. What if there are thousands, millions of mystical experiences, and each one is different? What then are you "possessed" by when you surrender control and let yourself be transformed? This is the Other-as-reason's greatest fear: *total* loss of control, a surrender not to an alien and mysterious force that is nevertheless somehow safe and predictable (as the surrender to the overwhelming power of sweet reason is supposed to be), but to the void, to chaos, to swirling mutability. And so deeply conditioned is our fear of this mystical surrender that it is almost impossible for us to dispense with rational control altogether: to translate, say, as blindly as the initiate experiences the mysteries, eyes closed in the dark; to transform the source text without a plan, without even a clue of what will come next, and also, inevitably, to be transformed by the experience of surrendering to mystical translation: "Whatever I've vouchsafed to the veracity of your verbality, keep safe with the tenacity of your taciturnity; store my simple story." This is still little more than a variation on Tatum's literal version above; but surrendering to the echoes in my head pushes *tenacity* toward *veracity*, *keep safe* toward *vouchsafe*, *store* toward *story*, and the new translation seems more English, somehow, seems to exude an echoic integrity that transforms it beyond the tired dualism of foreignism and domestication. The *veracity of verbality* doesn't exactly make the *tenacity of taciturnity* mean more, perhaps; but it does make it feel more at home rhetorically, domesticates it within the sentence without falling into the kind of flat reductive "ordinary language" that Larry Venuti calls domestication. As for foreignism: the *tenacity of taciturnity* is precisely the kind of foreignized phrase that Venuti and others call for, but then so is the *veracity of verbality*, and I made that one up. It's not in Apuleius. Neither is *store my simple story*, which sounds to me more like Shakespeare than any foreign author—though we could argue all day over just how foreign Shakespeare is, separated from us in time by four centuries and from me as a North American by an ocean but more under my skin than the latest novel by Dean Koontz, whose work I've never read.

In my next version of the passage I let go a little more, surrender to the transformative power of the words swirling around in my head, and, to my surprise, find myself making the leap out of archaism into computer hyper-drive: "I've saved it to storage, so stash it safely in a security program; protect my primary file with your prissiest password."

And so on. There are so many exciting possibilities here that I hesitate to continue, lest I find myself unable to stop. (Addiction to the speaking of the Other-as-mystery?) The more I get into the passage, the more enticing, and also profoundly frightening, total surrender to transformation becomes, and I backpedal furiously, trying to regain some control over what I'm doing by coming up with a *plan*, a *regime*, a—a—a dictionary, a thesaurus, an alliterative ABC of the passage, which helps a little but not much. It feels like I'm paddling a pogue in a storm with a popsicle stick—the verbal transformations threaten to swamp even my alphabetic regime:

> Always amass in august augmentation aught I allow into the alleys of your argumentative animosities, and ably adduce any arcane account of mine in arduous antivocality.
>
> But my bequests to the byways of your bonny bosom, broach them not, I beseech you, but bury my brashest bromides beneath bossiest brass.
>
> What I've cached in the certitude of your calm core, closet constantly in closest confinement, and coldcock clowns who'd clutter my cleanest counter.
>
> Don't divulge the doodle I've deposited in your dreamer's depths, I demand; dodge determinedly all dubious drives to dislodge it, and dam my dimpled dalliance up indefinitely.
>
> What I entrust to your elevated eminence I trust you'll ensconce in extraordinary evasion; ever encircle my effusive enthusiasms with eagles' eyes.
>
> Friend, fie if you fail to fence my fiery fanaticism within your feverish forehead, and favor my fictions' factuality with fortressed fortune.

Enough! But all right, two more:

> Once I've oozed on your orotundity, open not our orations to outsiders; own it only in orneriest ozone.
>
> Whatsoe'er I should secrete into the soggy soil of your soul, swear you'll stamp it with strictest secrecy, and succor my story's simplicity in stony silence.

Stop me, folks. But wait: what about the gnomic, the palindromic?

> Mind my stickling in mystical mind.

The Divided Self

CHAPTER 2

Assume for a moment that I'm right about *The Golden Ass* and the religious practices and attitudes it describes. Assume that there was a taboo on sacred texts and that the taboo had a significant impact on ancient thinking about translation. Assume, in other words—and I'll admit, even this is enough to swallow—that a person in antiquity who was *able* to translate a sacred text into another language would have been *afraid* to do so without various ritual or ceremonial precautions and without careful control over target readers' access to the finished product.

Now the question is, What does all this have to do with us? I want to devote this long chapter to an abbreviated answer to that question—abbreviated, because the full answer in some sense would constitute an intellectual history of the Platonic-Christian-scientific West. I want to cover a few bases in this history, the history specifically of Western rationalism and its continued uneasy entanglements with mystery and taboo, moving from Platonism's and Christianity's roots in the mysteries through the medieval taboo on (vernacular) Bible translation to the modern history of translation as empire. At each stage of my rather digressive argument, I want to explore the survival in the increasingly "modern" and "postsuperstitious" West of taboos such as Lucius faced in the temple when he was read to in Greek out of the Egyptian Book of the Dead.

I've already begun to build some bridges from these ancient taboos to our time; but for reasons that I'll be exploring in a moment, claims about the survival of "ancient" or "primitive" attitudes in our day awaken powerful resistances in many people, and the bridges are going to need a good deal of buttressing here. In chapter 1, I mentioned Robertson Smith's and James Frazer's Victorian effort to dig a deep cultural trench between "primitive" taboo-driven religions and "modern," "ethical" religions like Christianity; in a minute I want to quote Walter Burkert's attempt to dig a similar trench between the ancient mysteries and Christianity. But there are dozens of such trenches. The presocratics were irrational, Plato was the first rationalist; in Plato mystery ends and reason begins, like a guillotine falling, chopping off the modern rationalist regime (us!) from the dark misty past. The Middle

Ages were primitive, the Renaissance was modern. The Victorians were primitive, the twentieth century is modern. At some point between Homer and our own "enlightened" era, everything changed, the world was suddenly and irrevocably transformed. The old darkness was gone, banished forever (except perhaps in a few benighted souls, of whom the less said, the better) by the light of sweet reason. Whether the magical metamorphosis was accomplished by Plato and Aristotle, by Jesus and Paul, by Renaissance humanists, by Marx, Darwin, and Freud, or by Saussure and Chomsky, we are separated from the dark night of the primitive past—and thus also protected against its return in our midst, in our words and deeds—by a mighty historical gulf, a watershed of prodigious proportions.

Freud would call this gulf a defensive fantasy, an attempt to protect our repressions by projecting our own deep-seated atavistic primitivism back onto an earlier age. In translation studies this fantasy has proven particularly useful in mystifying mainstream thinking about translation as universal rather than historically grounded—grounded, as I argued in *The Translator's Turn*, in medieval theology, or, as I'm arguing here, in primitive religious taboos. The "commonsensical" notions that have informed most thinking about translation over the past three or four centuries—that translation is about equivalence; that equivalence is about rendering the meaning of whole sentences, not individual words; that sense-for-sense equivalence is attainable and its attainment is measureable—these notions are just *there*, givens, "obvious" and therefore almost certainly universal truths or truisms about translation, something to take for granted and build on. No need to question them, challenge them, historicize them; no need even to defend against those who would challenge them, because anyone who would make such a ludicrous case against the obvious is patently not a serious person.

And so even if I'm right, even if translators were once afraid to translate sacred texts, even as late as the sixteenth century, that's all in the past now. We're moderns, sophisticates, scientists, secular thinkers utterly untouched by ancient superstitions.

Just don't ask us to burn a Bible.

Here's Burkert:

> The basic difference between ancient mysteries, on the one hand, and religious communities, sects, and churches of the Judeo-Christian type, on the other, is borne out by the verdict of history. Jewish, Christian, and Islamic sects have demonstrated astounding capacities for survival, even as minorities in a hostile environment. . . . It was quite different with the ancient mysteries, whether those of Eleusis, Bacchus, Meter, Isis, or even Mithras, the 'invincible god.' With the imperial decrees of 391/92 A.D. prohibiting all pagan cults and with the forceful destruction of the sanctuaries, the mysteries simply and suddenly disappeared. There is not much to be said [at least not by Burkert] for either the Masons' or modern witches' claim that they are perpetuating ancient mysteries through continuous tradition. Mysteries could not go underground because they lacked any lasting organization. They were not self-sufficient sects;

> they were intimately bound to the social system of antiquity that was to pass away. Nothing remained but curiosity, which has tried in vain to resuscitate them. (53)

Ecstatic religion survives all over the world, but because we don't today have Isis or Dionysus cults practicing exactly the same religious mysteries as existed two millennia ago, the mysteries didn't survive. Never mind that the mysteries survive within Judaism in the form of Kabbalism, within Christianity in a wide variety of forms, including Haitian voodoo (an ancient African ecstatic religion subsumed into Catholicism), within Islam in the form of Sufism. Never mind that, as I want to show in a minute, Christianity inherited a powerful mystical strain from Mithraism, Orphism, and other ancient mystery cults—this strain can be dismissed as a third- and fourth-century corruption of the pure simplicity of the primitive church, which (the corruption) was fortunately eradicated in the Reformation. (This for those Protestants who want to situate the great watershed in the sixteenth century.) Never mind either that Christianity only survived the three-plus centuries between its invention and its elevation to the status of state religion (between 313, when Constantine converted, and 391/92, when paganism was banned) in the fragmented form of local groups who wrangled over questions of orthodoxy—the "stable" dogmatic and institutional structures that Burkert lauds are something of a nostalgic myth about the early church—and that the wrangling has continued unabated to this day.

What interests me most about this passage from Burkert, though, is his take on "going underground," because I believe that the mysteries and the taboos they channeled did indeed go underground—only in ways that Burkert doesn't quite comprehend. "Mysteries could not go underground," he writes, "because they lacked any lasting organization." Burkert sees only one way for a sect to go underground: it must possess a universalist theology and a carefully documented institutional structure that will survive political hostility from the surrounding society—which is to say, it must be a "major" (read "rationalist") world religion like Judaism, Christianity, or Islam. The mysteries "were not self-sufficient sects; they were intimately bound to the social system of antiquity that was to pass away." They were *purely* social in the tritest, most superficial sense of that word—they were things rich people did, like going to a therapist or enrolling in a self-help seminar. A Marxist might say that they were sheer superstructure, surface phenomena controlled by deep economic structures that were soon enough wiped out by the passing of time, taking all of their superstructures with them. Nothing survived the 391/92 ban on the mysteries—except "curiosity, which has tried in vain to resuscitate them."

But this is a telling exception. What was this "curiosity" that survived, and how do we explain its survival? Burkert seems to want to portray it as a low-level intellectual interest, perhaps like baseball fans wondering what the game was like "back in the olden days," before this or that rule was changed;

but how would anyone have known enough about the mysteries to remain curious about them? Burkert himself stresses the dearth of textual evidence that survives. And even if a few people did find evidence of the "vanished" mysteries, what could possibly motivate them to take a "curious" interest in things so utterly destroyed—let alone to try "in vain to resuscitate them"?

Clearly Burkert is aware that the mysteries have survived in a myriad of forms and is trying (in vain!) to thematize those survivals as mere idle curiosity, as a dilettantish mind-set that has generated "peripheral" social phenomena like the Freemasons and the Wicca movement—phenomena easily ridiculed for silly handshakes and such. But consider for a moment the possibility that the mysteries went underground *into* emotions like curiosity: that an unconscious or "felt" openness to mystical experience was itself the underground in which the mysteries survived the state church's attempts to eradicate them; that the Other-as-mystery continued to speak Western Christians after the fourth century but through new and less audible channels—for instance, through a general suspicion of or dissatisfaction with reason and alienation from an over-ritualized and over-theologized church. Mystics and mystical cults kept appearing throughout the Middle Ages (and continue to pop up today) out of curiosity, yes. But this curiosity was and is not about ancient archives—rather it is about experiential states peripheralized by the church.

Suppose, in other words, the mysteries went underground ideosomatically, into the deep layers of a whole civilization's bodily knowing, feared and craved like a taboo, repressed and denied like an addiction. Suppose the Other-as-mystery fled the ascendant Other-as-reason to the dark corners of the collective Subject but never went away—never even fell silent. Then mystical cults and experiences would keep "mysteriously" cropping up in the midst of an increasingly rationalist civilization; then "curiosity" about mysticism would never quite die out, never quite succumb to the calm planishments of the Other-as-reason and its many societal mouthpieces, especially fathers, teachers, scholars, and scientists.

The Divided Self

My conception of the battle between the Other-as-reason and the Other-as-mystery is loosely and shiftingly metaphorical—probably it has to be, since the Lacanian Other is not exactly something you put on the scales or rub between your fingers. It's a force, or a nexus of forces, that we only begin to feel once we metaphorize our existence in terms of a partly external and collective force that wields us from within.

For example, it's a political force and can be conceived on the model of the polis, the political realm: the dominant or ascendant Other (the Other-as-mystery in the ancient world, the Other-as-reason in the modern world) is like the ruling class, especially conceived collectively and dynastically, even though embodied in a succession of actual power-holders. It is never identical to an actual existing ruling class; the ruling class is the metaphor's vehicle, so that we can *imagine* the silent, invisible, and largely repressed working of the dominant Other by thinking about how a ruling class rules a society. But the ruling class is also one of the primary vehicles of the dominant Other itself, which is one of the main ways a ruling class does rule a society—by shaping and conditioning and channeling the dominant Other in(to) every citizen's body and behavior. This ruling Other rules in the lives of individuals and the groups they form partly by pulling together a coalition of like-minded Others (the Other-as-reason, the Other-as-patriarch, the Other-as-parent, the Other-as-capitalist, the Other-as-god, the Other-as-majority, the Other-as-intelligence, the Other-as-sanity, etc.); but partly also by controlling and silencing and marginalizing a whole range of antagonistic Others, Other-voices that are defined as "deviant" and thus "rebellious" by the very fact that they are not part of the ruling coalition. These would include, in our day, the Other-as-mystery, the Other-as-feminist, the Other-as-communist, the Other-as-child, the Other-as-devil, the Other-as-minority, the Other-as-stupidity, the Other-as-schizophrenia, all of which, as my names for them suggest, might be likened to (and in fact are metaphorically modeled on, and are often socially channeled through) a political opposition, or a group so marginalized politically (the young, the dumb, the crazy, the homeless) that it is not only powerless but virtually voiceless and invisible.

And my conception of the Other is primarily political, social, ideological—collective—even though, as I say, the Other wields us from within. The Other as I conceive it is not an innate force. We aren't born with it. It's not a psychic (let alone cosmic) "mechanism." It is pumped into us by our society. It is thoroughly saturated with social power. Embodied in individuals, it is designed to govern those individuals' behavior along collectively acceptable lines—with all the manifold conflicts that collective "acceptance" implies, some people wanting you to act one way, others wanting you to act another.

But because of the debilitating dualisms imposed on us by the ascendant Other-as-reason—self/other, inside/outside, political/psychological—readers of *Ring Lardner and the Other* have typically inclined unconsciously toward *either* a political *or* a psychological take on my Othering there, liberals reading it as a cryptomarxist attack on the autonomous bourgeois subject (I am *too* the author of my behavior!), Marxists reading it as a cryptoliberal retreat into the mystifications of psychoanalysis (you think everything boils down to the psychodynamics of the individual). Such is the power of the Other-as-reason that fighting these excluded-middle arguments is pretty much a lost cause. But one tries. Like this: the Other is *both* inside *and* outside your head/body/behavior. It's a political force that operates psychologically. It's an Other that's also a primary component of the Self.

Even after all these disclaimers, I hesitate to broach the metaphor for the Other-as-reason's ascendancy over the Other-as-mystery that will dominate this chapter: R. D. Laing's theory of schizophrenia from *The Divided Self*, from which, obviously, I've taken both my chapter and my section titles.

"Oh, so this is all just about individuals going crazy." No. Laing's psychiatry is perceived as radical in the Freudian tradition precisely because it is so political, so social—so grounded in the psychosocial dynamics of the group. *The Divided Self* is an early book (1960), but it already contains the germ of the radical notion that Laing was going to be hurling in the face of the psychoanalytical establishment all through the sixties and seventies: that we're a sick society, a schizoid society pretending to be healthy and normal (and defining "health" and "normality" in our own pathological image), and that the schizophrenic is actually closer to emotional health than we are because s/he has quit pretending, and so has taken the first (horrific) step toward regeneration, which lies on the other side of destruction.

I accept this characterization wholeheartedly and only want to radicalize it further: I am going to be arguing in this chapter that the schizoid condition Laing analyzes, the ostensibly "normal" precondition of schizophrenia, is the psychosocial normality created by the Other-as-reason. I'm going to suggest that the Other-as-reason *is* schizoid, terrified of the body, inclined to externalize, objectify, deaden, and finally to robotize the body, and that it is in fearful love with a precarious and ultimately self-destructive isolation or withdrawal that it idealizes as "mind," "thought," "abstraction," "transcendence"—even as "idealization."

As Laing conceives the schizoid personality organization, which I have been calling the reign of the Other-as-reason, it is built up in the child as a response to a threat to survival. This threat usually comes most proximately from the parents, or from the entire schizogenic family situation, which instills in the child an image of the world as hostile and uncaring, simultaneously invasive and indifferent—capable both of penetrating any psychic armor the child may erect and of turning the child to stone with a glance. As long as the schizoid condition is considered a rather rare anomaly, arising in a few unfortunate individuals as a result of bad parenting or emotional trauma or whatever, it's easy to point fingers at the mother (as most psychoanalysts before Laing tended to do) or at the individual family. But what Laing wants to do is to push this indictment onto a systemic level, to show how a schizoid society creates schizoid families who express sadness and shock and anger and disbelief when one of their members goes nuts, loses control of the sham life that the other members manage so successfully, acts out the sickness that permeates every cell of the family and the society at large. And what I want to do is to extend this systemic indictment from twentieth-century Anglo-American society to Western civilization as a whole, to the rise of reason as a schizoid response to the terrifying bodily experience of mystery.

Inside the family, the child experiences a threat to survival—emotional survival, survival both as an individual and as a functioning member of the group. Channeling this threat to the child is part of the parents' schizoid response to a similar childhood threat from their own parents—this is the "dynastic" aspect of the Other, that which guarantees its transmission from generation to generation. But the child doesn't know this; s/he only knows that life itself, survival, is radically uncertain. To protect him/herself against this threat, the child increasingly dissociates a mental "true self" from the physical and behavioral self that acts in the world, the self that everyone else sees, which the "true self" thematizes as a "false self." This Laing calls the "false-self system," since its complexity and conflictedness belies the implied unity of a word like "self." The child typically thinks of this false-self system as a creature of the external world, which is in league against the child's true self; all embodied action, everything the child's body does and the child's mouth speaks, comes from and is channeled through the false-self system, which is a sham maintained as a buffer between the world and the true self. But because that buffer is controlled by external forces, because it is both the child's only defense against the world's hostility and the most powerful expression of that hostility, the protection is slim, ultimately nonexistent; in fact, the false-self system repeatedly infects or contaminates the isolate true self, causing the latter to withdraw still further, until its isolation from the social realm, from the world as a shared social place, is almost absolute.

Compare this discussion of schizoid withdrawal, now, with the birth of reason in ancient Greece and its development since. Any of Laing's characterizations of the isolated "true self" could be applied equally well to the rational self, the thinking self, or, in the psychosocial body politic, the Other-as-reason, which withdraws fearfully from the embodied Other-as-mystery into an abstract, transcendental, disembodied realm of pure thought: "In the schizoid condition here described," Laing writes, "there is a persistent scission between the self and the body. What the individual regards as his true self is experienced as more or less disembodied, and bodily experience and actions are in turn felt to be part of the false-self system" (82). The body is dangerous, treacherous, a threat to the disembodied self, which exists in the pure realm of thought: "When the self partially abandons the body and its acts, and withdraws into mental activity, it experiences itself as an entity perhaps localized somewhere in the body" (78–79)—a "mind," which lives somewhere inside the physiological brain (the "head") or perhaps in the chest (the "heart"). "The self feels safe only in hiding, and isolated. Such a self can, of course, be isolated at any time whether other people are present or not" (79), because other people are part of the embodied physical/social reality that the schizoid self seeks to flee into mentality, ideality, transcendence, abstraction, reason.

This flight from the "world," as Christian theology puts it, gradually generates a crushing, numbing anomie. Embodied interaction with other people is one of our greatest sources of satisfaction, of pleasure, ultimately, of emotional health, and the fearful condemnation of that social realm as "unreal," as a world of shadowy "images" and "copies" (in the rationalist vocabulary of Plato), or as "carnal" or "evil" or "fallen" (in the rationalist vocabulary of Platonic Christianity), or as unanalyzed and therefore prescientific sense data (in the rationalist vocabulary of empirical science), condemns the "true" self to an increasingly unbearable existence. As Laing writes, in the schizoid organization

> a persistent, haunting sense of futility is the equally inevitable outcome, since the hidden shut-up self, in disowning participation . . . in the quasi-autonomous activities of the false-self system, is living only 'mentally.' Moreover, this shut-up self, being isolated, is unable to be enriched by outer experience, and so the whole inner world comes to be more and more impoverished, until the individual may come to feel he is merely a vacuum. The sense of being able to do anything and the feeling of possessing everything then exist side by side with a feeling of impotence and emptiness. The individual who may at one time have felt predominantly 'outside' the life going on *there*, which he affects to despise as petty and commonplace compared to the richness he has *here*, inside himself, now longs to get *inside* life again, and get life *inside* himself, so dreadful is his inner deadness. (78)

Terrified of the free-flowing world outside her or his mental prison, the schizoid self perceives that world as chaotic, a vortex or black hole that seeks to suck her or him too into its destruction. "His autonomy," as Laing puts it, "is threatened with engulfment. He has to guard himself against losing his subjectivity and sense of being alive. In so far as he feels empty, the full, substantial, living reality of others is an impingement which is always liable to get out of hand and become implosive, threatening to overwhelm and obliterate his self completely as a gas will obliterate a vacuum, or as water will gush in and entirely fill an empty dam" (80).

And so walls are erected: first between self and others, then, internalizing that first wall, between mind (the shrinking synecdoche of self) and body. The schizoid divided self that results is the source and the author of philosophical dualism—which we now, having been locked for centuries into the schizoid prison of rationalist civilization, being spoken continuously by the Other-as-reason, think of as "intrinsically human." Everybody dualizes! It's the way we—*we*—humans, we think—are made. But it's really only the way we rationalist humans are made. Dualism is a schizoid ideology, whispered to us as our only hope by an anxious Other-as-reason.

The Birth of Reason

All this seems natural to us now. We have been hearing about the mind or the soul trapped in the prison of the body at least since Plato, and the voices proclaiming this schizoid doctrine swelled to a crescendo with those Judeo-Christian Platonists Philo, Paul of Tarsus, and especially Augustine, whose early-fifth-century book *On Christian Doctrine* placed Platonic rationalism at the very core of Christian systematic theology. But how did this happen? Where did reason come from? What drove this flight from the body and material, from carnal life in the world into the abstract fantasy world of mind?

One answer to this question is that reason was invented by Plato. Before Plato, there was no reason; he thought and thought, and suddenly there was reason. I'm caricaturing, of course, but some admirers of Plato and Greek rationalism in general have depicted the birth of reason in very similar miraculous terms, reason sprung full grown from the head of Plato, *fiat ratio*. These are also the people who will be most offended by my portrayal of rationalism as a schizoid condition. But it seems reasonable to ask whether a philosophical ethos as momentous as reason could truly have been born *ex nihilo* in the head of one man—whether Plato was not rather the first great spokesperson of a cultural groundswell that took many centuries to reach even the fruition it found in Plato, let alone that of Augustine, or Thomas Aquinas, or Descartes, and whether the older, more "primitive" attitudes could have died out entirely even in those later thinkers, let alone in Plato.

If you're going along with my Other-model of the birth of reason, the Other-as-reason growing in opposition to the dominant Other-as-mystery and gradually superseding and displacing it, you will probably have considered a number of possibilities for the Other-as-reason's appearance in the psychosocial field dominated by the Other-as-mystery, sometime, presumably, between Homer and Plato—say in the first half of the first millennium before the Christian era. As numerous writers have shown, the transcendental, anticarnal impetus of rationalism would have been foreign to the Greek spirit of Homer and Hesiod, for whom the sensual pleasures of fighting, feasting, and fornicating were primary, and who thought of the gods and the afterlife as very much like human existence in the present. By Plato's time, the rationalist groundswell was strong enough to regard this world view as immoral, as Plato makes clear in the early books of the *Republic:* human behavior should be subject to rational control, and a theology that doesn't conduce to that control leads to atheism and should be shunned. In order to convince humans to think first and act later and to structure their thought along rationalist lines, the gods too must be subordinated to "reasonable" ethical codes. Somehow this very "un-Greek" notion took hold in certain segments of Greek culture by the late fifth century B.C.E. How? And where did it come from?

Nobody knows. Chances are, however, its sources lay outside Greece—whether in Egypt, where Plato may have traveled (one legend has him traveling to Egypt and bringing back reason like a trophy—or like a disease, depending on your point of view), or in the mind of the Christian God, who whispered it in Plato's ear in order to prepare the way for the rationalist theology that would grow up, largely thanks to Paul, around His radical pragmatist Son. Who can tell?

A theory that I find wonderfully wacky and poetic, and just plausible enough to be enormously attractive, is Julian Jaynes' thesis in *The Origin of Consciousness in the Breakdown of the Bicameral Mind* that the gods spoke to humans back in the early days of human history from the counterpart of Wernicke's area (the speech center just above the left ear) on the *other* side of the brain, in the right or nondominant hemisphere. Strikingly, when that area of the brain is stimulated electrically the subject hears hallucinatory voices that s/he is inclined to obey without thinking, and EEGs show remarkable electrical activity in that area in schizophrenics. At some point around 1000 B.C.E., however, these voices fell silent. Since this divine speech had provided humans with their most powerful (indeed, irresistable) form of social control—their "right-brain" gods typically told them to act in accordance with social authorities' wishes—the much-lamented "death" of the gods created a kind of social power vacuum, a political black hole that needed to be filled with some new source of psychosocial regulation. Consciousness, Jaynes argues, or reason, and its philosophical ethos rationalism, arose in response to that need. Because the brain, for whatever reason, stopped channeling political authority through the right lateral lobe and producing the reflexive and uncritical obedience that resulted, humans needed to evolve a mental technique for self-regulation—and reason was the result.

A related explanation for the rise of reason in ancient Greece is found in Eric A. Havelock's *The Muse Learns to Write*. Havelock shows that the Greeks were the first to invent an alphabet that could represent the full range of orality, not just syllables but individual sounds (phonemes); the Greek invention, most probably an Ionian invention circa 700 B.C.E., was not exactly the vowel, as some have claimed, but the "(pure) consonant" (60). Earlier scripts (such as Mesopotamian Cuneiform) had vowels; the Greeks were the first to isolate consonants and vowels as discrete elements that could be combined to represent syllables, previously the smallest unit represented in written scripts. "In so doing," Havelock argues, "they for the first time supplied our species with a visual representation of linguistic noise that was both economical and exhaustive: a table of atomic elements which by grouping themselves in an inexhaustible variety of combinations can with reasonable accuracy represent any actual linguistic noise" (60).

The importance of this invention for rationalism, Havelock suggests, is that it placed the power to encode and decode information in the hands of the individual, *any* individual, not just a member of the priesthood—and in so doing effectively *created* the individual, the "self." When scripts represent syllables rather than phonemes, as remains the case in numerous major languages even today—Hebrew, Arabic, Chinese, etc.—an ambiguity remains about the written representation of phonetics, requiring a class of experts to explicate written texts and rendering mass literacy problematic. Where a phonetic script like the Greek or the Roman democratizes, individualizes, and demystifies writing (or rather, the connection between writing and speech), a syllabic script tends to retain its original association with the sacred, with a divine writing that must be interpreted by a priesthood (and that is taboo to touch). Recall Lucius's comments on the Egyptian characters that protected the script from prying profane eyes: even had he been fluent in *spoken* Egyptian, the hieroglyphic script in which the Book of the Dead was written would have required the presence of a priest as translator. Havelock claims, therefore, that countries that still use syllabic script, even when their characters can be produced on typewriters and computers, even when their languages are used flexibly and effectively in the international development and dissemination of information, retain a much stronger connection with oralist culture (a living poetic and narrative tradition grounded in religion, a surviving belief in the importance of memorization, etc.) than do those that use a phonetic alphabet.

Havelock's speculations also explain a good deal of the conflict at the heart of the Platonic project, Plato's use of the "conservative" antiliterate figure of Socrates to promote literacy, logic, and prose over orality, myth, and poetry. (It also strikingly explains the relative modernity of Herodotus when compared with the younger Socrates. The Greek alphabet was probably invented "overseas" in Ionia, Herodotus' homeland, and all the early Greek prose writers, including Herodotus, wrote in Ionic: Pherecydes of Syros, Hecataeus of Miletus, Anaxagoras of Claxomenae, Protagoras of Abdera, Ion of Chios, Pherecydes of Athens, and Herodotus of Halicarnassus [Havelock 92]. Ionic writers had a head start over Attic writers not only in prose literacy but in rationalism as well.) Let me quote Havelock at some length, drawing special attention to his remarks on *psyche* as "ghost" or "shade," a connection that will become important in my discussion of the German romantics in chapter 3. Selfhood, Havelock claims, is an invention of the Socratic vocabulary:

> Aside from the reflexive pronouns (my-self, your-self, him-self) the chosen symbol of selfhood became *psyche*, often erroneously rendered as "the soul." The choice betrays an instinctive fidelity, on the part of those who exploited the word, to the continuing partnership between orality and literacy. For here was the symbol of the speechless thoughtless "ghost" of oral epic, able in Greek orality to discourse (and so "think") only after being revived by the warm blood of temporary human life, but now given a new dimension in the guise of the "ghost in me" which as it speaks also thinks and, through the new life of the intellect, achieves the only complete life of man.
>
> Once the reader found himself set free to compose a language of theory, with its abstract subjects and conceptualized predicates, he also realized that he was employing new mental energies of a different quality from those exercised in oralism. Pressure accordingly arose to give this mental operation a separate identity. One can say that the entire Athenian "enlightenment," assigned by historians to the last half of the fifth century B.C., revolved around the discovery of intellectualism, and of the intellect as representing a new level of the human consciousness. The linguistic symptoms of this radical shift away from oralism, which has ever since underlain all European consciousness, occurred in a proliferation of terms, for notions and thoughts and thinking, for knowledge and knowing, for understanding, investigating, research, inquiry. The task set himself by Socrates was to bring this new kind of terminology into close connection with the self and with *psyche*. . . . For him, the terminology symbolized the level of psychic energy required to realize thought of what was permanently "true," as opposed to what fleetingly happened in the vivid oral panorama. (114–15)

Yet a third (if still related) explanation for the rise of reason is Walter Wili's in "The Orphic Mysteries and the Greek Spirit." Wili traces the birth not only of reason but of the retributive eschatology that later shaped Christianity—heaven and hell, heaven a spiritual place that is our true home, far preferable to our sinful existence on earth, hell a place of divine punishment for indulging in the pleasures of that existence—to Orphism, which began to flow into Greek culture from Thrace between the eighth and the sixth centuries B.C.E.:

> Probably at the end of the eighth century, the god Dionysus had set out from his original Thracian home; first to Thessaly and Thebes, then to Attica, he had brought wild ecstasy, dark terror, the ideas of guilt and atonement, condemnation and election—forces and concepts which have usually been regarded as un-Greek and anti-Greek. . . .
>
> First to Thebes and Thessaly, then to the rest of the Mediterranean world, Dionysus brought the orgiastic cult of the Bacchantes—an accomplishment celebrated with striking frequency by the Greek tragic poets beginning with Aeschylus, and later by the Roman poets. Become milder, he brought to Attica the Orphic mysteries and the drama. The march of Dionysus in the seventh and sixth centuries was an astounding triumph. In contrast to the widely accepted view that this Dionysian revolution was un-Greek, it can be understood only if we assume that the god found in his path a kindred extra-Homeric, pre-Homeric religious substance, amenable to the doctrine of sin and atonement, stain and purification. The truth is that the Dionysian revolution had revived an archaic Greek sentiment that had lain dormant in the motherland. (66–67)

Who knows? Like Jaynes' and Havelock's books, this explanation is mostly speculation on very flimsy evidence; and Wili's postulation of a "pre-Homeric religious substance" that was revived in the Orphic mysteries (an "assumption" that a few lines later has suddenly become a "truth") sounds pretty far-fetched to me. What Wili's thesis does, however, is to stage a transitional encounter between the Other-as-mystery and the Other-as-reason, to suggest at least one way in which the latter might have risen out of the former. The Bacchantes bring "wild ecstasy, dark terror," an orgiastic cult that is steeped in the mystery of the body and its pleasures, the cessation of thought that comes through sex, drugs, dancing, chanting—and yet they also bring "the ideas of guilt and atonement, condemnation and election," early rationalist notions that sow not (only) the divine terror that sears through thought but the cautious controlling angst that fosters thought. The Bacchantes celebrate the transindividual pain and joy of divinity through carnal pleasures, but they celebrate specifically *divinity*, not carnality: the transformative *enthousiasmos* is an otherworldly rather than a worldly delight, a gift of the god to his elect, to whom he also promises release from this fallen world. Here is the beginning of a schizogenic double bind: carnal pleasures are good, but only when they lead past carnality to the spirit world; enjoy the flesh for the promise it brings of release from the flesh; understand your body to be, at least when possessed by Dionysus, the vehicle of your deliverance from the body. Wili tends to idealize this anticipation of Plato and Christianity, but striking parallels with Laing's discussion of the schizoid condition shine through his idealizations:

> All the richer was the ethical evaluation of the Titan myth. For in the Orphic view, when man rose from the ashes of the Titans, it was not only the evil Titanic nature that he inherited. The Titans had eaten the boy Dionysus; thus the ashes, and hence man as well, contained a divine, Dionysian part. The evaluation of man as a good and evil creature of Titanic and Dionysian origin is essential to Orphism and occurs here for the first time in Greece. Only recently a writer has called it the most original and far-reaching creation of the Greeks and spoken of the Titanic nature as the Orphic original sin. Rightly, in so far as this basic view led the Orphics to devaluate human life and brought them the conviction that man must redeem himself by fleeing the Titanic and saving the Dionysian in himself. The divine soul must strive to return to its source. The body becomes the tomb and prison of the soul, which seeks flight into transcendence: the myth of the Titanic-Dionysian origin of man created the belief that the body was the tomb of the soul, the *soma-sema* (σῶμα-σῆμα) dogma. This is the center of the Orphic Mysteries. It epitomizes the Orphic and un-Greek flight from the world. (74)

As Wili sums up the Orphic contribution to the rationalist Greek spirit, the Orphic revolution "dematerialized the soul, devaluated earthly life, and subordinated even the gods in heaven to a simple ethos" (80).

Orphism wasn't alone in instilling these values in Greek culture, of course. Many of the parallels between the Orphic and the Eleusinian mysteries, both of which were established in Attica during the age of the Peisistratids (sixth century), point ahead unmistakably to Pythagoras, Empedocles, and Plato, especially the focus in both on what Wili calls a "luminous 'other world'" (82) and on death and rebirth through purification. Catharsis, ritual purification, was central to both mysteries, and both had a profound impact on Attic tragedy, where, as Aristotle was to insist in the *Poetics*, the climax was always essentially a cathartic moment. The Egyptian/Pythagorean notion of metempsychosis, the transmigration of souls, combined with the conception of divine retribution, which controlled souls' progress from one body to another, may have been introduced into Greece by Orphism—though Plato's contemporary Isocrates says in the *Busiris* that Pythagoras went to Egypt and brought it back himself. In addition, other ancient scholars, like Diogenes Laertius and Diodorus, reported that Pythagoras had personally claimed to have remembered it from his many lives, going back to Hermes' son Aethalides, whom Hermes had granted the boon of never forgetting one life in his death and rebirth into the next (Barnes 86–87). And as Wili shows, Empedocles, a disciple of Pythagoras, attempted to restore to Pythagoreanism a "purer" and more ancient, prerational form of Orphism, regarding rationalism "as a downfall from the realm of piety" (85), though he also embraced and expanded the Pythagorean notion of metempsychosis as a "doctrine of the immortal aristocratic soul" (85).

This back-and-forth shuttling between "piety" and "reason," the grounding of the schizoid withdrawal from embodied life in either divine spirituality or human thought, finds its fullest expression in Plato. Wili reviews the Orphism of Plato's *Gorgias* (where "the souls, naked and removed from the body, are judged according to the virtue and piety of their lives" [88]) and the *Phaedo* (where "men, who think they are living on earth, actually live in misty hollows [Orphic note], while the true earth, the 'earth of ideas,' exists in the pure ether and sends only a feeble glimmer of its perfect beauty down into the hollows" [88], and "each soul is led to judgment in Hades by its daemon, which is its guide and guardian angel, and thence to its appropriate place of retribution" [88]). And he comments: "We pause in amazement. The 'Orphic' myth has been subordinated to a metaphysical pure substance, the idea. In this myth the supreme purification, the catharsis attained in the Mysteries, has indeed ceased to be Orphic, and yet the style of this ultimate thinking remains Orphic, and the injuction to purification continues to ring through. The concept of retribution is metaphysically transfigured by the idea" (89).

But the transfiguration is not univocal, or even unidirectional. If the Orphic mysteries are transformed by Plato's rationalist metaphysics, his rationalism retains a powerful dose of mystery. Wili notes this phenomenon, too, and calls it a "reciprocal sublimation," by which

> Orphic experience was purified in pure thought, and pure thought, through Orphic experience, attained to the spheres which can no longer be encompassed in logical discourse. It is safe to say that without Orphism and its Pythagorean variations Plato would not have arrived at anamnesis and pure ideas. And this may shed new light on Plato's so crucial statement of a truth which he experienced at the time of the *Gorgias*, which he intimated in his myths and openly professed in the seventh *Letter* (341d), saying that "the highest in philosophy cannot be stated, but after laborious thought arises suddenly as a fire in the soul, and then feeds on itself." (90)

In Laing's terms, the "true self" is in flight from the body and its passions, its connections and attachments to the embodied world of human interaction—but the farther and the faster the "true self" flees, the more its flight is contaminated and infiltrated by the all-pervasive enemy it seeks to escape. Bodily passion is the "irrational" spy in the supposedly impenetrable fortress of reason. And so the "true self" seeks to "turn" the spy, to get him/her/it to double as reason. As Wili writes:

> The Platonic Eros includes three basic irrational forces: the desire for the beautiful, sensory vision, and the common striving of those who love. These three basic forces might still belong to the best Attic conception of Eros, but Plato sublimates them in his passionate thought. For, inextricably intertwined,

> they become for him the impulsion, immanent in man, to gain pure vision and thought, to travel the road of knowledge and wisdom. . . . This is the holy ascent of philosophical knowledge; the road of Eros has become the road of pure thought. . . . [He does the parable of the cave as the prison of the body, then:] Now, all at once, it becomes evident that the parable of the cave was made possible by the soma-sema dogma of Orphism, and we see how a very ancient Orphic experience reappeared in the pure thought of the metaphysician Plato—as a sudden fire—and with the power of Eros forces its way from the tomb to the sun. The road of Eros and of Orphism are one and the same. It is the road from the mystes, who has closed his eyes, to the epopt, the seer, 'whose eyes have been opened'; it is the road from the *mysteria* to the Anakalypteria. (91)

The Detachable Soul

The defining fantasy in all this, the primary hope for post-Orphic rationalists who hope to build a mental place of safety in a hostile world, is the concept of the soul's detachability from the body. If, as Wili says, "the most original and far-reaching creation of the Greeks" is the notion that humans are mixed bags of good and evil, the necessary corollary to that belief, the substratum that made it possible to build an ethos of reason on top of it, is the possibility of *separating* the good and evil after death. For this one needed a divine dualizer or judge who would determine which part was good and which was evil and would send each part to its respective realm—the good part upward into pure spirit (or reason), the bad part downward into everlasting physical torment. And since the good part became inextricably intertwined with spirit, mind, soul, and reason, and the bad part with the body and its carnal pleasures, the belief in eschatological judgment went hand in hand with a doctrine of the soul's separability from the body—a brand-new idea in the history of world religion. Before, every human being had always been an indivisible unity, a person who lived on this earth and then, when s/he died, went to the afterlife, which was remarkably like this one. No judgment—no *diakrisis*, the Greek word for judgment that literally means a separation.

But by the time of Plato, the detachable soul was becoming not quite a commonplace, perhaps, but at least a thinkable cultural idea, a theory that came to mind and found articulation and was not immediately laughed out of court. When Plato introduces the idea in the *Gorgias* he has Socrates make a few anxious (or perhaps only campy) gestures toward the ridicule he half-expects his interlocutor Callicles to shower on it: "Give ear then, as they say, to a very fine story, which you, I suppose, will consider fiction, but I consider fact, for what I am going to tell you I shall recount as the actual truth" (523a). In the story he tells, Pluto comes to Zeus to complain about the way people are judged and sent either to the Blessed Isles (if they were good) or to "the prison of vengeance and punishment which they call Tartarus" (523b) (if they were bad). The wrong people are going to both places,

Pluto says. Zeus vows to put a stop to the misplacement, deciding that the problem must be that people are judged with their clothes on, which covers up their true natures, evil people coming in fine dress, good people in beggar's rags, and so on, which deceives the judges. The judges, too, are living beings who pronounce judgment fully clothed, which further distorts their perceptions, "their eyes, their ears, and their whole bodies acting as a screen before their souls" (523d). To solve these problems Zeus sets up an entirely new procedure: (1) people should be prevented from knowing how and when they will die; (2) the dead must be stripped naked (of both clothes and living bodies) before they are judged; (3) "And the judge must be naked too and dead, scanning with his soul itself the souls of all immediately after death, deprived of all his kinsmen and with all that fine attire of his left on earth, that his verdict may be just" (523e). From this story Socrates draws the following conclusions, which are so familiar to us from two millennia of Platonic Christianity that they almost go without saying:

> This is what I have heard, Callicles, and I believe it to be true, and from this story I infer the following conclusion. Death, in my opinion, is nothing else but the separation from each other of two things, soul and body, and when therefore they are separated from one another, each of them retains pretty much the same condition as when the man was alive, the body retaining its own nature, with all the marks of treatment or experience plainly visible. . . . And so I believe that the same thing is true of the soul, Callicles, once it has been stripped of the body, everything in the soul is manifest—its natural characteristics and the experiences which a man's soul has encountered through occupations of various kinds. . . . And it is proper for everyone who suffers a punishment rightly inflicted by another that he should either be improved and benefited thereby or become a warning to the rest, in order that they may be afraid when they see him suffering what he does and may become better men. Now, those who are benefited through suffering punishment by gods and men are beings whose evil deeds are curable. . . . (524a–525b)

Compare this fantasy now with the imaginings of R. D. Laing's schizoid patients, who rage inwardly at the worldly success of shamming hypocrites (including their own false selves!) and long for a day when all false fronts will be swept away and everyone's true self will stand revealed for judgment. Then, then the evil will pay dearly for their successes on earth, for the false fronts presented by their clothing and bodies and behavior will count for nothing, and their black little souls will cringe in the harsh light of the judge. Whereas I—the good and true and pure person hidden deep here inside, whom the world never sees—I will be rewarded for my sufferings here on earth and escorted to the Isles of the Blessed, where I will dwell in paradise with my kind forever. This is, in fact, the only way a schizoid individual can imagine free and easy intercourse with others: after judgment, after the stripping away of all false selves by a judge who is absolutely predisposed to the schizoid's true self because s/he is that self's fantasy projection. Or as

Socrates describes this paradise in the *Phaedo*, Plato's fullest treatment of the detachable soul: "But those who are judged to have lived a life of surpassing holiness—these are they who are released and set free from confinement in these regions of the death, and passing upward to their pure abode, make their dwelling upon the earth's surface. And of these such as have purified themselves sufficiently by philosophy [reason!] live thereafter altogether without bodies, and reach habitations even more beautiful, which it is not easy to portray . . ." (114bc). The schizoid thinks, "These are not my parents, this is not my true home, I was not meant to live this way, I am surrounded by boors and cads and hypocrites to the point that I am forced to become one myself just in order to survive; but all through my ordeal I maintain my inner purity, confident that one day I will be free of all this falsity and will be restored to the community of my peers, a paradise utterly unlike anything on this sinful earth, where all free souls, liberated from the prisons of our bodies, will mingle in eternal delight."

Socrates offers these fantasies diffidently, expecting ridicule; but the Hellenization of the Mediterranean world in the Alexandrian empire, borne on the wings not only of Alexander's troops but of Plato's and Aristotle's philosophies, disseminated them all across that world. By the intertestamental period—the two centuries or so before the Christian era—the Orphic/Platonic fantasy had gradually transformed Jewish eschatology as well, which had never had a day of reckoning or a detachable soul or a heaven and a hell before. Christianity was born out of this Hellenistic Judaism, heavily influenced by Plato and the Alexandrian Jewish philosopher Philo of Judaea—and by Paul of Tarsus, who had read extensively in both.

And as I showed at some length in *The Translator's Turn* (56ff, 141ff), the belief in the soul's separability from the body conditioned the mainstream Christian translation theory as well (perhaps by analogical extension), making it seem natural to dualize texts as the Hellenistic tradition had dualized bodies, into an evil fleshly part that passes away and a good spiritual part that remains—a part that above all can be popped out of the body in which it is trapped and popped into another at will. Hence we have sense-for-sense translation, invented by Jerome out of passing remarks by that Platonic popularizer Cicero and gradually, over the next millennium or so, instilled in the heads and bodies of Christian translators as the only orthodox method of translation—the method whereby the abstract meaning or "soul" of a text is separated from its carnal body (its individual words in their original word order, their original source-language connotations and collocations and mood and general source-language "feel") and transferred to another (target-language) body. Translation became a kind of metempsychosis, a schizoid metempsychosis, which might be thought of as the precursor to schizophrenic psychosis—in which latter translation is impossible because the division between body and soul or between true and false self breaks down, and it is no longer possible to tell word-meaning from sentence-meaning, syntax from semantics, source language from target. In metempsychotic translation these elements are kept strictly separate, schizzed, as Deleuze and Guattari would say—the superlinguistic meaning is liberated from the prison of the source-language words in their original sequencing and mood and so forth, and a new target-language prison is built around this "meaning," but without changing it, without contaminating it with the physicality of the new prison structures. No matter what linguistic body it is trapped in, the "meaning" remains pure, abstract, transcendental, ideal, stable, permanent—always itself, always detachable for one more transfer to a new prison.

Midrash and Translation

Ultimately, however, this repeated transfer of pure meaning from one prison to another begins to disturb Christian translation theorists. Why do we keep having to put meaning back in jail? There arises by the third or fourth century C.E. a mystical longing for meaning without words, for the absolute Logos, which is one and eternal and unchanging—a longing that generates on the one hand an animus against not only translation but all writing, all verbalization; and on the other a strain of translational perfectionism that I traced to Augustine in *The Translator's Turn* and want to return to when I get to Augustine again later in this chapter.

But these developments are both rationalized traces of mysticism. The oneness of the *Logos*-without-*logoi* is a displaced form of the mystical knowing-without-knowing, seeing-without-telling, and the imagination of perfect translation is a universalized form of the priestly control over translation in the ritual space. Because both subordinate the Other-as-mystery's craving for mind-numbing oneness to the muscular control of the Other-as-reason, these ideas are quite different from the pre-metempsychotic thinking of the ancient nature cults that conceived the body and soul as one. Metempsychotic translation becomes possible because the text's soul or meaning or "ghost" *(psuche)* is thought of as detachable from its verbal body and transferrable across *(meta)* to another verbal body. This is the sense in which the survival of the ancient mystical belief in the oneness of the body and soul in Islamic Sufism, Jewish Kabbalism, and similar religious movements has maintained in these traditions an ancient animus against translation—at least against the kind of reductive meaning-transfer that was canonized in orthodox Christianity.

In "The 'Conservative' Character of Mystical Experience," for example, Steven Katz discusses the problematic of translating mystical texts and especially of reading them in translation at some length (23–29). He begins with the superficial problem that a translation is always an interpretation, often an *over*interpretation (though what "degree" or progression is involved here isn't clear—I guess the idea is that an interpretation is okay, though only one of many possible readings, while an overinterpretation isn't even acceptable as one of many). Then he adduces three serious problems:

"First, the connotative senses of words are lost" (24). "When a learned Jew hears certain Hebrew words which appear in the text of the Song of Songs, he connects them to a whole world of rabbinic discourse and hence the words gain a depth, a richness that is lacking in their merely denotative, dictionary sense. This kind of connotative force is, in fact, one of the most striking features of midrashic exegesis, and a prominent element in Kabbalistic thought and reasoning" (24). That "whole world of rabbinic discourse," which Katz thematizes in terms of depth and richness, is the unity of body and soul that later Hellenized Judaism will reject, but that survives in Kabbalism.

Second, "Even when scrupulous care is taken, translators inevitably must use words in 'translation' which lead to fundamental problems of understanding" (25)—"*Brahman* becomes 'God', while *Mu* becomes 'Nothingness' as do the German *Nicht* and the Hebrew *ayin*. But the Chinese Buddhist *Mu*, the *Nicht* of Eckhart, and the *Ayin* of Lurianic Kabbalah are *not* equivalent to the English terms 'Nothing' and 'Nothingness'" (25).

These two problems are old news for the translation scholar. But then comes the kicker:

> Third, the translation of texts implies the adoption of a *principle of translation:* that languages are composed of 'arbitrary' signs which stand for given realities though no necessary connection exists between sign and reality, and thus any one of many signs can 'stand for' a given referent. However, religious texts are often, if not always, believed by the faithful, and especially by mystics, to be more than arbitrary signs. In several traditions, at least, religious texts are taken to be the *literal* revelation of God and hence, in principle, untranslatable in a very special way. For example, Jewish mystics took the Torah as a unique reality whose every jot and tittle had cosmic significance. Here the 'power of speech' is given its maximum sense: the Hebrew letters, words, and names possess the power of creation and more. It is through them—'God spoke'—that worlds are created, ordered and destroyed; there is a casual [*sic*] nexus between revelation—Divine speech—and creation. Special potency is found in the names of God, most of all in the Tetragrammaton, whose proper employment can achieve cosmic elevation, spiritual salvation, and all forms of practical magic. The Muslim interpretation of the Koran is virtually the same. Unaffected by any human consciousness—hence the importance of the traditional insistance [*sic*] on Muhammed's illiteracy,—the Koran is Allah's co-eternal wisdom. Thus, even one who knows scant Arabic and intones its words by rote achieves higher spiritual states in as much as he is held to be sharing in Allah's own wisdom. As the speech of Allah, the words have the power to bring God and man together by virtue of their point of origination, comprehension aside. Then again, among the most important Sufi spiritual exercises is the practice of *dhikr Allah*, the remembrance and repetition of Allah's sacred names, especially the traditional formula: *La ilaha illa'llah'*—"There is no god but Allah." (26–27)

The "principle of translation" is, of course, the principle of schizoid or metempsychotic translation, based, as Katz says, using a Fregean vocabulary, on the separability of sign and referent, or, as Augustine would have said, on the separability of thought *(cognitio)* and spoken words *(locutio)*. The metempsychotic translator has to be able to separate the meaning of a text from its actual verbal expression; if he or she can't do that, "translation itself" becomes impossible. Thus mystics who reject that metempsychotic theory of language or principle of translation, who insist that meanings are inseparable from their verbal expressions, typically reject translation also.

The only thing that bothers me about Katz's account is his flat-out insistence that "the translation of texts implies the adoption" not only "of a *principle of translation*" but specifically of *this particular* principle of translation. So successful has been the Christian formulation of translation theory that it has come to seem like the only possible one, the intrinsic "nature" of translation. This phenomenon is even clearer in a piece by Joseph Dan called "Midrash and the Dawn of Kabbalah," in which Dan pauses briefly in his exposition of the "spirit of midrash" (130) to contrast it with Christian exegesis, which is based on translation.

"The Hebrew midrash," Dan writes, "is alien to western literary, exegetical, and homiletical tradition because of the vast differences between the Jewish and Christian scriptures" (128). I want to explore in a moment the most problematic aspect of this claim, that the differences between Jewish and Christian interpretive traditions are "in" or "of" the scriptures themselves; it's clear from Dan's own description that the differences lie primarily in the interpretive traditions, in institutionalized *responses* to texts, rather than in the texts themselves. Because Jewish and Christian preachers interpreted their sacred texts differently, understood them in different ways, did different things to them, the texts themselves came to seem very different.

But for now consider Dan's portrait of the differences, specifically his portrait of the Hebrew Bible as what he calls a "total text" (128)—a conception manifestly based in the ancient Hebrew understanding of the total human being, the total and inseparable body-soul that lives for a time on this earth and then is "gathered to the fathers." Unlike Christian preachers, he says, for whom the message of their Bible lay "beyond" letters, syllables, and words in some transcendental realm of "meaning," Jewish preachers discerned a holistic message in the text, not only in the meaning but also in the sound and feel of individual words, in the shape of letters, in the frequency with which certain words and letters appear in a given verse or passage or chapter, in the numerical value of textual units from individual letters to whole verses, in the placement, shape, and sound of individual vocalization points, in the various musical *(te'amim)* and decorative *(tagin)* "diacritics" added to letters and words (like the leaves and tendrils Lucius saw on the Egyptian text in the temple of Isis), in acrostics spelled out in the initial or final letters of a section *(notarikon)*—generally, as Dan says, in "the countless ways other than ideonic content and meaning by which the scriptures transmit a semiotic message" (128).

This is unquestionably a far fuller, more inclusive construct of a sacred or other text than was normalized in the metempsychotic Christian West, which has tended to dismiss the "body" of the text as irrelevant to meaning. The rare Christian or post-Christian interpreter who has paid attention to supposedly "irrelevant" matters like the shape or sequence or frequency of letters in a text has almost invariably been considered unserious, a dangerous or harmless crank, childish or insane—and readers who pay attention to the feel or color of a word or a passage today are generally only tolerated when they are poets reading poetry. But these peripheralized responses to texts have long been central and crucial to rabbinical culture: "It should be emphasized," Dan notes, "that these methods are in themselves not mystical, and any message, even the mundane or humorous, can be and was reached in these ways. This kind of midrashic treatment is completely neutral on possible meaning and was used in the Middle Ages and modern times (relying on sources originating from the ancient period) by every Jewish preacher and exegete, each according to his own preferences and tastes. Pietists, philosophers, traditionalists, and mystics shared this same midrashic tradition" (128).

What makes this distinction between Jewish and Christian reading habits specifically interesting for a discussion of translation, however, is Dan's insistence that the distinction *stems* from rabbinical reliance on the Hebrew original and Christian reliance on translations: "The possibility of using the totality of the text," he writes, "is created by the nature of the original Hebrew language of the Jewish scriptures. This is in marked contrast to the fact that Christians in the Middle Ages and modern times have usually had to use a translated text. Some of the Christian scriptures were written originally in Greek, but in most Christian Bibles all of the Old Testament and most of the New are translations. In reading the Vulgata, most Christian preachers in the Western Church had a text which in many cases had undergone two translations. Such a text cannot preserve the sanctity of the shape of letters; at best, it can convey the ideonic meaning of the original" (128).

So far, so good. Dan begins to falter, however, when he tries to explain how this situation came about:

> Even in regard to the simple meaning of the text, there is a vast difference between reading a text in what is believed to be the language of revelation and reading a translation. Many, probably most, of the verses in the Old Testament, for example, can be translated in more than one way, because there are at least several shades of meaning, and sometimes even complete obscurities, in the text. A translator has to choose between all possible interpretations and present one of them, losing in this way the richness, as well as (from a religious point of view) the profundity of the original. The translated text thus conveys a sense of clarity which is completely missing from the original. The translator does not transmit the text, but one possible meaning of it, creating a new text which is much more flat and unequivocal than the original (especially so if it is a translation from a translation, as is the case with the Gospels). This is one of the reasons why the Roman Catholic Church could develop a set of dogma. Dogmatic thinking must rely on an unambiguous text. The Hebrew Bible does not lend itself easily to the formulation of dogma, because of the obscurities which haunt almost every biblical verse. (128–29)

To see what Dan is trying to do here, let's take that passage one proposition at a time:

1. "There is a vast difference between reading a text in what is believed to be the language of revelation and reading a translation." Note here the vanishing traces of individual readers: "reading a text," "believed to be the language of revelation." *Someone* reads, *someone* believes—and it will make a "vast difference" for Dan's claim whether the someone he has in mind really does experience an original differently from a translation. Do all readers really read originals and translations in just this way? Dan's ideal reader of the Hebrew scriptures might be imagined as anxiously respectful of the original's taboo energy (spoken by Yahweh into the human writer's ear, the human writer's hand guided by Yahweh), while his (counter)ideal reader of, say, a Latin or English translation of the Bible reads without affect—or, as he implies a few lines down, with the "flat" affect that is typical of schizoid patients. These are not, of course, to be taken as variable somatic responses to a text (which is what they seem like to me); they are objective textual properties that wield readers as their instruments. The differences lie in the scriptures—not in the readers. Otherwise Dan's idealization could be falsified by a single reader for whom an English translation was far richer, fuller, more alive than the Hebrew or Greek original—or, worse, by the actual history of hegemonic responses to sacred originals and translations in the West. For in the Western Church, translations like the Septuagint and the Vulgate came to be thought of as guided by the Holy Spirit and therefore purer, truer to God's Word than the originals, which were mostly written by men who didn't know Jesus, who hadn't been possessed by the Holy Spirit. Bible translations took on the taboo power of the originals and gradually displaced them—not because of their ideonic content but because they *terrified* their readers.

In fact it was an integral part of this Christian assault on the body, on the embodied "false-self system" of mystery and taboo and the "total text," to teach people to reify their—all right, *our*—responses to texts as the objective features of those texts and then to forget that this process was something they were taught, to think of it as something everybody just *knows*. Teach people to respond to texts as we want them to—reductively, abstractly—then help them repress their responses and think of their impressions of the texts as imposed on them externally by the texts themselves (*not* by an authoritarian institution). That way we won't have someone saying, "But wait, this translation feels *more* ambiguous to me than the original," or more alive, more creative, etc. If we play our cards right, all right-thinking people will agree with us that translation simply *is* the process of reducing complex texts to the stable univocity we need for (and that also arises out of) our systematic theologizing, and anyone who disagrees is just not a serious person. Certainly not a good Christian. Enforce the new orthodoxy with punishments for deviation: those who deviate are not only not serious, they're heretics, burn them at the stake. Gradually build the fear of excommunication, execution, eternity in hell into the normative (and eventually universal) structure or "principle" of "translation," so that, when Christian civilization becomes "civilized" enough not to have to burn "bad" or deviant translators at the stake, no one will *want* to deviate any longer; or if they do, they will do it blunderingly, as rank beginners, not knowing why they do it and submitting willingly to being taught by more experienced peers.

2. "Many, probably most, of the verses in the Old Testament, for example, can be translated in more than one way, because there are at least several shades of meaning, and sometimes even complete obscurities, in the text." And the Old Testament is the only book in the world of which this is true. It's not true of the New Testament, let alone a contemporary novel, least of all a business letter or technical document. Only the Hebrew Bible is this polysemous. Sure.

3. "A translator has to choose between all possible interpretations and present one of them, losing in this way the richness, as well as (from a religious point of view) the profundity of the original." Note here how a metempsychotic restriction placed normatively on translators is thematized as intrinsic to translation: a translator *has* to choose, not because someone forces her or him to, not because translation has been defined this restrictively in the Christian West, but because that's what translation *is*. Translation as total or infinite interpretation, as midrash, would simply not be translation. Translation is *e pluribus unum*. Translation is loss. Translation, in Dan's (also Katz's) wealth-and-depth metaphors of "richness" and "profundity," is impoverishment and superficiality.

4. "The translated text thus conveys a sense of clarity which is completely missing from the original." A translation that doesn't convey that sense of clarity is a bad translation. It is not just that a bad translation is *more* ambiguous or polysemous than the original; a bad translation is also *as* ambiguous or polysemous as its original. The procedural norm of moving from lesser to greater clarity, once imposed on translation as an ideal, something for translators to strive for, is here portrayed as an impairment, a regress, a negative ideal; but it has clearly become established as "natural" or intrinsic to translation, part of translation's universal nature, not a restrictive norm.

5. "The translator . . . creat[es] a new text which is much more flat and unequivocal than the original." Here all the repressions begin to converge: translators don't create vibrant texts, texts that live, texts that provoke a variety of interpretations, because translators move from lesser to greater clarity, because translators move from many interpretations to one, because translation is a process of reducing polysemous texts to univocity, because . . . well, why?

6. "This is one of the reasons why the Roman Catholic Church could develop a set of dogma. Dogmatic thinking must rely on an unambiguous text." And now the whole thing flips over on its head: yes, "dogmatic thinking must rely on an unambiguous text," hence we'd better reduce the polysemy of our sacred texts; hence we'd better translate them into an unambiguous idiom;

hence we'd better train our translators to translate for clarity rather than, say, for creativity or vibrancy or whatever; hence we'd better thematize (and regulate) translation as intrinsically a movement from lesser to greater clarity. First the dogmatic pressure; then the need for translation; then the need for a carefully circumscribed conception of translation that feeds dogmatic uniformity. Dan gets it exactly backwards—because that is how he is *supposed* to get it. That's how mainstream metempsychotic translation has been constructed in the Christian West: by first instituting restrictive norms, then repressing and naturalizing them as universals, as part of translation's intrinsic nature, and finally "explaining" the flat uniformity of orthodox words about god (theology) as a *consequence* of translation.

Metempsychotic Translation and Taboo

But there's a conflict to be resolved. On the one hand, Bible translations terrify their readers; on the other, they induce a schizoid flat affect in their readers. This conflict is at the core of the survival of ancient taboos within Christianity, and it's going to take me the rest of this chapter (if not longer) to work it out. Though in all likelihood the conflict lies in the tensions of taboo itself: designed to protect people against holy things, to keep them safe, it generates terror in them. The terror keeps them safe—though not perhaps *feeling* safe.

In a translation like the Septuagint or the Vulgate, for example, the translation *isn't* the words of the deity; hence, it is a safe (displaced or "euphemistic") version that can be used and abused in lieu of the original. Jerome, for example, can tear the Septuagint to shreds in his letter to Pammachius, sarcastically exposing all its "errors" and additions and deletions without fear of heresy. It's only a translation. But it's specifically a translation of a taboo text, and, by the extreme contagiousness of taboo, by its volatile transmissibility, it, too, quickly becomes taboo and is eventually privileged over the original on the grounds that it was guided by the deity (the Holy Spirit). As I'll show in a moment when I return to the problem of Christian asceticism, this was Augustine's take on the Septuagint, following a long line of authors beginning with Philo Judaeus and including Pseudo-Justin, Irenaeus, and Epiphanius. Philo's fiction that the translators worked in isolation and still produced identical translations through divine inspiration was not discredited until the sixteenth century, when it was assaulted by writers like Juan Luis Vives, Joseph Scaliger, and Humphrey Hody.

And I don't know how other readers feel, but when I read Jerome's letter to Pammachius I feel a bit uneasy as he tears into the Septuagint. Hey, man, this is the *Bible* you're talking about! Augustine revered the Septuagint so highly that he was as shocked at Jerome as I still am and warned him against translating from the original Hebrew—use the Septuagint! (But use it worshipfully.) And the same thing happened to Jerome's Vulgate: written as a safe vernacular *surrogate* for the Bible in its taboo original languages, it gradually displaced the original text and became so taboo that Luther shocked sixteenth-century Germany by "adding" a word to it, translating "Arbitramur hominem justificari ex fide absque operibus" (Romans 3:28) by "Wir halten, daß der Mensch gerecht werde ohne des Gesetzes Werke allein durch den Glauben"—adding "allein" to a sentence in which Jerome (the translator!) had *not* written *sola*.

I'm suggesting, then, that metempsychotic translations are attempts to displace and repress the ancient taboo on sacred texts, attempts to demystify them, to bring them out of the terrifying realm of the divine and into the ordinary human sphere—into the marketplace, as Luther insisted in 1530: "man muß die Mutter im Hause, die Kinder auf der Gassen, den gemeinen Mann auf dem Markt drum fragen, und denselbigen auf das Maul sehen, wie sie reden und darnach dolmetschen" (21)—"you've got to go out and ask the mother in the house, the children in the street, the ordinary man at the market. Watch their mouths move when they talk, and translate that way." (All translations from the German, except where otherwise noted, are my own.) Metempsychotic translations are attempts, to put it differently, to achieve what we've achieved today, the Bible rendered so common, so ordinary, that I can own a dozen different translations in Latin, German, Finnish, and English, along with a Greek New Testament, and I can pull any one of them off my shelf any time I want to check something—even if I'm planning to say something unorthodox about it. (Just don't ask me to throw it on the floor and trample on it.) And I suggest that this displacement proceeded along two pathways:

1. By shifting from alien word to own word. Hebrew becomes Greek, Greek becomes Latin, Latin becomes German and French and Spanish and English and a hundred or more other vernaculars. But even those vernaculars are quickly rendered alien through contact with taboo: the Greek of the Septuagint, the Latin of the Vulgate, even the German of the Luther-Bibel and the English of the King James. When I taught the Bible as literature a few years ago I shocked several of my Baptist students by encouraging them to compare translations (a radical idea first suggested by that notorious freethinker Augustine, in *On Christian Doctrine*). For them the King James Version *was* the Bible. In *The Translator's Turn* I called the King James Version a soporific, preferred by many devout church-goers because its rhythms and phrasings are so familiar from childhood, a consideration that will usually take precedence over minor details like metempsychotic equivalence with the Hebrew and Greek originals (225). But I missed an important point, which is that people cling tenaciously to a translation like the King James not just because it feels familiar, but because its familiarity is shot through with the intensity of taboo. I portrayed the King James there as a kind of textual tranquilizer, Valium for the masses, and I still think that's accurate; what I missed was that the survival of taboo has the masses *hooked* on Valium, addicted to it, so that they fight the introduction of new Bible translations like a junkie deprived of a fix.

2. By shifting from body and letter to spirit and sense. Every new Bible translation fights the old taboos by claiming to be closer to the spirit and sense of the original than all its predecessors. It is, after all, the embodied letter of the original that is taboo: the way people feel when they read it, the intensity of their somatic response. The somatics of taboo is intimately tied up with the feel of a text, the taste of words and phrases on the tongue, the way they caress the ear, the textual rhythms that the whole body feels and internalizes. A more "spiritual" (sense-for-sense) translation is thus (temporarily) a less taboo text than the original, because it has (as yet) generated no powerful somatic responses in its listeners and readers. But if the translation catches on, these responses will come. The taboo exists not in texts but in listeners' and readers' bodies, in their responses to the text, and quickly begins to infect the way they read and hear the new words and phrases, effectively making the new translation over into the somatic mold of the old one (or, in bilingual readers, of the original).

This somatic "fit" is then idealized rationally as textual equivalence, and schizoid scholars go off searching for formal structures of equivalence between the two texts, determinedly repressing the tabooed somatics that make the two texts *feel* equivalent. That equivalent "feel" is, after all, part of the false-self system from which the schizoid rationalist mind is in full-tilt flight. No, no, it's much better to look for equivalence in "safe," because abstract, mental things like structures.

What is tabooed in the mainstream tradition, then, *is* the body, the carnality of speech and, by extension, of writing as well. The mystical power of sacred texts is (felt as) invested in the body, in somatic response, in being-embodied-in-the-world, so the schizoid Other-as-reason creates for itself a kind of mentalist enclave *in* the body but (supposedly) not *of* it, or even, if it can pull it off, outside the body's "true" confines (which are a synecdochic reduction of the whole). The schizoid Other-as-reason is a kind of Apollonian Lucifer figure, banished to mentalist darkness but casting its own light about until that enclave seems to be the only place of sanity, the only order in chaos, a kind of *panrationeum*.

The mystical experience is a full-bodied participation in the taboo energy that ordinary mortals quite rightly fear—without readiness, such an experience can kill you. As long as the Other-as-mystery ruled in culture, this energy was managed both through overt institutionalized taboos (on touching, seeing, doing, saying certain things, collectively enforced avoidance behaviors) and through mass participation in folk festivals, seasonal rites, vegetation ceremonies. Merging with that energy under certain ritual conditions, either through mystical exaltation or through death, was a widely accepted social good. As the Other-as-reason took over, the energy was increasingly managed through an expansion and repressive rationalization of the taboos, of the avoidance behaviors that kept people away from the forces that might kill them but also gave them life. The Other-as-reason fled the energy into an isolated place called "thought" or "individuality" or "self," into an increasing sense that one should avoid all contact with the energy, should divorce the perceiving self from the experiencing self and increasingly treat the latter as alien, other, inert.

The Christian Mysteries

And again Laing's description of the schizoid condition is apt:

> The self then seeks by being unembodied to transcend the world and hence to be safe. But a self is liable to develop which feels it is outside all experience and activity. It becomes a vacuum. Everything is there, outside; nothing is here, inside. Moreover, the constant dread of all that is there, of being overwhelmed, is potentiated rather than mitigated by the need to keep the world at bay. Yet the self may at the same time long more than anything for participation in the world. Thus, its greatest longing is felt as its greatest weakness and giving in to this weakness is its greatest dread, since in participation the individual fears that his vacuum will be obliterated, that he will be engulfed or otherwise lose his identity, which has come to be equated with the maintenance of the transcendence of the self event though this is a transcendence in a void. (84)

Push this "transcendence in a void" far enough, of course, and the whole flimsy structure collapses. What the schizoid needs to sustain the structure is a metaphysics of transcendence, either a secular metaphysics like rationalism or a Platonic theology like orthodox Christianity. Then transcendence is no longer (perceived as) taking place in a "void." Rather, the void is expanded to contain and become all reality, ideal reality, transcendental reality, Plato's "true earth" or "realm of forms," Jesus' "kingdom of heaven," which is within us, if we could only cling more tightly to it, and all around us, if we could only see it and enter in. Then there is a transpersonal force that lives in our hiding place with us and also permeates the entire transcendental cosmos, a loving personal God, or, less personalized and thus less consoling as well, an Other-as-reason, the Logos as logic. Then the world that we suffer in, the embodied world of other people, drops away as sheer illusion, the dross that is sloughed off when the divine *diakrisis* arrives and things are finally revealed for what they are.

And so schizoid Christianity develops a whole ritual of oneness with God to protect the isolated self from engulfment by the false-self system. "What may happen," as Laing puts it, "is that an experience of losing one's own individual isolated selfhood can be tolerated in certain circumscribed situations without too much anxiety. It may be possible to lose oneself in listening to music, or in quasi-mystical experiences when the self feels it is merged with a not-self which may be called 'God,' but not necessarily" (98). Thus the Catholic mass was held (until the 1960s!) in a language that few understood because understanding was not important: the important thing was sustaining the isolated schizoid self through a ritual enactment of unity with other people, that which the isolated self most needs to survive, but unity removed to a transcendental realm where it is not with *people* (the enemy!) but with a loving personal God, thus sustaining the very principle of schizoid isolation. The body's senses could even be drawn into this enactment through music, drama (liturgical ritual), scent (incense), etc.—but only very cautiously, so as not to awaken the anxieties of the mentalist self.

As numerous students of the ancient mysteries have shown, this ritual sacramentalism of the medieval church was largely borrowed directly from the surviving mystery religions of the first three centuries C.E., especially Mithraism, which had achieved the status of a state religion when it was finally banned in the edict of 391/92—after being reinstated as the official religion of the Roman Empire by Julian the Apostate in the 360s. Hugo Rahner, for example, a Jesuit priest who has his own ax to grind in studying the mysteries—rather different from the ax I'm trying to sharpen here—puts the scholarly consensus in the form of a rhetorical question: "Did not—from the second to the fifth century at any rate—a broad stream of Greek piety force its way into the Church, transforming Christianity's pristine biblical simplicity into the mystic sacramental form that lives on in the worship of the Russo-Byzantine Churches and to a more limited extent in Latin Christianity? If so, may not an apparent affinity between Christianity and the cults have been rather more marked at the end of this period than at its beginning?" (3).

Rahner is intent on preserving Christianity from the appearance of having been *modeled on* the mystery cults; it's okay for the cults to have influenced Christianity after Jesus, but the true core of Christianity must be seen to have been revealed by Jesus. This is an important question for Christian dogmatists, of course, who are concerned with that "true core": was it a "pristine biblical simplicity," or the "mystic sacramental form" that prevailed until the Reformation and beyond? Protestant scholars, for obvious reasons, have preferred the former explanation, beginning with Isaac Casaubon's *Exercitationes de Rebus Sacris* (1655), which Rahner (6) characterizes as a Calvinist attempt to discredit Catholicism by tracing its sacramental system genetically to the mystery religions. The eighteenth century reacted against the excesses of this approach and ignored the mysteries altogether; and it has remained for our century to explore the impact of the mysteries on Christianity. Rahner is one of the chief figures in this movement, and while his book is a bit gushy for academic tastes, he ends up taking a moderate, if still unquestionably metempsychotic, position on the controversy:

> The Church was not fashioned in a vacuum; it is the continuation of God's becoming man; it must therefore turn to man with the revelation that Christ entrusted to it—and that means that, at the time, it had to turn to the men of the Graeco-Roman world with their distinctive speech and culture. These were the media through which it had to work, the flesh in which its spirit had to be clothed; for the history of the Church is essentially the putting on of a body by the Word of revelation. The soul inhabiting that body—we call it the Church—is from heaven, but the blood thereof is Greek and its speech the

> speech of Rome. Is it surprising that these things should have left their characteristic marks? (13–14)

For me, less driven than Rahner to justify a specific version of Christianity as its "true core," the interesting thing here is the complex dance of two opposing impulses in medieval (and later) Christianity: the "pristine biblical simplicity" of the early church and the Reformation, pushed by the Other-as-reason to resist the bodily blandishments of the Other-as-mystery; and the "mystic sacramental form" of the Roman Catholic and Eastern Orthodox Churches, in which the Other-as-mystery manages to gain back territory lost to the Other-as-reason through the very insecurity of reason's beleaguered position. In order to triumph over the body and mystery, reason has to feel utterly isolated, totally self-sufficient, physically and emotionally unneedy—and it can't do it. It needs the body, needs other people, needs the mystical experience of unity, to survive. This lets the Other-as-mystery get its foot back in the door, and medieval "reason"—the theological tradition from Augustine to Aquinas—is flooded with mysticism. But the mysticism that floods in is also transfigured by the ascendant Other-as-reason, as Orphism once was transfigured by Plato.

This dialectical tension is everywhere visible in the history of mystery and reason; any historical period one chooses to cordon off for close study, whether ancient Greece or Rome or the early church or the Middle Ages or the Reformation or today, reveals archaic impulses seeking to flood reason with the body and modern impulses seeking to hem the body in with rational control. We are far more rational today than any civilization before us, and we produce far more schizophrenics as a result; but we are still in love with mystery, still powerfully drawn to its dark force, its ability to transform us beyond the mind's control. Hugo Rahner sees some of this ongoing battle in the period he studies, but mistakenly, I think, he sees the battle as long since won (or lost, depending on your point of view):

> We can best assess their [the mystery cults'] unique and almost anomalous quality as historical phenomena by contrasting them with the spirit of Homer and with that poet's essentially Ionic preoccupation with the things of the present world. This last was a spirit that did not easily succumb. Even as late as the fifth century the religion which it informed was to produce the Apollonian brilliance of Greek sculpture, yet it was never able to overcome the "Orphic fears" that filled the souls of pious men with dark unease, for, as Prümm has said, "the fair fashioning of the gods of death does not resolve their riddle or make them weigh more lightly upon men", and the more the acids of Attic comedy, and later the rationalism of the Stoa, dissolved the traditional belief in gods and goddesses, the greater the disquiet that led the Greek increasingly to seek refuge in the eerie realm of the cults. The temperature of piety began to rise—indeed piety became overheated, and to express these new feelings man began to reach back to supposedly ancient things, to Orpheus and Pythagoras. Latte describes the change in religious feeling that took place between classical

> and Hellenistic times in these words: "A new vital rhythm, a clamorous enhancement of the ego, replace that self-effacement in thought and word that till then had been accounted the distinguishing mark of a civilized human being. What man now seeks among the gods is the bizarre, the note of overcharged pathos, as against the Olympian calm of classical times."
>
> Meanwhile the boundary-walls of the Greek spirit, breached since Alexander's day, were falling into ruin, and across them flooded the un-Greek mystery cults of the East. Even the black fetish stone of the *Magna Mater* travels from Pessinus to Rome; it is followed by the mild Isis of the Ptolemies, and everywhere pious women bewail the dead Adonis. Thoughtful Greece and sober Republican Rome seek to guard against the thing, but in vain; for all these foreign cults—though we should not always lightly equate them with the actual mystery cults themselves—give better expression to the religious needs of men than the official cult of the national gods. Cumont is certainly right when he says: "Even though the triumph of the Oriental cults sometimes creates the impression of a reawakening of aboriginal barbarism, they nevertheless represent a more advanced type of piety than that of the national religion. They are less primitive, less simple and better equipped with organs than the old Graeco-Italic idolatry." (17–18)

There is a lot of mythologizing going on in this passage. It channels a Renaissance or neoclassical myth full of Hellenic nostalgia, which insists on positing a "true," "pure" soul or spirit of ancient Greece and Rome—"Thoughtful Greece and sober Republican Rome"—that is then contaminated by foreign influences from the East, or that is destroyed by a reaction against emergent rationalism. (Rahner has an implicit servosystem model for this process: apparently the true spirit of Greece was balance, and when rationalism was artificially injected into the system, the system reacted by producing [or importing] far too much mysticism, throwing the system off balance and leading to the downfall of classical civilization. Classical thinkers and poets grew addicted to rationalism, which began to deprive their compatriots of mystical contact with gods and goddesses, leading to a mystical flooding that increased antiquity's tolerance for reason.)

Still, there is a lot to work with in Rahner's characterization of the process. There may not have been an "Olympian calm of classical times," as Latte eulogizes, but it is undeniable that the older forms of the mysteries were simpler and more heavily grounded in seasonal nature worship than the later forms; in this sense Rahner is right to stress the "Ionic preoccupation with the things of the present world." Latte also underscores the importance of the ego, the new individualism that arose concomitantly with the new mysticism and the new rationalism (with the somatizing of reason/mystery as an addictive dialectic). A seasonal nature religion has no individuals, only aggregates, and immortality is achieved *in* the aggregate: you and I will die, but our children and grandchildren will live on. The birth of the ego is tied both to the new rationalism, in the slippage between collective beliefs and individual experiences (empiricism as an individualistic testing of communal norms), and to the new otherworldly mysticism, in the pressure for individual survival beyond the grave (eschatology as an individualistic transcendence of the communal sphere). Latte's nonsense about "that self-effacement in thought and word that till then had been accounted the distinguishing mark of a civilized human being" is sheer neoclassical nostalgia, Latte's projection of his and his friends' aversion to capitalist ego back onto an earlier and supposedly more pure and pristine age. Even his diction sounds more eighteenth century than classical: "accounted," "distinguishing mark," "civilized human being." Latte's is an upper-class male vision of paradise imagined as a Golden Age at the dawn of civilization in (where else?) ancient Greece.

Rahner takes pains to distinguish Christianity—"true" Christianity, rationalist Christianity—from the mysteries, which he calls "essentially a religion of emotion" (21). The mysteries, he says, "did not address themselves to the thinking, let alone the enquiring and reflective mind. They proclaim no doctrine or dogma and the fact that the cult legend takes a thousand forms in no way affects the quality of the act of piety itself" (21), which is "directed at the instinct for sombre awe in the devotee; indeed in some forms they may be said to be directed at his very nerves" (21). If the ancient mysteries are thus a religion of the body, Christianity is a religion of the mind and the spirit. If the mysteries are a religion of myth, Christianity is a religion of history; as G. Kittel writes in 1932 in a passage that Rahner quotes approvingly, "The Gospel of Christ crucified is wholly unmythical; it is not a song, nor a sound, nor a thought, nor a myth, nor a symbol. It does not tell of some dim legend but of a completely realistic, completely brutal, shameful, frightful event in history, that took place within the immediate experience of living men" (32–33).

And yet through all this, Rahner can't quite shake the old mystery taboos and finds himself having to claim that they are somehow innately human:

> At this point we may usefully consider yet another phenomenon which to the superficial observer might suggest that there had been borrowing from the cults but which in reality is simply due to the essentially universal character of religious psychology. I refer to the tendency to make a secret of matters of religion, a tendency that amounts not merely to a psychological but to some extent to a sociological law.
>
> The deeper and more moving the religious perception of a pious man becomes, the more such experience inclines him chastely to guard it from the non-initiate, and his anxiety to do this increases if there is any danger of the profane multitude breaking in on this holy ground. (38)

A most interesting claim! Rahner attributes religious secrecy to "the essentially universal character of religious psychology," not to a survival of ancient taboos. Christianity is history, not myth, mind, not body—yet it can't shake some age-old bodily impulse to taboo its holiest truths. And why? Rahner skirts uneasily over this awkward question, which I want to address in a moment; still, his description of the Christian mysteries, the sacramental secrets, is eloquent:

> Now this psychological law begins to operate actively within Christianity as soon as the appropriate external circumstances have come into being. However public the Christian message may be, however much it may be "a mystery preached from the housetops" and addressed to all mankind, yet from the third century onwards, as Christianity became more widespread and popular, a need is felt for safeguarding it against the breaking-in of the mass. That is why it is now—and only now—that the so-called *disciplina arcani* is born and indeed it was not till the fourth century that it became fully developed. It is, indeed, not surprising that the Church Fathers who came to Christianity from Neoplatonism [including Augustine] should have used a manner of speaking of these things that was certainly formed within the religious world of the moribund cults. The mysteries of baptism and of the altar of sacrifice were wrapped about with awful, reverent and concealing rites, and soon the iconostasis was to make the merest glance into the holy of holies impossible for the non-initiate. They turn into φριχτὰ καὶ φοβερὰ μυστήρια—the dread and awful mysteries. "This is known to the initiates" is a phrase to be found in all Greek sermons and even the Pseudo-Areopagite warns the initiated Christian who has passed through the mystagogia against careless talk: "See that thou be not a babbler concerning the most holy things, guard the mysteries of the hidden God so that none who is not initiated may partake therein, and to make this sure, speak of the holy only to holy men and speak in holy illumination." (39)

Bible Translation and Taboo

"However public the Christian message may be, however much it may be 'a mystery preached from the housetops' and addressed to all mankind, yet from the third century onwards, as Christianity became more widespread and popular, a need is felt for safeguarding it against the breaking-in of the mass"—this passage presents a puzzle that lies somewhere near the heart of my project in this book. Specifically, in a religion founded on exoteric openness, on the importance of welcoming everyone—Greek and Jew, man and woman, slave and free—into the fold, Bible translation was tabooed, banned, and prohibited both tacitly and by law for well over a thousand years. How is this possible?

Implicit in my argument so far has been a history of *don'ts*, the shifting forms the taboo on translation has taken through the centuries; and perhaps this is the place to spell out these *don'ts* as clearly as possible.

1. *Don't translate*. A translation for outsiders is pointless; only a small group of insiders would understand it; the outsiders would only distort and pervert the translated text. This is the blockage I explored in chapter 1 through my discussion of the imposition of a taboo on translation, or perhaps only on "handling" the sacred text. As the mystery religions spread from Egypt to Greece and Rome and beyond, there is, naturally, pressure to

assimilate the cultic rites to the languages and cultural norms of the new worshippers, but this pressure is resisted. Some assimilation, some translation does take place; in chapter 1 we watched Herodotus tell the story of how the Egyptian mysteries of Amon-Ra spread from Thebes to Dodona and became the Greek mysteries of Zeus. But in every such geohermeneutical migration, the mystery texts themselves remain in Egyptian. These texts are translated ritually only for initiates, never for outsiders, and only by priests, never by lay initiates. Every "translated" cult retains the taboo on translation, often in slightly altered form. The god or goddess wrote the sacred text in his or her own language, Egyptian or Hebrew or Greek or (for the medieval and early modern church, by that curious twist I explored a moment ago that, through the contagion of taboo, renders a *translation* God's holy writ) Latin, and any attempt to "dilute" God's word by translating it into another language will incur the god's or goddess's wrath.

But then, later:

2. *Don't translate accessibly, "openly," so that your target text is easily understandable by a target reader*. By clinging closely to the source-language syntax and semantics you not only do homage to the original, you prevent the target text from falling into the wrong hands—uneducated Bible readers, say, who might think that since Jacob had four wives, they can too.

And, of course, as a corollary to that last one:

3. *Don't add anything to or subtract anything from the source text*—upon pain of, well, I'd rather not say (but *something* terrible).

And then, gradually, after a long process of social assimilation:

4. *Don't present translations as translations*. Always make them sound like and pass for target-language originals without ever cutting yourself off from the original's power to dictate the terms and frameworks for "correct" interpretation. (Though Willis Barnstone argues that this impulse has been present from a very early period, at least since the compilation of the Hebrew Bible in around the sixth or fifth century B.C.E.)

And all along, strangely, uneasily:

5. *Don't talk about translation*. If you have to theorize translation, restrict yourself to restating the obvious, to reminding people of what everyone should already know. Never poke and prod at repressions. Never try to demystify existing "theories." Laugh easily at translation theories that tie current orthodoxies to medieval theology or the ancient mystery religions: such theories are concocted by people trying to be clever, to get published, to make a splash. Translation is patently (*everyone* knows this) a matter of reproducing in the target language more or less exactly what the source text is trying to say. It has nothing to do with religion or taboos or any of that other fancy stuff. The very idea.

Obviously, some of these taboos conflict; some even conflict internally. When the medieval and early modern church interdicted Bible translations, they meant to prevent translations from Jerome's Vulgate into the vernacular. Translation was okay for Jerome because God guided Jerome's hand and rendered his version more pure than the Hebrew and Greek originals; translation of that translation is taboo. There are also patent conflicts between the taboo on translation (1) and the taboo on communicative translation (2), and between that latter taboo and the taboo on what Juliane House calls overt translation (3), translation that draws attention to its own translated status. These conflicts partly reflect historical shifts in the social recuperation of the ancient taboos: different periods (and different factions in the same period) behaviorize the ideosomatic pressures on translation in different ways, with different emphases, so that in the 1520s, say, we have both Thomas More's reluctance to have the Bible in English at all and William Tyndale's and Martin Luther's determination to have the Bible read as if it had originally been written in English or German.

Freud suggests a possible reason for these shifts and conflicts and overlaps in *Totem and Taboo:* "The instinctual desire is constantly shifting in order to escape from the *impasse* [imposed by taboo] and endeavours to find substitutes—substitute objects and substitute acts—in place of the prohibited ones. In consequence of this, the prohibition itself shifts about as well, and extends to any new aims which the forbidden impulse may adopt" (30). Luther's "openness" to translation is steeped in the same taboos as More's "closedness"—Luther just shifted ground; he found substitute objects and substitute acts.

But in part, the conflicts also run much deeper than such historical shifting and reflect an important aspect of taboo's ideosomatic survival through the centuries. *All* of the *don'ts* I listed, in all their conflictedness, remain in force today. The stratification of ideosomatic programming means that no taboo is ever lost. No version of a taboo is ever lost. The ancient taboo on sacred texts remains with us today—it is much weakened, perhaps, but with us nonetheless. Every time a translator hesitates before translating some great poem or decides not to translate it at all—because, say, it's "untranslatable," its beauties would be lost in translation, it would feel like desecration even to try to render it in the target language—s/he feels some of the force of that taboo. It seems likely to me that the preference linguistic translation theorists show for "ordinary" source texts like weather reports, business letters, technical documentation, and the like over "special" source texts like poems is grounded in a survival of that ancient taboo as well. It's okay to translate and study "marketplace" texts, since they never possessed the hieratic aura of mystery that the gnomic texts of various religious and poetic traditions once had and perhaps still have. But subliminally, poems are off-limits for translation; they are taboo and thus "difficult"; finally they are non- or extraordinary or "special" uses of language that are unrepresentative of "the language" and therefore beyond the scientific pale. This may explain why Eugene Nida, considered so conservative and conventional in translation theory circles, is regarded as such a dangerous radical in religious circles: he treats the Bible as if it were a marketplace text, a weather report or a business letter, a text to be translated for mere communicativity without the slightest concern for its sacrality, which is to say, for the terrors of its tabooed mysteries.

The really clear examples of the taboo on translation within the metempsychotic tradition, however, are from the Middle Ages and the Reformation: Aelfric's tenth-century anxiety when asked to translate Genesis into Latin; the persecution of the fourteenth-century Lollards, which was accompanied by legislation prohibiting possession of a vernacular Bible; the sixteenth-century prosecution of one Richard Hunne for possessing an English Bible and his mysterious hanging, supposedly done in jail by his own hand and with his own belt; the 1536 execution of William Tyndale for translating the Bible into English; Luther's flight into anonymity as the "Junker Karl" in the Castle Wartburg when it began to look likely that his life was in danger. Of these, I want to look closely at two, Aelfric's letter to Aethelweard and Thomas More's defense of the Hunne prosecution in his *Dialogue Concerning Heresies* (1529).

Aelfric

Aelfric (c. 955–c. 1010) was an English abbot, writer, and translator whose efforts to instruct monks and spread medieval learning have become emblems of tenth-century England. He was probably born into a middle-class family in Wessex, where he seems to have lived all his life; scholars have speculated that his father was a court official or a merchant. All we know of his childhood is that he had a Latin tutor whose Latin was weak and that he entered Aethelwold's monastic school in Winchester, the hub of the intellectual reform movement of the late tenth century, in the early 970s, probably while he was still in his teens. He was sent to the newly founded monastery of Cernel in 987, where he spent eighteen years as a simple priest. In 1005, at the age of 50, he was appointed abbot at yet another newly founded monastery at Eynsham.

Aelfric was brought to Cernel to teach the monks, and his writings grew organically out of this pedagogical program. Like King Alfred a century earlier, he was concerned about the decline of learning in England (a decline now attributed to the Danish invasions), and he concocted a plan similar to Alfred's for providing in English, specifically for monastic students and monks ignorant of Latin, a compendium of the knowledge essential to faith. Interestingly, however, everything he wrote about this project trembles with his fears that he is revealing mysteries to the profane. In 989 and 992, for example, he wrote the *Catholic Homilies*, a collection of eighty sermons geared to the liturgical year whose subjects spanned sacred history from Creation to the Last Judgment. Because his Biblical quotes in these sermons were carefully selected and presented in an explanatory context that anchored them dogmatically—a context that serves as the Christian equivalent to the priest Mithras's ritual preparation of Lucius and that in some sense displaces the taboo by framing it in commentary—Aelfric was not as nervous about this work as he would be later about his translation of Genesis. Even so, he addresses the first book of homilies to Bishop Aethelwold with an anxious glance over his shoulder:

> However rashly or presumptuously undertaken, I have nevertheless formed this book out of Latin writers and from Holy Scripture, translating into our ordinary speech, for the edification of the simple, who know only this language both for reading and for hearing; and for that reason I have used no difficult words, but only plain English; so that our message might the more readily reach the hearts of those who read or hear, to the profit of the souls of those who cannot be taught in any other tongue than that to which they were born. (quoted in Hurt 42)

"Presumptuously" refers to Aelfric's sense of his position in the Catholic hierarchy: should a lowly monk be doing this work? "Rashly" refers to taboo: am I treading on dangerous ground here?

What's interesting in these remarks and even more so in his prefatory letter to his translation of Genesis, however, is the manifest tension they reflect between ancient taboos, which bid him *not* to translate, and emergent exoteric rationalism, which bids him not only to translate but to translate as accessibly as possible. Aelfric's patron Aethelweard, the father of his abbott and the ealdorman or governor of the territory, the powerful man to whom Aelfric addresses his prefatory remarks, commissioned the translation because he wanted to participate in the great tenth-century renaissance of "learning" (read "rationalism") but needed a translator's help to do so. He had no Latin. And so he called upon loyal Aelfric to help him: the learned monk at his son's monastery had done the *Catholic Homilies* a few years before, so maybe he would translate part of the Bible. Aethelweard must have known Aelfric would resist; the recalcitrance of monks when it came to rendering scripture into the vernacular was well-known, and Aethelweard had only been able to persuade another monk to translate the second half of Genesis. In the church's eyes, as a layman, Aethelweard was an outsider. He was someone to whom the *mysteria* should not be divulged. As the royally appointed governor of the region, however, who happened also to be the father of an abbott, he could do virtually anything he wanted; and if he wanted an Anglo-Saxon translation of the Book of Genesis, he would get it.

This, then, is the preface to Aelfric's translation:

> When you desired me, honoured friend, to translate the Book of Genesis from Latin into English, I was loth to grant your request; upon which you assured me that I should need to translate only so far as the account of Isaac, Abraham's son, seeing that some other person had rendered it for you from that point to the end. Now, I am concerned lest the work should be dangerous for me or any one else to undertake, because I fear that, if some foolish man should read this book or hear it read, he would imagine that he could live now, under the new dispensation, just as the patriarchs lived before the old law was

> established, or as men lived under the law of Moses. At one time I was aware that a certain priest, who was then my master, and who had some knowledge of Latin, had in his possession the Book of Genesis; he did not scruple to say that the patriarch Jacob had four wives—two sisters and their two handmaids. What he said was true enough, but neither did he realize, nor did I as yet, what a difference there is between the old dispensation and the new. In the early ages the brother took his sister to wife; sometimes the father had children by his own daughter; many had several wives for the increase of the people; and one could only marry among his kindred. Any one who now, since the coming of Christ, lives as men lived before or under the Mosaic law, that man is no Christian; in fact, he is not worthy to have a Christian eat with him. If ignorant priests have some inkling of the sense of their Latin books, they immediately think that they can set up for great teachers; but they do not recognize the spiritual signification, and how the Old Testament was a prefiguration of things to come, and how the New Testament, after the incarnation of Christ, was the fulfillment of all those things which the Old Testament foreshadowed concerning Christ and his elect. Referring to Paul, they often wish to know why they may not have wives as well as the apostle Peter; but they will neither hear nor know that the blessed Peter lived according to Moses' law until Christ came to men and began to preach his holy gospel, Peter being the first companion that he chose; and that Peter forthwith forsook both wives and goods, and followed Christ's teaching to that new law and purity which he himself set up. . . . Now I protest that I neither dare nor will translate any book hereafter from Latin into English; and I beseech you, dear earl, not to urge me any longer, lest I should be disobedient to you, or break my word if I should promise. God be gracious to you for evermore. Now in God's name I implore, if any one should transcribe this book, that he will strictly follow the copy, since I cannot help it if an inaccurate scribe introduces corruptions. In such case he does it at his own risk, not mine; and the careless copyist does much harm, unless he corrects his mistake. (lxx–lxxi)

Watch Aelfric at work setting up hedges against the charge of heresy, the charge of doing dangerous work, a charge that is "only" in his head (or in his body's continuing response to ancient taboos) since he is *commanded by his lord* to do this dangerous work. He insists, I didn't translate the whole book of Genesis, only half, so that if my translation should fall into the wrong hands, the danger would be minimized; and I'm not going to translate another word, so don't ask me to, lest I have to disobey you or break my word; and if some scribe introduces corruption into my translation, that's his problem, not mine, so don't come hurling your accusations at me. Aelfric, a medieval cultural hero who dedicated his life to the spread of learning in the vernacular, an early harbinger of the (rationalist) Renaissance, was terrified of the old taboos—terrified enough to translate the bare text of Scripture (unframed by protective commentary) into Anglo-Saxon only once, and then to do so with great misgivings and only upon the express command of his powerful patron Aethelweard, father of his abbott and governor of the territory.

Of course, it could be argued that what he reacted to was not some deep-seated taboo but a specific theological and ecclesiastical concern, a fear he mentions explicitly of leading more ignorant readers astray—his sense that "foolish" readers untrained in dispensationalist theology would read the patent "immorality" of Genesis as a *carte blanche*, giving them license to commit bigamy and incest and anything else they desired. As a senior monk in his monastery, entrusted with educating the younger monks in the doctrines of the church, he was accountable before God for the immortal souls of the men in his trust. And his concerns were very real, and even today continue to haunt dispensationalists—fundamentalist Christians who "explain" the "immorality" of God's people in the Old Testament as Aelfric does by saying that the Jews were allowed more leeway before the coming of Christ (a nice touch: Jesus came to "free" us from the law by imposing an even stricter one). Baptists, for example, rarely encourage the reading of Genesis and rarely take scripture lessons from it in Sunday worship. And when they do, they hem it round with severe dispensationalist strictures that limit all the immorality to the old dispensation, before Christ.

But there is more going on in Aelfric's protests than systematic theology. He is patently *afraid*. His words surge with scarcely suppressed fear, a fear that overrode even a direct command from his bishop, so that even in obeying it, he wheedled the command down to a mere half of the original (translate Genesis), did that half under polite but anxious and insistent protest, and stated flatly that he refused to do any more. If he was mainly worried about being held accountable for his readers' immorality—you translated the book, you exposed them to the Bible without proper preparation—surely he was aware that, by the hierarchical rules of the Catholic Church, doing the translation at his lord's command relieves him of accountability (as Hitler's command relieved the Nazis of responsibility for the Holocaust—or so they were led to believe by nearly two millennia of ecclesiastical hegemony in the West). If on the Day of Reckoning the Judge says to Aelfric, *hey buddy, look what you did*, all he has to say is *I was only following orders*, and Jesus will go after Aethelweard. But this reassurance still wasn't enough for Aelfric. He still was terrified. He still felt his translation was not *right*, was dangerous.

And maybe his fears were justified. This justification may be difficult for us modern readers to see, steeped as we are in the culture of rationalism that Aelfric helped create, but Aelfric addresses a very real concern. How *do* you account for all the lying, cheating, stealing, raping, and deceiving that God's chosen do in the Book of Genesis in the name (and with the explicit or implicit approval and blessing) of Yahweh? The problem isn't just a matter of explaining this immoral behavior away, sweeping it under the rug, as it might seem to us; it's a matter of developing some form of institutional protection against the terrible wrath that God will direct against anyone who misinterprets his word. The bold, resolute, almost heroic "sinning" of the Old Testament patriarchs and their families presented a ghastly temptation for medieval cenobites and did so only partly because these stories might entice the monks into breaking their ascetic regimens against fornication and mendacity and the rest. The lure of behavioral transgression is strong, no doubt about that, but the lure of interpretive translation is stronger still—and in the eyes of medieval theologians, it was far more dangerous. It is one thing to lust after women—even after four wives like Jacob—and quite another to come to see God as a petty, childish, insecure tyrant who throughout the Book of Genesis constantly bullies his creations into doing his bidding and threatens to destroy them if they don't obey.

Such tendencies are easy to see in Genesis. The difficult thing, the thing that requires incessant ascetic vigilance, is *not* to see them and not to anger a wrathful legalistic God by seeing them. And so medieval theologians developed rationalist prophylactics against this dangerous vision of God—notions of the different dispensations, for example, according to which more is expected of people who have heard of Jesus than of those who haven't. The question then became, how do you best protect the "common people," the still largely illiterate lay masses, from this sinful vision: through knowledge (inducting them into the mysteries) or through ignorance (guarding the mysteries against "profane prying")? Do you protect your own anxieties by protecting others from "dangerous" knowledge, as the medieval church did? Or do you, like "Protestants" from the fourteenth-century Lollards to the sixteenth-century Reformers, disseminate your institutionalized prophylactics to everyone in the form, say, of carefully regulated Bible translations accompanied by catechistic teaching?

Thomas More

Ironically enough, Thomas More's 1529 *Dialogue Concerning Heresies and Matters of Religion*, the result of a 1528 commission from Bishop Tunstall to read all of the heretical writings in English and pronounce upon them, was a staunch defense of political and ecclesiastical authority against the forces of social change that More felt all around him. When the changes came, they came not from below, from the masses, as he had feared they would, but from above, from his king, Henry VIII, who ordered all England to convert to the heresy More had attacked and, in 1535, had More himself executed for treason. The arch-heretic William Tyndale, then a fugitive from Catholic justice in Germany, replied to More's charges in *Answer unto Sir Thomas More's Dialogue* (1531), and More wrote his longest book, the two-volume *Confutation of Tyndale's Answer* (1532–1533), in response; he also defended his own enforcement of the antiheresy laws in two further books in 1533. In another rich irony, Tyndale was captured and executed for heresy in 1536—outliving his "orthodox" accuser by a year.

More's *Dialogue* is a fascinating transitional document for a study of the ascendancy of reason over mystery, since the old taboos so clearly survive in More's calm modern voice. Like Aelfric, More clearly didn't want the Bible in the vernacular and nervously imagined the restrictions that would need to be placed on dissemination if a vernacular Bible ever became readily available. But More was a highly articulate modern rationalist who justified his esoteric fears with brilliant casuistry. Above all, he wrote his attack on heresies in the "modern" form of the dialogue—as modern as Plato—which enabled him to give voice not only to his own orthodox position but to that of his opponents as well. His interlocutor, called only the Messenger, gives a highly persuasive articulation to the tabooed "seditious" or "heretical" notions More attacks—thus introducing into the argument its own potential "confutation." The Messenger, whom More modeled on a tutor to the children of one of his friends just outside London, has come in contact with Lutheranism at the university and comes to More with his questions and confusions; he remains a Catholic but is strongly drawn to the Protestant idea that the written word of the Bible supersedes even the ancient practices of the church. The Messenger voices what we would have to call the rationalist wave of the future, the spirit of the pragmatic, commonsensical, demystificatory middle class that was steadily to expand its hegemony until it more or less ruled the world; and in this historical sense, despite the argumentative bludgeoning he takes from More, the Messenger triumphs "in" (or beyond) the dialogue: the history of the last four centuries has conditioned More's readers to take the Messenger's side.

Significantly, however, this "triumph" is partly, even largely, More's; the Messenger is, after all, no real person but a fictional character in More's *Dialogue*. More could have caricatured the Messenger beyond all hope of reader identification, but he didn't. More set up the possibility of the Messenger's sociopolitical triumph—perhaps out of a deep-seated "literary" (or political-unconscious) awareness of the social forces that would soon lead to his own downfall and death. More worked hard to make his Messenger come alive, to make him speak eloquently for the forces of Protestant sedition; and if that hard work gave him a subliminal foreknowledge of his own defeat, it also gave his *Dialogue* the political resonance that would help it survive the death of its author.

Another significant factor in all this is that in the *Dialogue*, *both* More and the Messenger are sixteenth-century rationalists, humanists, modern well-educated men engaged in questioning the wisdom of the ages—and while More comes down on the side of tradition, specifically, in terms of Bible translation, on the side of the mystificatory tradition that tabooed sacred texts and sought to keep them from the profane, he does so in a rationalist vein that subtly undermines the tradition as well. In his desire to make his defense of orthodoxy seem reasonable, he does not ban *all* vernacular Bibles, only those vernacular Bibles that do not meet certain institutional criteria for approval. He makes an attempt to mystify the ancient taboo through reasonable argumentation—although his argumentation is easily overturned when the powers that control institutional approval change their minds, as they did soon after England turned Protestant only a few years after More wrote. If the Bible must be kept in Latin because it's taboo, because terrible things will happen to lay readers who attempt to approach it in the vernacular, then the church authorizes vernacular translations at its peril. But if, as More suggests, the obstacles to vernacular Bible translation are not divine wrath but the heresy of previous translations, the heretical inclinations and lack of education of those who now clamor for a vernacular Bible, and the absence of adequate controls on who will be granted access to vernacular Bibles and for how long, then all you need to do to overcome these obstacles is to control the translation process, to educate the populace, and to regulate distribution. And these remedies, especially the first two, became realities in the decades following More's death.

The Messenger first asks More to justify the late-fourteenth-century Constitution Provincial, written by Archbishop Thomas Arundel, which said, in part (the English modernized by More's editors):

> We resolve therefore and ordain that no one henceforth on his own authority translate any text of Holy Scripture into English or any other language by way of a book, pamphlet or tract, and that no book, pamphlet or tract of this kind whether already recently composed in the time of the said John Wyclif or since, publicly or privately, under pain of the greater excommunication, until the translation shall have been approved by the diocesan of the place, or if need be by a provincial council. (quoted in More 684)

And here is the relevant passage from More's *Dialogue*, beginning with the Messenger's voice:

> Bvt now to the matter we were in hande with. Ye sayd ye wold make answere for the law / wherby the clergy of this realme have forboden all the peple to haue any scrypture translated into our tonge / which is as I sayd in my mind an euill made lawe.
>
> Mary quod I that is sone answered. Lay the charge to them that made it.
>
> Mary quod he so I do. For who made y^t constytucyon but they?
>
> Surely quod I no body els / nor they neyther.
>
> No quod he? what euery man knoweth it.
>
> Verely quod I many men talke of it / but no man knoweth it. For there is none suche in dede. There is of trouth a constytucyon that speketh of suche matter / but no thyng of suche fassyon. For ye shall vnderstande that the great archheretyke Wyclyffe / where as the hole byble was longe before his dayes by vertuous & well lerned men translated into ye englysh tonge / & by good and godly people with deuocyon & sobernes well & reuerently red / toke vpon him of a malycious purpose to translate it of new. In which translacyon he purposely corrupted y^t holy texte / malycyously plantyng therin suche wordys / as myght in ye reders erys serue to ye profe of suche heresyes as he went about to sow / which he not onely set forth with his own translacyon of ye byble / but also with certayne prologes & glosys which he made therevpon. And these thynges he so handeled (which was no great maystrye) with reasons probable & lykely to ley people & vnlerned / y^t he corrupted in his tyme many folke in this realme. (314–15)

There is, in other words, no law forbidding vernacular Bible translations—only one forbidding maliciously corrupt Bible translations, such as Wyclif's, which lead ignorant readers astray. Actually, what the Constitution Provincial specifically forbids is the making of *unapproved* vernacular translations: theoretically, as More keeps insisting all through these chapters (14–16 in book three) of his *Dialogue*, it would be possible for someone to translate the Bible into English, get the translation approved by the ecclesiastical authorities, and then have it carefully distributed by those authorities, one copy at a time, to specially vetted lay members of the congregation and collected back after a reasonable period, say, twenty-four hours, lest it be passed illicitly from hand to hand. We're moving, here, toward the relative "freedom" of the rationalist demystification of the ancient taboos, which enlightened souls from Aethelweard through Wyclif and Jan Hus to William Tyndale and Martin Luther had been advocating for centuries—but this movement is very slow, very cautious, very fearful. Indeed, it was not until the 1580s, half a century after Catholicism had been criminalized in England, that the Catholic Church would actually approve the translation of the Bible into English. The Douay-Rheims Bible (New Testament 1582, both Testaments 1609–10) was the product of that approval.

More writes:

> For I trowe, y^t in this lawe ye se nothynge vnreasonable. For it neyther forbedeth the translacyons to be red that were all redy well done of olde before Wyclyffys dayes / nor dampneth his bycause it was newe / but bycause it was nought / nor prohybyteth newe to be made / but prouydeth that they shall not be redde yf they be mysse made / tyll they be by good examynacyon amended / excepte they be suche translacyons as wyclyffe made & Tyndall / that the malycyous mynde of the translatoure had in suche wyse handled it as it were labour lost to go aboute to mende them. (316)

And so at last the Messenger, after a long discussion of the case of Richard Hunne, who was arrested for possession of an English Bible and found mysteriously hanged by his own belt in prison, comes to agree that More does truly want to see the Bible in English. But, the Messenger says, More is not typical of the clergy of the day:

> I am sure quod your frende ye doute not but that I am full and hole of your mynde in this matter that the byble sholde be in our englyshe tonge. But yet that the clergye is of the contrary and wolde not haue it so / that appereth well in that they suffer it not to be so. And ouer that I here in euery place almost where I fynde any lerned man of them / theyr myndys all set thereon to kepe the scrypture frome vs. And they seke out for that parte euery roten reason that they can fynde / and set theym forth solemply to the shewe / though fyue of those reasons be not worth a fygge. For they begynne as far as our fyrst father Adam / and shewe vs that his wyfe and he fell oute of paradyse with desyre of knowlege and connynge [learning]. Nowe yf this wolde serue / it muste from the knowledge and study of scrypture dryue euery man preste and

> other / leste it dryue all out of paradyse. Than say they that god taught his dyscyples many thyngys a parte / bycause the peple sholde not here it. And therfore they wolde the peple sholde not nowe be sufferd to rede all. Yet they say further that it is harde to translate the scrypture out of one tonge into another / and specyally they say into ours. Whiche they call a tonge vulgare and barbarous. But of all thynge specyally they say that scrypture is ye fode of the soule. And that the comen people be as infantys that muste be fedde but with mylke and pappe. And yf we haue any stronger mete it must be chammed [chewed] afore by the nurse and so put into the babys mouth. But me thynke though they make vs all infantys / they shall fynde many a shrewde brayne among vs / that can perceyue chalke fro chese well ynough and yf they wolde ones take vs our mete in our owne hande. We be not so euill tothed but that within a whyle they shall se vs cham it our selfe as well as they. For let them call vs yonge babys and they wyll / yet by god they shall for all that well fynde in some of vs y^t an old knaue is no chylde.
>
> Surely quod I suche thynges as ye speke / is ye thyng that as I somewhat sayd before putteth good folke in fere to suffer the scrypture in our englyshe tonge. Not for the redynge & receyuinge / but for the bysy chamming therof / & for moche medlyng with suche partys therof as lest wyll agre with theyr capacytees. For vndoubtedly as ye spake of our mother Eue / inordynate appetyte of knowlege is a meane to dryue any man out of paradyse. And inordynate is ye appetite when men vnlerned though they rede it in theyr langage / wyll be bysy to enserch and dyspute the grete secrete mysteryes of scrypture / which thoughe they here they be not able to perceyue. This thynge is playnly forboden vs that be not appoynted nor instructed thereto. (332–33)

And More goes on to instantiate the traditional defenses of keeping the Bible from the unlearned masses:

- In Exodus 24 Moses went up the mountain but left the people behind at the bottom, signifying "y^t the people be forboden to presume to medle with the hygh mysteryes of holy scrypture / but ought to be contente to tary bynethe & medle none hygher than is mete for them / but receyuing fro the heyght of the hyll by Moyses that y^t is delyuered them / that is to wytte the lawes and preceptes that they must kepe / and the poyntes they must byleue" (a reading he attributes to Gregory of Nazianzus, the fourth-century church father).

- Drawing upon Paul's promise in Ephesians 4:11 that Christ "wyl haue some reders and some herers / some techers & som lerners / we do playnly peruerte & tourne vp so downe ye ryght order of Crystes chyrch / whan ye one parte medleth with ye others offyce" (334).

- Plato forbids the masses from "embysy[ing] theym selfe in reasonyng and dysputynge vppon the temporall lawes of the cyte / whiche wolde not be reasoned vpon but by folke mete therefor and in place conuenyent" (334), lest they learn to dislike and condemn those laws and call for their removal. The next passage presents a nice irony, given the change not only in the laws of England but in More's fate over the next few years: "For tyll a lawe be chaunged by authoryte / yt rather ought to be obserued thanne contempned" (334).

When the laws governing the state church are changed by the authority of King Henry, and More is asked to recognize his king as the head of his church, he refuses—which authority should he obey, his king or his pope?—and is imprisoned for treason and ultimately beheaded. In less than a decade, without changing his views or his behavior, the scourge of heretics has become a heretic; the man who helped condemn Richard Hunne to death for possession of a vernacular Bible is himself condemned to death for refusing to aid in the social transformation that would a few years later decriminalize the possession of vernacular Bibles, that in fact would even encourage their production and distribution.

Besides, More goes on, if ordinary uneducated people started reading the Bible in their own language, they would soon (especially when drunk, a state More assumes is pretty common among these lewd folks) debase it into just another marketplace text—a charge that is leveled against vernacular translators of sacred texts right up to and including Eugene Nida in our own day: "And there whan the wyne were in and the wytte out / wolde they take vppon them with folyshe wordys and blasphemye to handle holy scrypture in more homely maner than a songe of Robyn hode" (335), resulting in "sedycyouse sectys and heresyes / whereby the scrypture of god shold lese his honoure and reuerence / and be by suche vnreuerent and vnsyttynge demeanour amonge moche people quyte and clene abused / vnto the contrary of that holy purpose that god ordayned it for" (335).

This passage is More's strongest expression of the taboo: a sacred text must be kept *sacred*, which is to say, taboo, apart, holy, venerated (from a distance) with a mixture of respect, awe, and dread. The Bible is not just some book, some story or song of Robin Hood, to be bandied about by ordinary drunks in a tavern, profane louts who know nothing of Latin or Church doctrine or any of the other "grete secrete mysteryes" that More so jealously guards. The Bible is "the scrypture of god," God's Word, written by the very hand of God, and to be protected against such "vnreuerent and unsyttynge" abuse. In the end, all More's rationalizations, all his sophistry, all his careful open-mindedness can be traced to a visceral fear that surges with the most primitive emotions in religious history, a holy terror before the things and the words of the god.

One of the most chilling moments in More's take on translation comes in his *Confutation of Tyndale's Answer*. More had taken Tyndale to task for rendering the Greek word *ecclesia* as "congregation" rather than "church" and for thus apparently implying that the Roman Catholic state church was not the true *ecclesia* named in the Bible. Tyndale had replied in his *Answer unto Sir Thomas More's Dialogue* that Erasmus had translated *ecclesia* into Latin as *congregatio*, adding snidely that this translation didn't bother More because Erasmus was More's darling. All this is interesting enough; but Tyndale then went on to wish that Erasmus's *Praise of Folly* or *Encomium Moriae* were written in English so that ordinary people could see that More had had very different opinions at the time that work was written! More was properly amazed at this suggestion: not only is there nothing in the *Encomium Moriae* to warrant Tyndale's wish, but More didn't even write the book. The Moria figure who narrates it is Erasmus's fictional creation, just as the Messenger in More's *Dialogue* is More's creation—Moria is based loosely on More, perhaps, and certainly refers humorously to More, in whose house Erasmus wrote the *Encomium Moriae*, but actually signifies not More but Folly.

In any case, something about Tyndale's bizarre wish troubled More deeply—so deeply that he decided it was a very good thing the *Encomium Moriae* was *not* in English and that the same was true of a number of other Latin books as well:

> And therfore in these dayes in which Tyndale hath (god amende hym) wyth thenfeccion of his contagyouse heresyes, so sore poysened malycyouse and newfangle folke / that the kynges hyghnes and not wythout the counsayle and aduyce not of his nobles onely, wyth his other counsaylours attendynge vppon his gracys person / but also of the ryght vertuouse and specyall well lerned men of eyther vnyuersyte [university] & other partyes of the realme specyally called thereto, hathe after dylygent and longe consyderacyon hadde therein, ben fayne for the whyle to prohybyte the scrypture of god to be sufferd in englyshe tonge amonge the peoples handes / leste euyll folke by false drawyng of euery good thynge they rede in to the colour and mayntenauns of theyr owne fonde fantasyes, and turnynge all hony [honey] in to posyn [poison], myght both dedly do hurt vnto theym selfe, and sprede also that infeccyone farther a brode: I say therfore in these dayes in whyche men by theyr owne defaute mysseconstre [misconstrue] and take harme of the very scrypture of god, vntyll menne better amende, yf any man wolde now translate Moria in to Englyshe, or some workes eyther that I haue my self wryten ere this, all be yt there be none harme therin / folke yet beynge (as they be) geuen [given] to take harme of that that is good / I wolde not onely my derlynges bokes but myne owne also, helpe to burne them both wyth myne owne handes, rather then folke sholde (though thorow theyr own faute) take any harme of them, seynge that I se them lykely in these dayes to do so. (1:178–79)

As long as there is any chance at all that someone might misread a Latin book, whether Scripture or a secular piece like Erasmus's *Encomium* or More's *Utopia* (the most likely referent for "or some workes eyther that I haue my selfe wryten ere this"—More didn't write that much in Latin), *even burning is preferable to translation*. This is a highly educated man of the early sixteenth century, a modern rationalist with whom many of us were encouraged to identify through Robert Bolton's play from the sixties, *A Man For All Seasons*—could he have been this afraid of popular access to Latin works? Could the taboo run this deep? You'll notice that More doesn't advocate the burning of Latin Bibles to prevent the likes of Tyndale from translating them into English: the Bible is so taboo that one must even risk its translation rather than burn it. The *Encomium Moriae* and *Utopia* are ordinary enough, everyday enough, to burn—and yet they are also taboo enough to make burning them preferable to releasing them for popular access. In this same period, the early 1530s, More was literally engaged in the burning of heretical books, though not with his own hands; he is here saying, almost self-sacrificially, that he is willing to burn even his own books and those of his friends, good books, nonheretical books, if they are likely to be read in a heretical fashion. Such is the "contagiousness" of heresy (or taboo), as he says, that it spreads like a plague, like an infection, from one carrier to another; and in an evil age such as More's, an age in which "euyll folke" clung to heretical "fonde fantasyes" in place of the truth, the only safe thing to do with potentially heretical books in English was to burn them. Fire purifies books and bodies of disease. Books in Latin were still fairly safe, since most of the heretics didn't read Latin; but with learned heretics like Tyndale running around translating Latin books into English and attempting to spread his heresies across the land, More says we'd better be ready to burn Latin books, too, if they seem in danger of being translated into the vernacular.

Esoteric Mutations

Indeed one of the most striking aspects of the schizoid condition, as Laing describes it, and of esoteric religion, as scholars of the mysteries describe them, is what we might call a culture of protective possession. The Bible is mine, ours, the prize possession of my small group of specially trained priests or scholars—this is one of the subtexts in Aelfric and in the Constitution Provincial and in More and in the writings of dozens of other authors. No one else shall have it. "The isolation of the self," as Laing says of the schizoid personality, "is a corollary . . . of the need to be in control. He prefers to *steal*, rather than to be given. He prefers to give, rather than have anything, as he feels, stolen from him; i.e. he has to be in control of who or what comes into him, and of who or what leaves him" (88). The "good things" that everyone needs—love, affection, admiration, laughter, togetherness, joy, religious experience—do not flow freely, but are possessed and jealously guarded against theft. And because they are possessed, because they become possessions and thus inert *things*, they become shams, pathetic imitations of the true enlivening emotions: you experience love as an ethos, affection as a checklist of "nice" things to say and do, admiration as sycophancy, laughter without pleasure, togetherness without connection, happiness without joy, religious experience as obedience to social authorities. You have a feeling and are immediately afraid that someone is going to take it away from you or that sharing it with someone else will diminish it for you—so you guard the feeling. You tuck it away and don't let anyone else know you've got it. And, ironically enough, you *don't* have it, because hiding the feeling kills it. But you pretend not to notice this loss. Maybe you succeed and really believe you still have it. But you remain wracked with doubts: what if you have it but haven't hidden it carefully enough, and someone is stealing it right now? What if you had it, but someone stole it when you weren't paying attention? (But you were paying attention *all the time!*) (Even when you were asleep?) (Omigod!) What if you never had it in the first place and only thought you did?

I'm suggesting here, perhaps rather circuitously, what I broached briefly in chapter 1: the much-vaunted secrecy of the mystery religions may have been tied closely to the rise of reason—to the whispering of the ascendant schizoid Other-as-reason, which infiltrated the mysteries early on in order to subvert their drive toward ecstatic bodily experience. The Bacchantes seek orgiastic unity with the god—and, well, guilt and the devaluation of human life. The Mithraists, convinced that the soul is stained by its dwelling on earth in the body, seek to wash away the stain through repeated ablutions, practice strict vegetarianism, and abstain from all sexual contact. Isis too enjoins upon her initiates absolute sexual abstinence. We know that the Greek word *mysteria* originally meant folk festivals and that these festivals often involved initiations (which the word eventually came to mean), but these initiations were open to everyone. The word only began to be associated with keeping things secret in the sixth or fifth century B.C.E., at precisely the same time that reason began to rear its head. Taboos existed in these cults long before it became taboo to disclose the holy secrets; could the taboo on disclosure have been only a passing phase in the Other-as-reason's assault on mystery and the body? The Other-as-reason gets in, looks around, sees people generally having a good time but afraid of touching certain things, afraid of doing certain things, afraid of saying certain things; then it's a simple matter, really, of gradually shifting their fears from the old taboos (silly things like sacred objects and the king's body) to new ones, like bodily pleasure (sex, eating), death and the afterlife, and open communication with other people.

Why? What is gained? *Cui bono?* The obvious benefit of this shift is increased control—over one's environment, one's associates, one's own body and behavior. A side benefit for participants in the mystery religions, though in Laing's terms a highly problematic one, was membership in a group—a group defined specifically in terms of a self-protective withdrawal from a larger group, so that the mystery cult would have served as a macrocosm of the schizoid self. This idea casts two related but rather different lights on the whole process. On the one hand, membership in an esoteric cult raises in-group self-esteem by thematizing the possession of arcane knowledge in terms of *deserving* (you've done something to earn your special knowledge, you're *in here*, you're better than those who lack it) and *not-deserving* (they're inferior, they're *out there*, they couldn't handle it). On the other hand, membership escalates power games by thematizing the possession of that knowledge in terms of *defense* (if your enemies on the outside got hold of this knowledge they could hurt you, gain power over you) and *offense* (your possession of the knowledge yields you power over them—as long as you keep it inviolate, safe from their spies).

Both of these thematizations serve to generate anxiety and fear, of course, which is the massive drawback in this regime—the fear that you'll slip and reveal what must never be revealed and as a result will be diminished as a person (loss of self-esteem, loss of in-group status) and will probably be overrun and crushed by your enemies. This fear in turn generates anxious vigilance, self-control, discipline, repression, ascesis. The ban on communication has the advantage of drawing the lines clearly, of telling you exactly who is going to share your knowledge and who isn't (secret handshakes, signals, etc.). Another advantage of such a ban (which may come to seem a disadvantage, from some points of view, in some circumstances) is that the possibility of flows across boundaries is taken out of your hands, placed in the hands of a priesthood. If someone else tells you not to tell, you bear no responsibility in maintaining the sense of *rightness* in not telling. It's an institutional thing, written up in the rules, surrounded by a dense network of punishments and rewards, ultimately internalized as "second nature."

Grant me, then, my assumption that "mystery" in the sense of esoteric secrecy (including the ban on making sacred texts available to out-groupers through translation or other means) was a passing phase in the Other-as-reason's rise to power that emerged in the mystery religions a century or two before Plato and died out (not entirely, but largely) by the late seventeenth or eighteenth or nineteenth century. Or, if my insistence on dragging the Other-as-reason into it is too tendentious for you, grant me that this esoteric secrecy was a passing phase in the history of Western religion, which peaked in the pagan cults in the early centuries of the Christian era and in Christianity a few centuries to a millennium later, then gradually surrendered to intensified exotericism. Either way, how do we explain it? What made "mystical" secrecy so common as to seem to Hugo Rahner to be a universal law of religious psychology—and then displaced it enough in the cultural unconscious so that most Christians today have very little sense of secrecy about their faith (at most a sense that religion is a private matter)?

Consider once again the schizoid individuals R. D. Laing describes, individuals who are possessed by not only taboo but by a nerve-wracking sense that they are themselves taboo—that they channel a powerfully destructive energy that they dare not loose on society. I would suggest that what survives in these individuals is an earlier stage of the Other-as-reason's assault on the body and human connectedness—a stage, in fact, that sounds remarkably like what we read about in Apuleius or Aelfric, the fear that disclosure of the mysteries will be literally destructive. (This is not to say that most of us no longer harbor such fears, but only that the Other-as-reason has succeeded in getting most of us to master and repress them, to live as if we didn't feel them.) Certainly Laing's patients sound like the many thousands of mystical devotees, inside and outside Christianity (monks and priests to this day), who have abstained from sex for a myriad of different reasons, all of which revolve around a sense that sex and the carnal body is polluted and any indulgence in its pleasures will draw divine wrath like a lightning rod. Schizoid Christianity, one might say, institutionalizes the fear that sexual love will electrocute the lovers and through them electrocute all society—it taboos sexuality and enshrines asexual love, spiritual love, what Augustine in the *Confessions* deified as Continentia, which is a way of idealizing isolation, glorifying the self's withdrawal into the protective enclaves of reason (philosophy) or God (theology). Hence we also have the Other-as-reason's imposition of sense-for-sense translation, which flattens language into abstract meaning or rational content, taboos the carnality of both literalism and free imitation, and renounces both of these "sinful" temptations.

The only way "out" of these burdensome restrictions, clearly—so it seems to us—lies through increased rational control. We teach small children not to touch hot stoves and not to play with the ignition switch in a car because we know that they lack both the knowledge and the bodily control to use these things safely, although we handle them daily without a single thought of danger. As children grow older we loosen the restrictions, moving from outright bans on certain kinds of behavior to defined parameters for this behavior accompanied by warnings and other "information" about how best to proceed—until finally the children become like us, able to negotiate the erstwhile "dangers" with unconscious ease. And the same pattern must have occurred within the "mysteries," with the schizoid secrets that the Other-as-reason tabooed and forbade initiates to disclose to outsiders: avoidance behaviors had to be prescribed and strictly enforced until avoidance became second nature, and initiates began to enforce it in themselves. Then, gradually, as self-enforcement began to take hold, avoidance displaced the ban altogether. It doesn't really matter what rule you obey, so long as obeying it gets you in the habit of obeying the rules. Once you've mastered that skill, a whole legion of individual rules drop away, no longer necessary. These rules only needed to be enforced while rational self-control was under construction.

Still, the achievement of increased freedom through enhanced self-control indicates that what is achieved isn't really freedom, but a new form of slavery, what Nietzsche called "internalized mastery"—and that the lifting of the bans on sexual pleasure and human communication would not necessarily entail healthy human intercourse. Certainly the prevalence today of seminars and self-help books on sexual and verbal communication—how to really make love to your partner, how to really talk with your partner, sexual/verbal intercourse by the numbers—suggests that the schizoid Other-as-reason still runs the show, just with greater outward success. The difference between a schizoid and a schizophrenic, remember, is that the schizophrenic can no longer masquerade as a "normal," "healthy" person—a sham the schizoid generally pulls off with apparent ease (and the expenditure of enormous quantities of psychic energy). All the anxieties remain to torment the schizoid behind the scenes; success is an "effect" achieved only through great effort. Nothing is natural. Nothing flows easily from or to the schizoid person.

If, then, the early imposition and later gradual rescinding of bans on communication, the movement from overt prohibitions to outward freedom based on self-control, represent the Other-as-reason's "child-rearing," so to speak, then the historical shift from esoteric to exoteric religion should demonstrate some of the schizoid's anxiety-ridden efforts to *seem* free and easy and natural. I want to spend the rest of this chapter tracing these efforts, moving through asceticism and culminating in a discussion of the attempt to export the Other-as-reason to the "savages" of the New and

Third Worlds—the explicit colonialism of much translation theory and practice over the past three or four hundred years.

But for now, let me offer a schematic representation of that shift: the processes by which the esoteric structures of the mystery religions were reproduced, in altered and often disguised forms, in the exoteric structures of a religion like Christianity. What kinds of people desired a change, and how did they work to bring it about? What did they want, what did they think they were achieving, what did they fear?

I suggest that the shift was brought about over nearly two millennia by three kinds of people, all acting on whispered instructions from the Other-as-reason: (1) people in power in the mystery religions or in positions of esoteric power in Christianity who wanted to open the mysteries of their faith up to greater numbers; (2) people in power in competing (less well established) mysteries, Christians before the fourth century C.E. when Constantine declared Christianity the official religion of the empire, and scholastics and scientists from Roger Bacon and Thomas Aquinas in the thirteenth century to Galileo in the seventeenth who wanted to win widespread acceptance for their ideas; and (3) people cut off from the avenues of established power, disenfranchised people who wanted some of the benefits that the powers-that-be withheld. Each kind of person might have followed several different pathways to increased openness:

1. *Those who already possess the arcane knowledge and want to make it available to a larger public.* This process involves a continued respect for the mysteries but a rethinking of the taboos surrounding inclusion and exclusion (and continuing repression of all others). The options:

a. Reconceive the knowledge so that it's less dangerous to divulge it. It's not harmful information. It's good, beneficial information. Everyone should have access to it. Argue that it was originally intended to be readily available to all. If it still seems dangerous, translate it into a safer form—so it will be simpler, clearer, less open to misinterpretation—or translate carefully selected portions of it into an orthodox commentary that frames and sanitizes it.

b. Reconceive human nature, or the nature or "readiness" of the excluded groups, so that revelation poses no (or at least a smaller) threat to them. The uninitiated are not as stupid, as resistant, or as emotionally fragile as we had thought. They will not be destroyed by access to the mysteries.

c. Institute an educational regimen designed to prepare the excluded groups (ultimately, everyone) for the mysteries. (This was the Protestant solution to the problem of access to vernacular Bibles.) Thematize the current in-group, especially the priests (and all other mystai as lay priests), less as gatekeepers (though they remain exactly that) than as helpers, facilitators, Prometheus bringing fire to humans (idealize the condescension involved here). Stigmatize those conservative members of the in-group who would punish you for divulging secrets as ignorant, behind the times, unmodern.

2. *Those who possess a competing knowledge and want to make it available to a larger public*—a public including both those who are currently devotees of

the older mysteries and those who have been socialized to think of themselves as lesser humans because they are not devotees. This process involves a continued respect for mysteries in general combined with competitive rejection of a certain set of (well-established) mysteries. The options:

a. Set up the new mysteries as equally arcane (i.e., retain the distinction between those who know and those who don't) but as simultaneously *easier* to gain (all you have to do is say these words, anyone can do it) and *more important* to gain (the new mysteries contain the truth about life after death, the old ones are merely superstitious lies). (This was the method used by the early church fathers.)

b. Make sure, or discover, or don't realize that there remain mysteries in the new group, too, things that only priests know, things that only become available to members at certain hierarchical levels. Defend these mysteries (if awareness of them is even tolerated) on pragmatic grounds: people below a certain level really don't need to know this stuff—it would only make them unhappy or dissatisfied. (This was the position of Thomas More and many other "enlightened" Christians during the three or four centuries when vernacular Bible translations gradually won widespread acceptance.)

c. Promulgate propaganda images of the older mysteries as silly or dangerous or both (because only the new mysteries are grounded in the truth) and/or of the older mystagogues as immoral or illegal or both (they are Satan-worshippers, they sacrifice infants, they use drugs, they have orgies). (This is a time-tried Christian method that is still very much in use today in relation both to unsanctioned cults at home and to indigenous religions in the mission field.)

3. *The disenfranchised who want to break down the barriers blocking their access to the benefits.* This process may involve some vestigial respect for the mysteries themselves, but it concerns itself more with the social fact of inclusion than with actual knowledge. The options:

a. Steal the knowledge and hand it out free to other out-groupers in the belief that the knowledge is good but its social restriction is bad (e.g., the Bible translations of Wyclif, Luther, Tyndale; Timothy Leary and drugs in the sixties).

b. Steal the knowledge and use it in a smear campaign against the exclusionary practices and silly beliefs of all religions.

c. Steal the knowledge and explore it in demystified but not necessarily antagonistic ways in order to understand the taboos we've internalized, to live with them without being victimized by them, and possibly to retain some awe before mystery itself, some sense that the universe withholds knowledge from all of us (e.g., this book).

The Christian Ascesis

One of the most powerful educational regimes devised by the Other-as-reason to train Western civilization in rationalist self-control is asceticism, which emerged during the first centuries of the Christian era as *the* dominant Christian discipline. The first Christian ascetics, anticipated and to some extent inspired by the writings of Origen early in the third century C.E., began to appear in Mesopotamia and Egypt toward the end of that century in the decades before the conversion of the Empire (313 C.E.); by the middle of the fourth century, Athanasius had written the enormously popular and widely imitated *Life of Anthony*, who was at the time still alive; and by the end of the fourth century, Augustine and others were forging a new monastic or "cenobitic" Church based on a communal "ascesis" or discipline that included sexual abstinence, fasting, silence, and the systematic eradication of "worldly" personality.

Askesis is the Greek word for *training* and was originally used by the Greeks to mean athletic training, especially that involving abstinence from the pleasures of embodied human existence and submission to various arduous physical tests. This physical discipline was of particular importance for athletic competitions like the Olympic Games and war. Later the word came to be used in an extended sense to signify various intellectual and moral disciplines as well, most notably as the Stoics' attempt to subject the emotions to rational control. The Sophists also incorporated intellectual and moral asceses into their pedagogical system, and much of their practice carries over into the antisensual teachings of Socrates and Plato. The early Christian ascetics were familiar with the ascetic doctrines of Plato and the more recent neoplatonist Plotinus (third century C.E.), but ascetic influences also flowed into the Near East during this period from other Hellenized mysteries, especially the Orphics and the Pythagoreans, and from Hinduism and Buddhism.

Christian asceticism can be read as a kind of *Aufhebung* or transcendence of classical civilization, a storing of social structure and order and "reason" in the most condensed form imaginable to survive the "barbarian" millennium ahead. Ascetic Christians in the fourth century pared Roman culture down to its barest minimum, to an antiworldly core that yet preserved in ideal form all the best (as they conceived it) that the "world" of their era had to offer: self-discipline, stoic endurance, suppression of decadent emotionalism and individualism, rigid hierarchical order. In Laing's terms, the ascetics constituted a kind of cultural "true self," which abstracted out of a dying false-self system everything it thought it could use and then squirreled this useful material away for future use.

This core yielded the monasteries that maintained it a powerful weapon against the dominant territorialism of the feudal lords—a right-makes-might, to put it aphoristically, to oppose to feudalism's might-makes-right. Because the territorial lords did have the worldly might that makes right, the monastic "right" made only a kind of otherworldly might; but the ideological survival of the Roman Empire in that otherworldliness gave it enormous worldly power, and that power was systematically extended throughout the Middle Ages. The ascetic imperialism of the medieval church was first channeled through superstitious fear of an angry deity monopolized by the clergy; and in some sense, despite an escalating series of bourgeois demystifications throughout the modern era, this imperialism of the spirit is with us still today. Gradually, however, the monasteries extended their worldly sway into overtly sociopolitical spheres, for example, through the amassing of vast ecclesiastical land holdings—a kind of parallel or mirror image of feudalism that is informed not by territorialism but by an ascetic ideology that structured even decadent opulence in schizoid and totalitarian ways. Toward the end of the Middle Ages, during the fifteenth and sixteenth centuries, the monastic opposition to the territorial ideology of might-makes-right began to assume political form in the rise of the absolute state, which can be seen as the socio-ideological extension of monastic rule. Finally and most importantly, though also most indirectly, ecclesiastical asceticism "seized power" in Western society through the rise of a secular but insistently ascetic bourgeoisie dedicated to monetary profit through a new ascetic regimen—for the best study of this process see Max Weber's *The Protestant Ethic and the Spirit of Capitalism*. As Benjamin Franklin's late-eighteenth-century list instructs, this regimen included temperance, silence, order, resolution, frugality, industry, sincerity, justice, moderation, cleanliness, tranquility, chastity, and humility. This transformed ascetic ideology has been so successful in the past few centuries that Franklin's (or we could say Augustine's) ascetic "virtues" have become naturalized in Western society, inscribed in what we unthinkingly take to be human "nature," in a discipline that (we believe) it is only "natural" for all humans to undertake.

I am arguing, in other words, that asceticism, and specifically the Christian asceticism of the Middle Ages, is not simply a rather ludicrous fanaticism that was popular for several centuries long ago and then happily died out, but that it is one of the dominant strains in our civilization—in schizoid Western ideology. As such, asceticism has been inscribed on our bodies, etched into the deepest strata of our being, and written on the backs of our foreheads by the Other-as-reason so that it seems natural, for example, that "maturity" be defined as the ability to delay the gratification of desires, or that leisure-oriented consumer society be portrayed as a decadent falling-off from an earlier work ethic, or that the translator be expected to empty him/herself of personal desires in order to achieve the neutral, impersonal transfer of the author's meaning to a reader in another language. The sheer ordinariness of these assumptions, that they are so familiar as to attract no attention whatsoever, is the strongest evidence of the continuing ideological sway of medieval ascetic ideology in our time.

Certainly the importance of asceticism for the history of Western translation theory cannot be overemphasized. "Normal" translation as it has been imagined in the West for sixteen centuries and continues to be imagined today is hegemonically ascetic. It's difficult to recall (or even to imagine) a Western definition of translation, simple or complex, old or new, conformist or maverick, that doesn't immediately betray its ascetic aims. Consider only the "renunciations" that are now and have long been expected of the translator: the renunciation of source-language syntax and "color" or "feel" or "mood" in the reduction of the source-language text to an abstract "sense"; the renunciation of personal biases, predilections, preferences, and opinions in the translator's training as a neutral transfer-machine. Consider the diatribes launched at "word-for-word" and "free" translations, and notice the temptation good translators feel and resist to indulge these pleasures: temptations to cling "too" closely to the source-language text, to trace its contours lovingly in the target language by translating word for word, or to strike off "too" boldly in a new direction, to sever ideologically controlled ties with source-language meaning by translating freely. Consider the discipline required of the translator to renounce all this, to resist such temptations, and the institutional support (translator training, translator organizations and conferences, legal and financial sanctions) provided to back up that discipline. The history of Western translation theory is many things, but above all it is a history of ascetic discipline. Following Jerome and Augustine, even the worldly rebels against ascetic translation typically only modify the prescribed ascesis.

Christian asceticism begins in a double tradition, eremitic and cenobitic, and the history of Western translation theory reflects this split right from the beginning. The eremite was the hermit who took drastic and dramatic steps—starvation, motionlessness, sleep deprivation, refusal to lie or sit down, sitting on poles—to still the lure of the world in himself. The cenobite was the monk or nun who submitted to monastic discipline, who surrendered all decision making to the father or mother superior and to the founder of the order in the form of a monastic "rule." Laing would call both forms of asceticism schizoid assaults on the body and the entire embodied world, including the false-self system that the schizoid harbors like a traitor under her/his own skin. Eremitism and cenobitism are simply the dialectical poles of schizoid "adjustment" to a hostile world—the eremite attempts to kill the false self, to be rid of it by one means or another, to banish it, to put it to flight; and the cenobite attempts to quell it, to subjugate it, to reduce it to an obedient extension of the rationalist "true self."

True, nearly all of Laing's descriptions of schizoid patients seem to be of eremites rather than cenobites, of lone crazies rather than rigidly disciplined group-thinkers; but that is almost certainly because cenobitic schizoids don't end up in Laing's office. They end up in the armed forces, or in terrorist cells, or on professional sports teams, or at universities, or in actual monasteries and convents, places where the exoskeleton of the institution's rules serves as the individual's rationalist "cure."

In *The Ascetic Imperative in Culture and Criticism*, Geoffrey Galt Harpham usefully places the two forms of Christian asceticism in a mutually complementary relation: "Each remembered what the other had forgotten—the eremite, that the grace of God dwelt within each person; and the cenobite, that the dead weight of sin stood between the human and the divine. If the eremite courted temptation in order to achieve the sharpest possible definition of himself, the cenobite sought not to be led into temptation so that the self would grow indistinct in its outlines, and would, ideally, simply cease to be" (28). This split had important consequences for the ideological survival of ascetic discipline: "But for the cenobite, the goal was not to protect one's vital selfhood, but to extinguish whatever spark of temptability lay within. Eremites renounced the world; cenobites renounced themselves. Accordingly, eremites gained themselves; and cenobites, through the monasteries that exerted their powerful influence until the Reformation, gained the world" (29). But the self that the eremite gained was a schizoid self, a controlling self that constantly threatened to implode into the black hole of the world, a self swarming with phantoms that undermined its precarious ascesis. And the world that the cenobite gained was a false-self system governed by rules of external behavior.

Since the worldly success of cenobitism has rendered both the ascetic tradition in Western translation theory more hegemonically cenobitic than eremitic and the ideal translator more a disciplined monk or nun than a self-dramatizing hermit—as Harpham says, the cenobite, like the ideal translator, is "faultless rather than excellent, a subtracted rather than an achieved self" (28)—it's tempting to set the eremitic tradition to one side and focus on the development of translation theory out of cenobitism. The exclusion of the eremite—the maverick, the bullheaded loner, the individualist, the Hölderlin, the Pound, the Nabokov—is in fact one of the great temptations of mainstream Western translation theory, one that I'm going to have to resist if I'm going to explore the complexities of ascetic translation. Although it's true, for example, that most Western translators have received overwhelming instruction of one kind or another in cenobitic invisibility (the "subtracted self") and have more or less successfully resisted the temptation to enter into eremitic self-dramatizations, the two most famous theorists of translation in the West were eremites: Jerome, the Illyrian hermit who ended his life in a monastery in Bethlehem, and Martin Luther, the Augustinian monk who broke free of the monastery and became one of the first modern eremites, a famous ascetic who ate and drank and married and clamored for attention. Jerome's "Letter to Pammachius" (395) and Luther's "Circular Letter on Translation" (1530) are powerfully eremitic documents that have shaped translation theory from the ideological periphery; they are wild, shaggy letters aflame with the passionate tempers and animal fears of their writers, documents that have been more quoted than read precisely because they are so embarrassingly unkempt and uncouth.

Calm, rational, presentable (cenobitic) translation theory begins in book two of Augustine's *On Christian Doctrine*, his discussion of signs (this section was written in 396, the year after Jerome's letter; the entire book was finished around 427). Augustine was the founder of a monastic order that bore his name, and during the course of the Middle Ages, a hundred or more other orders would either adopt or adapt his monastic *Rule* as their founding document. The *Rule* was read aloud to the assembled brothers or sisters (Augustine wrote masculine and feminine versions of the *Rule*) once a week; it constituted the order's social contract, and a brother or sister could be punished or expelled for an infraction by reference to it.

Where Jerome's eremitic translation theory is personal, pragmatic, and riddled with internal contradictions, Augustine's cenobitic one is impersonal, perfectionist, and systematic; where Jerome's is rhetorically hot, Augustine's is cool. Jerome's letter is ad hoc theory, a practicing translator's anecdotal attempt to rise above "mere" untheorized practice by systematizing his own translation decisions for others' emulation—but an attempt that resulted in a model for translation theory that Martin Luther and later practicing translators have cultivated when asked to pronounce on translation right up to our own day. Augustine's treatise is a scholarly semiotic that only veers incidentally into translation by way of illustration, then examining a highly idealized and impractical form of translation that is more dogmatic myth than institutional reality—a theoretical model that Leonardo Bruni and later linguistic theorists would cultivate when asked to pronounce on translation, again right up to our own day. In Laing's terms, Jerome is the schizoid individual just before psychotic breakdown—just before the total collapse of the false-self system and the onset of schizophrenia. Augustine is the "well-adjusted" schizoid individual who has managed to subject his entire false-self system to the rationalist control of his "true" self.

For all their differences, however, Augustine and Jerome did formulate a more or less coherent theoretical "core" or "center" that organizes all later translation theory into an ascetic/metempsychotic tradition. Both theorists insist that the source-language text be reduced to (or conceived as) its transcendental "meaning," an abstract semantic content that has been stripped of all "carnal" specificity (the feel or color of words, word order) and can therefore be transferred without change to a target language. Both caution the translator against insufficient knowledge of the source language and reading individual words out of context. Both teach the translator piety toward the source text and submission to the authority of the institution that maintains it (controls its interpretation, commissions its translation)—although in this respect the cenobitic Augustine is by far the more "reliable" guide. Jerome, the fiery eremite, counsels piety and submission in tones that ring with barely suppressed impious revolt.

Jerome

Jerome writes to Pammachius in 395 because he has been charged with "ignorance and falsehood . . . by an inexperienced, bumptious tongue [probably Rufinus, his one-time friend, now enemy]. This tongue, it seems, claims that I have made mistakes through misinterpretation or carelessness when I translated into Latin a letter written by another in Greek" (132). He continues: "my enemies tell the uneducated Christian crowd that Jerome falsified the original letter, that Jerome has not translated word for word, that Jerome has written 'beloved friend' in place of 'honorable Sir,' and that—more disgraceful still—Jerome has maliciously condensed by omitting the epithet 'most reverend'" (134). Jerome takes pains to defend himself against these charges—to show that they are based on ignorance and inexperience of translation—and lashes back at his enemies with his own "bumptious tongue." Compared with his slightly younger and infinitely more authoritative contemporary Augustine (Jerome was born circa 347, Augustine seven years later in 354; Jerome died around the age of 73 circa 420, Augustine at the age of 76 in 430), Jerome is a quirky, crotchety hothead whose blood boils throughout the letter: "At the very beginning, before I defend my translation, I wish to interrogate those men who call cunning and malice prudence. Where did you obtain your copy of my translation? Who gave it to you? How dare you display something obtained by your fraud? What place will be safe when a man cannot keep his secrets even behind his own walls and in his private desk?" (134). He rants on for a page or two about legal and scriptural precedents for this sort of deceit and fraud, calling Rufinus a Judas and a heretic, imagining him belching while offering up lame excuses for the theft of the letter, portraying the attack on his translation as a subterfuge to distract Church authorities from Rufinus' own black heresies, and generally venting his spleen at a political opponent. "If I happen to be a poor translator, does that absolve you from being a heretic?" (136).

In the defense that follows of his sense-for-sense Latin translation of a Greek letter from Epiphanius (Bishop of Constantia in Cyprus) to John (Bishop of Jerusalem), Jerome vacillates tellingly between eremitic self-dramatizations as an experienced translator who *knows* the right way to translate and cenobitic submission to the authority of a whole string of classical and Christian authors (Cicero, Horace, Terence, Plautus, Caecilius, and Bishop Evagrius of Antioch, who translated Athanasius's *Life of Anthony* into Latin). Here, for example, is an eremitic passage, which Jerome quotes from his own preface to a translation he did of Eusebius of Caesarea:

> "In the following sentence composed by another man, it is difficult not to diverge somewhere; and in translating it is hard to preserve the beauty of idiom which in the original is most distinguished. Each particular word has a significance of its own. Possibly I have no equivalent by which to express some word, and if I then must go out of my way to reach the goal, miles are spent to cover what in reality is a short city block. To this difficulty must be added the windings of word transpositions, the dissimilarities in the use of cases, the varieties in figures of speech, and, most difficult of all, the peculiar vernacular marrow of the language itself. If one translates each and every word literally, the passage will sound absurd; and if by necessity I change anything in the order and wording, it will seem that I have abused the function of translator." Then, after a lengthy discussion, which would be a bit boring to follow here, I added the following: "If anyone does not see how translation adulterates the charm of the original, let him squeeze Homer word for word into Latin—I will go even further and ask him to render Homer into Latin prose: the result will be that the order of the words will seem ridiculous, and that the most eloquent of poets will be hardly articulate." (138–39)

This is the first in a long string of such complaints, the most familiar (indeed almost *de rigeur*) complaints in the history of Western writing about translation. What the familiarity of Jerome's protests may conceal, however, is their implicit asceticism. "It is difficult not to diverge somewhere": this is the fulcral ascetic claim, and in its flaunting of difficulty, its intensification of the temptations that must be resisted and the pitfalls that must be skirted, it is specifically eremitic. Although as I say Jerome wrote the letter to Pammachius from a monastery in Bethlehem, he was temperamentally never a cenobite. His two years in the Egyptian desert, short as that time was in eremitic terms, had molded his self too sharply for such. His letter glows with visionary certitude, the rock-hard confidence and irascible stubbornness that comes from having discovered these "tenets" of translation for himself, the hard way; and he defends his certainty with the arrogance of the old hand, saying only *if you don't believe me, try it yourself; I don't need to explain myself to you.*

Jerome does not stick to this rhetorical stance throughout, however; he sandwiches these particular eremitic claims, for example, between quotations from Cicero and Bishop Evagrius that establish his cenobitic credentials as the submissive follower of a "Rule" ("for this practice I have behind me the authority of Cicero himself" [137], "now if my own opinion seems to lack authority . . . read and consider this short preface from a biography of St. Anthony of Egypt" [139]). Indeed, the remainder of the letter is devoted to a close reading of the Seventy's sense-for-sense translations from the Hebrew and the evangelists' free interpretations or misreadings of the Old Testament in order to show that the greatest authorities of all, the Greek translators of the Old Testament (whom Jerome at this writing, following Philo, still believed to have been divinely inspired) and the writers of the four gospels, tacitly approved of his translation practice and thus lent him their considerable exegetical weight.

Tellingly, however, the cumulative effect of Jerome's citations from the Septuagint and the gospels is subversive of cenobitic discipline—the citations undermine his implicit self-presentation as the submissive follower of a Rule. As I suggested earlier, the impetus of his citations, which are ostensibly submissive and honorific, is almost invariably accusatory: "though the sense is identical with that in the Septuagint, the words are dissimilar, and are quite differently arranged" (141); "even greater discrepancies may be discovered in another passage from Matthew" (144); "similar trifling mistakes occur in the Apostle Paul" (146); "one of the most striking misquotations is made by Stephen, Christ's first martyr" (147). Jerome is supposedly defending the writers and translators in question; but rhetorically his enumeration of their failings is carefully balanced between praise for sense-for-sense equivalence and blame for word-for-word deviation:

> Should one accuse the Apostle Matthew of adulterating his translation? It agrees neither with the Hebrew original, nor with the Greek Septuagint, and, worse than that, one could claim that Matthew has mistaken even the author's

> name, attributing the passage to Jeremiah instead of Zechariah.
>
> Far be it from Jerome, however, to speak like this about a follower of the Christ. The truth is that Matthew made it his business to formulate dogmas rather than scurry after words and syllables. (141–42)

It is a canny move: at the simplest level, Jerome provides a model for both praise and blame, hoping to force his accusers into an extension of their attack on him to the Seventy and the authors of the New Testament and thus, since such an attack is politically untenable (i.e., heretical), to force them back into praise for his own position.

But there is another, more devious (more eremitic) side to Jerome's claims—or rather, not a "side," but an ascetic tension between opposed resistances. Jerome does blame the Seventy and the evangelists, it seems to me, for their inaccuracies; and he also praises them for their creative deviances, their eremitic wanderings beyond the faceless cenobitic discipline of the scholars. He takes a fierce pleasure in enumerating the "defects" in the translated texts, the slippages from the Old Testament Hebrew to the Greek of the Septuagint and the New Testament, and the pleasure seems to me to be steeped in an eremitic imitation of Christ. This mimetic pleasure in effect conflates Jerome's implicit praise and blame for the Seventy and the evangelists, for it suggests simultaneously that the writers of the Greek Bible are nothing compared with Christ (and hence are as subject to blame as anyone else) and that their greatness, like Jerome's own, lies in their imitation of Christ (hence they are to be admired and emulated). "Far be it from Jerome, however, to speak like this about a follower of the Christ" renders "sed absit hoc de pedisequo Christi dicere" (7.4), or literally, "but go-away this about footman of Christ to speak," i.e., let this claim about a follower of Christ (that Matthew falsified his version) go away. This passage at once associates ("hoc") and disassociates ("absit") the potentially heretical claim with Jerome, making Jerome at once the bold utterer and pious banisher of the idea that Matthew made mistakes.

This reading of Jerome's duplicitous letter would corroborate Harpham's claim that, "conceiving of himself as a direct or primary imitation of Christ, the eremite actually stands in the position of the transcription of the spoken Word. The highly mediated nature of even this posture undercuts any pretension to true originality on the part of the eremite, but this is not the real point. The eremite had predecessors but not intermediaries; he placed himself in direct relation, if it can be called that, to the Mediator" (43). The eremitic Jerome has predecessors—Cicero, Horace, Bishop Evagrius, the Seventy, the evangelists—but they are not intermediaries in the sense of mastering or mediating his understanding of the source-language text (especially in the most radical Christian sense, of Jesus as the divine Source Text or Word). They are only humans like himself, predecessors in the sense of having gone before, having attempted (like himself) to place themselves in an unmediated relation to Jesus. Faced as translator and Bible scholar with the textual traces of their imitations, Jerome sees the inadequacies of those traces (as he sees the inadequacies of his own), and is not impressed—certainly is not silenced by them. But because he is attempting to achieve the same unmediated relation through his translations, he also recognizes the visionary power of their failures, the courage and determination that led them to deviate from mediated models of understanding and strike off on their own, hoping to transcribe the transformative Word on and through their own bodies by wandering like Jesus in the desert.

That Jerome doesn't actually come out and say this—that he doesn't openly identify himself with the Word incarnate and contemptuously set aside the mere human words of previous translators—suggests that the visionary model of translation his letter implies isn't so much the overt eremitic project of Western translation as it is the resisted eremitic *temptation* of Western translation. Jerome himself resists this temptation stoutly all through the letter, only giving out aural echoes of its siren call in, for example, his tonal contempt-cum-admiration for the evangelists.

This crisscrossing of temptations and resistances is inscribed within Jerome's own eremitic translation regimen, in what may be the oddest note in the letter: "Now I not only admit but freely announce that in translating from the Greek—except of course in the case of Holy Scripture, where even the syntax contains a mystery—I render, not word for word, but sense for sense" (136–37). Given the absence of support for (or later recurrence to) this "exception," Jerome's insistence that he renders the Bible word for word sounds superficially like knee-jerk piety—perhaps an attempt to protect himself against charges of heresy. Read this way, the "exception" becomes Jerome's claim to resist the eremitic temptation to "deviate" from the sense of the original.

But the situation is more complicated than this. Word-for-word translation is "normal" for esoteric ecclesiastical authorities ignorant of translation—for people who believe that piety toward the source text requires piety toward every word in it. This belief renders word-for-word translation an ideological haven for those afraid of heresy charges—and Jerome writes his letter precisely in order to defend himself against such charges. At the same time, however, word-for-word translation is "deviant" for ecclesiastical authorities with experience in translation who believe, metempsychotically, that the translator should show piety not toward the source *text* but rather toward its transcendental *meaning*. This tension renders word-for-word translation a temptation to be resisted, a delight in the felicity of the source text that the ascetic translator must renounce. As Jerome's claim that "even the syntax contains a mystery" suggests, word-for-word translation remains at least implicitly grounded in the taboos of the ancient mysteries: it reveals too great an attachment to the "world," to "fleshly" utterances, to the bodily "mystery" of specific articulations. The schizoid/metempsychotic/ascetic translator is expected to resist this temptation through idealization, abstraction, the transcendentalization of meaning, and especially through sense-for-sense translation, in which the "sense" to be translated is regarded as dwelling not in individual words or even utterances, but beyond all natural language in the mind of God (as "interpreted" or circumscribed by the Church) and is perceived by the pious translator only *through* the source text as through a glass, darkly.

Inscribed in the temptations and resistances of Jerome's letter, therefore, is a whole mutually defining system of theoretical oppositions that has informed translation theory until our own century. On the one hand, there is "humble" or "self-effacing" or cenobitic translation, predicated on the translator's pious submission to the source author's intention as defined by the ecclesiastical (or other social) institution; on the other, there is "arrogant" or "self-dramatizing" or eremitic translation, predicated on the translator's assumption that s/he knows best and will translate any way s/he sees fit. Each of these positions is then divided into a sense-for-sense/word-for-word opposition: the ignorant cenobite translates, or requires that others translate, word for word, while the learned cenobite translates, or requires that others translate, sense for sense; and the orthodox eremite translates (etc.) sense for sense, while the kabbalistic eremite translates (etc.) word for word.

As the ascetic tradition insists, these oppositions function not through sheer logical differentiation (this or that, A or not-A), but through the tension between temptation and renunciation: each translation model is a temptation that is renounced and resisted binarily by each of the other three. Thus Rufinus as a word-for-word cenobite and Augustine as a sense-for-sense cenobite both renounce or resist Jerome's sense-for-sense eremitism—Rufinus because Jerome has added to or subtracted from the source text; Augustine because Jerome has stepped beyond ecclesiastical control by using the Hebrew Bible (rather than the Church-approved Septuagint) as his source text. Thus Jerome as sense-for-sense eremite renounces or resists the cenobitic temptation to submit to ecclesiastical authorities (especially the Seventy and the evangelists) but simultaneously feels tempted by word-for-word translation for reasons both cenobitic (political security) and eremitic (delight in source-cultural mysteries).

Ascesis and Addiction

Before I move on to Augustine, let me digress for a moment and consider the ascetic tradition and the problematic of addiction, which I broached only briefly in chapter 1. Asceticism might usefully be seen as an addiction—an addiction to the quest for the perfected self, or, in the term I used in *The Translator's Turn* to describe one of the ideosomatic strains of mainstream Western translation, an addiction to perfectionism. Dualism and instrumentalism, the other two strains I discussed there, are addictive too—and somewhere along the line Western culture got hooked on all three. Taboo, as I said in chapter 1, is an addiction to avoidance behaviors; and the taboo on translation is a textual avoidance addiction, an anxiety about approaching or handling a text in a hazardous way. (Dualism, instrumentalism, and perfectionism might even be read as addictive rationalist methods of controlling taboo-addictions, as philosophical methadone treatments.) Where Kenneth Burke says in *The Rhetoric of Religion* that "man" is "(1) The symbol-using animal, (2) Inventor of the negative, (3) Separated from his natural condition by instruments of his own making, (4) And goaded by the spirit of hierarchy" (40), I would say that humans are *addicted* to symbolism, negation, reason, hierarchy, perfectionism, and the rest. The implication is that somewhere along the line we *got* addicted to those things, which in turn implies that our attachment to them isn't in our blood; in this light, what I have been doing in this chapter is tracing the genealogy of our becoming-addicted.

The reason I bring this up now, in the shadow of Jerome's impressive argumentative twists and turns, his attempts to position himself correctly so as both to vent his spleen at his enemies *and* to avoid heresy charges, is that addiction is precisely a balancing phenomenon, a constant attempt to find just the right balance between extremes. Neurologically, addiction is caused by an imbalance in the body's biochemical servosystem; this imbalance creates the phenomenon of tolerance, the need for more and more of the addictive substance, because the more of the addictive substance you ingest, the harder your body works to produce the antidote to it. Reading asceticism as a psychosocial addiction thus enables us to read Jerome's waffling in the letter to Pammachius as the operation of that servosystem: the more he attempts to mime orthodoxy (or ascetic perfection), the angrier he grows not only at his enemies who, he thinks, are less orthodox or perfect than he but also at those authorities who would force him into an orthodoxy that he *knows* is experientially false. The schizoid quest for perfection locks him into an addictive servosystem that keeps him shuttling between other people's perfection(ism) and his own, other people's falsity and his own, other people's truths and his own. The more orthodoxy or doctrinal purity or perfection he achieves, the greater his "tolerance" for that perfection—tolerance not in the sense of smiling indulgently on it but rather in the sense of taking it for granted, of not feeling its effects, of growing numb to it, so that it becomes impossible for him to take pleasure in it. If anything, his addictive tolerance makes him attitudinally *less* tolerant of the imperfections that he sees in others and himself so that he becomes progressively less able to take pleasure in his own and others' perfection. Hence he attacks the Greek translations of the Seventy and the evangelists for failing to measure up to his own perfectionist standards for translation (they're not as good as me!); he defends these same translations as good examples of the sense-for-sense translation he himself practices (I'm as good as anybody!); and he furiously backpedals whenever he senses that he is leaving himself open to charges of heresy (far be it from me!).

Indeed the entire ascetic dialectic of temptation and renunciation might be thought of as an addictive tolerance servosystem of this sort—as might the taboo dialectic of approach and avoidance and, as we'll see in a moment, Augustine's dialectic of fortitude and despair. The greater the temptation, the stronger the need for ascetic renunciation; the greater the renunciation, the more tolerance for renunciation (i.e., the less the ascetic *notices* her or his own renunciation, the more it comes to seem like no effort at all and thus itself like a kind of low-grade temptation), and the stronger the need for new temptations to renounce. Similarly, the more you avoid the taboo object, the more you develop your tolerance for avoidance, and thus the less avoidance *feels* like avoidance: it begins to feel like indifference, like a kind of flouting of the taboo. To keep a taboo alive one has to approach *and* avoid the taboo object frequently—as tolerance builds up, more and more frequently, with less and less emotional return.

There is, however, an important difference between psychosocial addictions and chemical addictions: the biochemical servosystem already exists for neurotransmitters, so that the introduction of an opiate, for example, into this system triggers it instantly. The system recognizes the opiate as an analog of chemicals already functional within it. For a sociopolitical addiction to take hold, the *whole dialectic* has to be attached ideosomatically, has to be somatized, neuralized *as* a normative social dialectic. There is no physiological reason why the renunciation or avoidance of a taboo object should generate enhanced temptation—or why, to anticipate Augustine again, the determination to do something impossible or enormously difficult should generate despair, let alone why that despair should generate a redoubled determination to complete the difficult task anyway. These dialectics are examples of social servosystems, not biological ones; to become addictions they have to be programmed into our ventral-tegmental systems (let fortitude trigger inhibitory impulses, let despair trigger excitatory ones). Or in Gregory Bateson's pithy remark, the alcoholic "cannot elect 'sobriety.' At best he could only elect 'sobriety—not drunkenness,' and his universe remains polarized, carrying always both alternatives" (319). Sobriety/drunkenness is an addictive servosystem only for the alcoholic; *any* addictive dialectic is a servosystem only for the addict, for the person who (or the society that) has somatized it as addictive. It's easy enough—in the abstract—to imagine a failed determination leading not to despair and enhanced fortitude, but to an easy laughter and a shrugged "oh well." In specific circumstances, circumstances already locked into the dialectic of fortitude and despair—I'm determined to install a dishwasher, dammit, despite everything the manufacturer has done to make it impossible for the ordinary homeowner—the possibility of laughing off one's original determination is usually unthinkable, and even if thinkable, undoable. Only a counterascesis, such as yoga (or a pharmaceutical intervention such as Valium), can free the trapped ascetic.

And that's what the Other-as-reason is to the Other-as-mystery, a counterascesis. Continue attaching taboo as an addictive avoidance, but subordinate it to a new philosophical ethos, a new set of life practices. Let taboo remain operative, for example, but socially invisible; repress it collectively, so that it becomes ludicrous even to think about addictive avoidance behaviors in terms of taboo. Thematize the death and resurrection of Jesus not as a cyclically recurring seasonal and symbolic and mythic event like the death and rebirth of Osiris or Mithras, but (with Kittel and Rahner) as a once-only historical event, sheer brute realism. (While making this argument, repress the rich mythic symbolism of Easter and generally the seasonal cycles of the liturgical calendar. Repress especially any bodily participation—through emotion or even physical movement, say, during music—in ceremonies that celebrate pure spirit.) Thematize your veneration for a source text and your desire to translate it so as to reflect that veneration, as motivated not by taboo (fear, addictive behavior) but by a simple value-free intention to convey the information contained in it to a target reader. (What could that possibly have to do with addiction?) Impose the new ascesis on the old addictive behavior so effectively that you repress, "forget" not only that it *is* an addiction but that the addiction was once thematized differently.

Augustine's Semiotic Ascesis

If Jerome allowed the ideological forces at work in nascent schizoid translation theory to explode into mutually repellent stances, Augustine exerted quite the opposite influence: his cenobitic approach to translation was a dogmatic straitjacket into which he attempted to fit a field that he didn't really understand very well. Augustine was one of the pivotal thinkers in the Western tradition: he not only formulated but instituted, politically, a synthesis of Plato and the New Testament that informs most of our deepest "intuitions" about ourselves and our world today. As the chief architect of medieval theology, which defined intellectual orthodoxy for over a thousand years, he has presided—though often not in name—over philosophical and scientific "correctness" well into our era. *On Christian Doctrine* in particular has been foundational for modern science, including the mathematical sciences (see 2.31.48–2.32.50) and especially linguistics and semiotics. Due to the Renaissance myth according to which "science" rejected and displaced "theology," however, Descartes and Galileo and Saussure and others are given credit for methodological innovations that are spelled out clearly by Augustine.

Jerome instituted translation theory almost by accident, individualistically, eremitically, in situational self-defense and self-creation; the cenobitic Augustine took a larger, more dogmatic view. Augustine instituted translation theory as a systematic undoing of the scattering of tongues at the Tower of Babel by identifying the *translatum* or tranferred message with the unitary Word of God and then policing the transfer. Translation may seem to be a mere ineffectual crossing of linguistic barriers carried out by imperfect, fallible humans; it may seem to partake of the marketplace (the bartering of meanings, this for that) or of the nomadic life (the constant reinscription of culture on a shifting geography, flux as the nomad's only stability). But for Augustine these are mere appearances, mere surface; in the depths lies true translation, perfect translation, ideal translation, the perfect transfer of a stable meaning from one language to another by the ideal interpreter. Such a perfect translation must exist for Augustine: Augustine's political optimism requires the possibility of bounding, if not binding, sin; of at least controlling if not remedying the damage wreaked on linguistic understanding at Babel. If "true" or "perfect" or "ideal" translation is not possible, if perfect communication between God and humans, Hebrews and Greeks, Greeks and Romans, Romans and Arabs and Berbers and so on is not possible, in some sense the Church is not possible. Then the most that can be hoped for is a proliferation of visionary monads, eremitic mystics, perhaps, who experience God's truth but cannot convey it to others.

In order to envisage perfect translation, then, and thus the Church, Augustine charts out a dual ascesis, a cenobitic purification at once of the *translatum* and of the translator. Everything in language that is not pure, simple, stable, and permanent must be excised; living language use, especially speech, must be derogated and dismissed as mere dross, a distortion of stable *logoi* (which are themselves distortions of the divine *Logos*) that is in turn subject to further distortion by listeners. And everything in human response that proliferates individuated meanings—all interpretive idiosyncracies, inclinations, and impulses—must be silenced from within and without: all this must be renounced by the interpreter and denounced by the monastic institution. Nomadic translation, marketplace translation, translation as a free-flowing series of encounters with other speakers in a fluid social sphere—these must be thematized as a temptation to be resisted, a sickness to be purged, an evil to be exorcised. The ideal translator for Augustine was a monk in a cell, someone purified of personality, perfectly conformed to cenobitic rule, wholly spoken from within by the voice of God—the perfect schizoid self.

Augustine begins book two of *On Christian Doctrine* with a definition of signs as solely directed at "bringing forth and transferring to another mind the action of the mind in the person who makes the sign" (2.2.3). His is a relational definition of signs that at once grounds their efficacy in and makes them the enabling condition of community. For the cenobite, danger lies not so much in the "world" as in the "self": community, relation, the "world" of social interaction that is anathema to the eremite is the cenobite's defense against the isolated ego. But this defense does not necessarily come from any social world—not, say, from the marketplace. No. Defense against the isolated ego requires an idealized community, an ideally unified community in which all speakers are themselves spoken by a higher unifying voice (Augustine would say God, I would say the Other-as-reason) and share the same signs as vehicles of their communication. The giving and taking of signs is the next best thing to the paradisal state of being "one mind," *of* one mind, one in mind, one through mind.

In Augustine's formulation the sign is the vehicle not only of the transfer of mental actions from one mind to another, but also of the elicitation or evocation of mental actions, of their "bringing forth" from the shadowy depths of inner being—what R. D. Laing would call the schizoid "true self." Signs are the "publication" of private thoughts, the rendering public of what was isolate, individual, incommunicado. Implicit here is that signs are also the rendering permanent of what was fleeting, evanescent: signs are the stabilization of the flux of mental actions, the freezing solid of what William James calls the stream of thought.

As both R. D. Laing and Geoffrey Galt Harpham make clear (Laing in his discussion of schizoids, Harpham in his discussion of ascetics), this conception of signification as exteriorization of the inward, communalization of the individual, publication of the private, and stabilization of the fleeting is caught up in a mortification of life, an attempt to "idealize" or "transcendentalize" the flux of life by killing it, by reducing its multiplicity and mutability to the fixity of death. In the same way, the evanescence of speech is "mortified" through writing: "But because vibrations in the air soon pass away and remain no longer than they sound, signs of words have been constructed by means of letters. Thus words are shown to the eyes," Augustine continues, extending the stabilization of the mutable to the visualization of the aural, and adds, "not in themselves but through certain signs which stand for them" (2.4.5). What is heard falls away; what is seen remains. (In the *Confessions* Augustine predicts that in heaven the saints will be able to see their thoughts.) What is "in itself" is carnal, worldly, individuated, false, and therefore subject to death-as-decay; what is represented in signs is ideal, transcendental, true, and therefore subject to death-as-perfection.

Unfortunately, however, "these signs could not be common to all people because of the sin of human dissension which arises when one people seizes the leadership for itself. A sign of this pride is that tower erected in the heavens where impious men deserved that not only their minds but also their voices should be dissonant" (2.4.5). "For itself": this is as impious as the "in itself." The sin, for Augustine, is not the will to power over other people—his own authoritarian formulations in his monastic *Rule* and throughout his writings and political activities consolidated the first successful political application of Plato's totalitarian designs from the *Republic* in the thousand-year reign of the medieval church—but rather the gathering of power into the prideful *self*, even when that self is collectively defined ("when one people seizes the leadership for it*self*"). It is selfishness that causes dissension, not the will to power. To put that differently, dissension arises when humans refuse to channel God's power—or (more secularly) when they refuse to wield power in God's name. The gathering of power into the self in effect blocks God's instrumentalization of humans as his agents and thus the transcendentalization of power: it is acceptable, indeed essential, that one "lead" or wield power over others as long as one is in turn "led" or instrumentalized by a rational, and therefore reasonable, higher power. Only God's "condescension" to human leadership can prevent human "dissension."

When selfishness bred dissension at Babel, then, that dissension led to vocal dissonance, which led to the need for translation; but in the "scattering" of Bible translations across the world Augustine sees a potential reversal of the Babelian scattering of tongues:

> Thus it happened that even the Sacred Scripture, by which so many maladies of the human will are cured, was set forth in one language, but so that it could be spread conveniently through all the world it was scattered far and wide in

> the various languages of translators that it might be known for the salvation of people who desired to find in it nothing more than the thoughts and desires of those who wrote it and through these the will of God, according to which we believe those writers spoke. (2.5.6)

The aporias that drive Augustine's idealization run deep: the scattering of translations allows all humans to hear "nothing more" than the single and unified voice of God. More is less: more languages, more translations, more voices mean less dissension, less plurality, less selfish individuation.

Augustine can only envisage this transformation of more into less through the ascetic regimen that he outlines in chapter 7, the seven-step path to "wisdom" (possession by the Other-as-reason, a.k.a. God) that enables the Bible reader (and thus also the translator) to renounce the "selfish" impulses that proliferate interpretations and preclude hegemonic understanding. I devoted a section of *The Translator's Turn* to a close reading of this regimen in terms of translational instrumentalism (52–54), and I don't want to repeat the argument here; just let me quickly list the seven steps as they apply to the cenobitic translator and comment:

1. *Fear*. Be afraid of critical censure, and let your fear guide you to obedience. In this first step, obey the rules (translate only the intended sense of the source text as that sense is defined by the relevant institution) out of sheer self-protection.

2. *Piety*. Respect the source author enough to set aside your own personal opinions and translate his or hers.

3. *Knowledge*. Familiarize yourself with the source author and text, historically, biographically, and terminologically.

4. *Fortitude*. Recognize that you will never know enough about the source author and text and will never be able to translate the text adequately, but do not despair. Keep trying to do the impossible; keep thinking of it *as* impossible, but also as absolutely essential.

5. *Mercy*. Remember the poor target reader, who could not understand the text if you did not translate it and will not understand it *as intended* if you add to it or subtract from it.

6. *Cleansing*. Purify yourself of all personal idiosyncracies that might distort the target reader's view of the source author's intention. Make yourself a window—a *clean* one—for the target reader to see through.

7. *Wisdom*. Attain peace and tranquility by clinging to what you know is right and sloughing off everything that does not contribute to that "right" state of mind—including the intermediate steps en route to this goal. Forget that you once translated "correctly" out of fear or fortitude or mercy. Let hegemonic translation become "second nature."

What makes this ascetic regimen so successful (witness how well it still works for us today, sixteen centuries after Augustine invented it) is partly that each step in some sense erases the last, so that the pious translator no longer needs to be afraid, the knowledgeable translator no longer needs to conceive his or her quest for knowledge in terms of piety, and so on, until the arrival at "wisdom" or perfect submission to cenobitic discipline erases everything that has gone before, leaving only (at least ideally) the perfectly neutral translator, the translator as robot, the "machine" translator that continues to practice all seven ascetic disciplines but has *forgotten* that it does so (has forgotten that it has been programmed and believes that it is "free"). This is the sense in which machine translation, the great cenobitic project of twentieth-century translation studies, would be the ultimate fulfillment of Augustine's ascetic program. Or, as Laing puts it, in the schizoid personality "The false-self system tends to become more and more dead. In some people, it is as though they have turned their lives over to a robot which has made itself (apparently) indispensable" (111).

Perfection, Enforcement, and the Alien Word

But this forgetful internalization is only part of the reason for the program's success. Another part is institutional enforcement, the maintenance of *communal* discipline that provides for sanctions when ideological programming fails. It is not enough to internalize and then forget fear, piety, knowledge, fortitude, mercy, purification, and wisdom; one must be repeatedly guided by institutional authorities to the proper fulfillment of those steps. Augustine uses his third step, knowledge, to illustrate the importance of submission to institutional guidance, insisting that readers (and translators) of the Bible limit themselves to certain books:

> In the matter of canonical Scriptures he should follow the authority of the greater number of catholic Churches, among which are those which have deserved to have apostolic seats and to receive epistles. He will observe this rule concerning canonical Scriptures, that he will prefer those accepted by all catholic Churches to those which some do not accept; among those which are not accepted by all, he should prefer those which are accepted by the largest number of important Churches to those held by a few minor Churches of less authority. If he discovers that some are maintained by the largest number of Churches, others by the Churches of the weightiest authority, although this condition is not likely, he should hold them to be of equal value. (2.8.12)

Note that at no point in this hierarchical regress is the Bible reader asked to make up his or her own mind; even in judgment calls, as when there is a discrepancy between number and weight, the cenobitic reader is to make the decision prescribed for him or her by Augustine (and indeed to recognize the need to make that decision only in circumstances defined by Augustine).

As we saw V. N. Voloshinov arguing in the last chapter, this institutional authority is traditionally vested in, justified by, and transmitted through the "alien word," a foreign word that is just domesticated enough to be almost understandable but still alien enough to be elevated, solemn, sacred, powerful, taboo. All priests, Voloshinov suggests, rely on the alien word for their otherworldly aura, for the impression they give of being in contact with a higher level of being—a higher level associated with the supernatural and borrowing ideological support for that association from a venerated foreign language.

Augustine is no exception. In a trivial example of his veneration for the alien word, he lists Hebrew words that Latin translators of the Bible do not translate, such as "amen" and "alleluia," due to their "holier authority" (2.15.22); because Augustine himself had no Hebrew, however, he clearly did not consider that language to carry much institutional weight. The alien words that patently carry "holier authority" for Augustine are Greek: the words of the Septuagint and the Greek New Testament, which he was able (albeit with great difficulty) to read. The most pressing of these for Augustine and the Christian Middle Ages was *logos*, of course, the Greek word for *word* and especially, after the first chapter of John's gospel, for *Jesus Christ*, the creative Word whom God spoke in the beginning and will speak in the end. Revealingly, *logos* is not a word native to either Jesus himself, who spoke Aramaic, or Augustine, who spoke Latin; rather, it is a word native to Plato and Philo Judaeus, the ghostwriters, as it were, of the New Testament and the presiding classical authorities for the Christian Middle Ages, largely due to the military conquests of Alexander the Great, student of Aristotle (student of Plato), founder and namesake of the city in which the Septuagint was created and in which Philo wrote. More broadly, and more significantly for the metempsychotic tradition of Western translation theory, the alien words of Augustine's dogmatic system are the Greek words of the Alexandrian translation that he too, like Philo and Jerome, believed to be divinely inspired:

> And in emending Latin translations, Greek translations are to be consulted, of which the Septuagint carries most authority in so far as the Old Testament is concerned. In all the more learned churches it is now said that this translation was so inspired by the Holy Spirit that many men spoke as if with the mouth of one. It is said and attested by many of not unworthy faith that, although the translators were separated in various cells while they worked, nothing was to be found in any version that was not found in the same words and with the same order of words in all of the others. Who would compare any other authority with this, or, much less, prefer another? But even if they conferred and arrived at a single opinion on the basis of common judgment and consent, it is not right or proper for any man, no matter how learned, to seek to emend the consensus of so many older and more learned men. Therefore, even though something is found in Hebrew versions different from what they have set down, I think we should cede to the divine dispensation by which they worked. (2.15.22)

This passage presents the perfectionist ideal of cenobitic/metempsychotic translation theory: the subordination of not one but seventy-two translators, in seventy-two monastic cells, to a single alien word, the word of the Holy Spirit ("many men spoke as if with the mouth of one"), with the result that the translation they produce actually supersedes the original text. "Who would compare any other authority with this?"—even a Hebrew authority, even the source text, believed by kabbalists to have been written in the language of heaven, in God's own hand. Implicit in this preference for a Greek translation over the Hebrew original, as I began to suggest above in my discussion of Joseph Dan and the Hebrew rabbinical tradition, is a preference for the schizoid/rationalist/ascetic regimen by which the translation was achieved. The Hebrew Bible was written over many centuries by sundry hands, spoken by a hodgepodge of voices without benefit of cenobitic discipline, and thus (though Augustine will not say this openly) is less reliable than a cenobitic document like the Septuagint: "even though something is found in Hebrew versions different from what they have set down, I think we should cede to the divine dispensation by which they worked." Even if the translation was not divinely inspired, Augustine clings to this notion of a surreptitiously political "divine dispensation": "even if they conferred and arrived at a single opinion on the basis of common judgment and consent, it is not right or proper for any man, no matter how learned, to seek to emend the consensus of so many older and more learned men." The "consensus of so many older and more learned men," spoken by the Other-as-reason if not by the Holy Spirit, constitutes a locus of authority that "it is not right or proper" to challenge. This passage shows the cenobitic ideology at its strongest: the subtracted self in search of a master whose command will render its expressions faultless. If the subtracted self can believe that the master is divine, so much the better; barring that ultimate transcendentalization of authority, however, any authority will do, especially one lent credence by the alien word and collective consensus, which together banish (or help *resist*) the demystifying effects of ordinary speech and the atomizing effects of the isolated self.

This insistence on the centrality of the alien Greek word to Augustine's cenobitic semiotic may seem to be undermined by the close attention Augustine pays to Latin translations; but actually there is no conflict. The key for Augustine is not the *use* of an alien language, but the *alienation* of whatever language one uses. Nor is this alienation entirely at odds with familiarity, for in some sense Augustine requires that both the alien and the familiar be resisted: neither the utterly alien nor the utterly familiar has any real impact, the former lacking impact because it is not understood, the latter because it is unremarkable. By domesticating the foreign and alienating the familiar, the user of language creates a kind of ascetic Esperanto, an "alien word" that is at once familiar and strange, understandable and shot through with awe. Here, for example, is Augustine's discussion of "impediments":

> For either an unknown word or an unknown expression may impede the reader. If these come from foreign languages we must consult one who speaks those languages, or learn them ourselves if we have leisure and ability, or make a comparison of various translations. If we do not know certain words or expressions in our own language, we become familiar with them by reading and hearing them. Nothing is better commended to the memory than those types

> of words and expressions which we do not know, so that when one more learned appears who may be questioned, or when a passage appears in reading where the preceding or following context makes their meaning clear, we may easily with the aid of the memory refer to them and learn them. Such is the force of habit even in learning that those who are nourished and educated in the Holy Scriptures wonder more at other expressions and think them poorer Latin than those used in the Scriptures, even though these do not appear in the writings of the Latin authors. (2.14.21)

These impediments might be thought of as survivals of mystery in Augustine's increasingly rationalist theology, as things that block reasoned understanding and must therefore, for the sake of Augustine's rationalism, be overcome through learning. At the same time, however, when they are memorized without understanding, these impediments can channel ascetic resistance to the force of habit and open the cenobite to a master ("one more learned") and thus to what Bakhtin calls the authoritative word, or what I'm calling the speaking of various authoritarian Others:

> The authoritative word demands that we acknowledge it, that we make it our own; it binds us, quite independent of any power it might have to persuade us internally; we encounter it with its authority already fused to it. The authoritative word is located in a distanced zone, organically connected with a past that is felt to be hierarchically higher. It is, so to speak, the word of the fathers. Its authority was already *acknowledged* in the past. It is a *prior* discourse. It is therefore not a question of choosing it from among other possible discourses that are its equal. It is given (it sounds) in lofty spheres, not those of familiar contact. Its language is a special (as it were, hieratic) language. It can be profaned. It is akin to taboo, i.e., a name that must not be taken in vain. (342)

But Augustine is transected by two such words, two authoritarian Others: the Other-as-mystery, the authoritative word of knowing-without-knowing, and the Other-as-reason, the authoritative word of knowledge-as-power. "And the first rule of this undertaking and labor," Augustine writes, "is, as we have said, to know these books even if they are not understood, at least to read them or to memorize them, or to make them not altogether unfamiliar to us" (2.9.14). Like many a Sunday school teacher today, he wants the authoritative word of reason, of understanding, but will settle for the authoritative word of mystery, or rote memorization: *know* these books even if you don't understand them.

We should recognize this dual and doubly bound "alien word," this complex mixture of the alien and the familiar, of ritual surrender and rational understanding, of mystery and reason, as the interlanguage into which translators are systematically encouraged to render their source texts—even by theorists like Eugene A. Nida, a vocal advocate of not making the translation sound like a translation. Nida disapproves of alien Bible translations, such as the radically literal renditions of Buber and Rosenzweig or Chouraqui and the outdated English of the King James Version, and calls for easily understandable colloquial translations; but he also disapproves of overly assimilated translations, slangy translations, modernized translations, and so on. The translation should be familiar but not too familiar—and alien, but not too alien.

Of course, this dialectical resistance to both the alien and the familiar means in practice that, depending on the readership for whom the translator is translating, the ascetic alien word may take any number of forms: from the carefully flattened colloquialism of a Nida translation to the stylized literalism of David Rosenberg in *The Book of J* to the jazzy modernization of Clarence Jordan's Cotton Patch Version; from the radical plainness of a Pound translation to the radical ugliness of Nabokov's *Eugene Onegin* (which his biographer Brian Boyd tells us he liked to pronounce "You-Gin One-Gin" [112]). Augustine says explicitly that he is addressing his remarks to Latin-speaking men (2.11.16); this requires him to posit an alien/familiar interlanguage between Greek and Latin. For later writers, who did not speak Latin themselves and did not address Latin-speaking men, this interlanguage had to shift: for many English writers in the eighteenth and nineteenth centuries, for example, who increasingly began to address not only men ignorant of Latin but women as well, the interlanguage switched to a space between Latin and English, a Latinized English that carries the authority of Augustine's Latin and the understandability of contemporary English.

In any case, what Augustine's vision of translation underscores is that the "alien word" of the translator's interlanguage or translationese is hegemonically the "authoritative word" that subjects both the translator and the target reader to a cenobitic discipline—to the masterful speaking of an authority who coaches the translator and the reader in submission to the ascetic command. Whether this means that the Bible reader can "trust" (and conform to) a Bible translation because the translator has been so thoroughly conformed to God's source-language intention or that a consumer can "trust" (and conform to) a translated advertisement or business letter because the translator has been so thoroughly conformed to the source writer's intention, translation since Augustine has been, and it remains to this day, normatively a cenobitic discipline. It is steeped in social regulation, mastery and subjection, command and conformity: perfection as power.

Metempsychosis Perfected

The metempsychotic conception of translation as the transfer of an unchanging soul from one body to another here achieves perfection as well. As I argued in *The Translator's Turn* (56–57), Augustine's model for perfected metempsychotic translation was Paul's doctrine of the spiritual body:

> But some will ask, "How are the dead raised? With what kind of body do they come?" You foolish man! What you sow does not come to life unless it dies.

> And what you sow is not the body which is to be, but a bare kernel, perhaps of wheat or of some other grain. But God gives it a body as he has chosen, and each kind of seed its own body. For not all flesh is alike, but there is one kind for men, another for animals, another for birds, and another for fish. There are celestial bodies and there are terrestrial bodies; but the glory of the celestial is one, and the glory of the terrestrial is another. There is one glory of the sun, and another glory of the moon, and another glory of the stars; for star differs from star in glory.
>
> So it is with the resurrection of the dead. What is sown is perishable, what is raised is imperishable. It is sown in dishonor, it is raised in glory. It is sown in weakness, it is raised in power. It is sown a physical body, it is raised a spiritual body. Thus it is written, "The first man Adam became a living being"; the last Adam became a life-giving spirit. But it is not the spiritual which is first but the physical, and then the spiritual. The first man was from the earth, a man of dust; the second man is from heaven. As was the man of dust, so are those who are of the dust; and as is the man of heaven, so are those who are of heaven. Just as we have borne the image of the man of dust, we shall also bear the image of the man of heaven.
>
> I tell you this, brethren; flesh and blood cannot inherit the kingdom of God, nor does the perishable inherit the imperishable. Lo! I tell you a mystery. We shall not sleep, but we shall all be changed, in a moment, in the twinkling of an eye, at the last trumpet. (1 Cor. 15:35–52)

Gone now is the dreary repetition of Greek metempsychosis, the schizoid soul leapfrogging wearily from body to body, each body as perishable as the last, birth-reproduction-death, birth-reproduction-death, over and over again, an unending cycle. In its place Paul theorizes a Christian metempsychosis, a perfectionist metempsychosis, in which the soul leaps from an imperfect body to a perfected one, from a perishable body to an imperishable one, from a body of dust to a body of heavenly glory—from a physical body, *soma phusikon*, a body made out of nature, a carnal false-self system, to a spiritual body, *soma pneumatikon*, a body made out of wind, spirit, a body made of intellect and ideas, a body tailor-made to fit the needs of the disembodied "true self." Here the Other-as-reason takes a tremendous philosophical leap forward: no more of the ancient Greek same ol' same ol'—bring on the perfect Platonic body, built to outlast eternity!

Of course, this mythic process doesn't work. It's an ideal straitjacket for translation that real translators can never quite don because its success is predicated on the intervention of the Holy Spirit, and the Holy Spirit really only works in retrospect (it's a lot easier to declare an existing translation perfect than it is to do a translation perfectly). As an ascetic regimen for Bible *readers*, therefore, Augustine's metempsychotic perfectionism was a huge success well into the Reformation, when it was most powerfully challenged (Jerome's Vulgate is *not* the word of God, Latin isn't the divine idiom, the Vulgate is just a translation), and even beyond, when it was transformed into the unconscious perfectionist principle that whatever Bible translation you grew up with (the King James, say) is infallible.

As an ascetic regimen for Bible (and other) *translators*, however, Augustine's metempsychotic perfectionism was a miserable failure, as it perhaps inevitably must have been. No ascetic regimen can truly succeed because the goals of such a regimen are necessarily unachievable. In truth, asceticism would never have gained its nervous grip on the Western psyche had its goals been attainable. Even the success of the readerly ascetic regimen was never perfect; the Reformation assault on the Vulgate was conditioned by the sheer impossibility of forcing a human translation into the mold of perfection, and the King James has been inundated by competing English translations for centuries. Augustine's quasimystical ethos of perfect translation only really "succeeded" in romantic theories of what Goethe called the "mystical interlinear version," the radically literal translation that somehow managed to capture not only the spirit but the body of the original and so transformed the target text into a kind of redemptive spiritual body.

Schizoid Translation as Empire

The one essential aspect of the rationalist ascesis that I've neglected so far is its expansionist nature—its participation in an imperialism of the spirit that all too often, when translated into the political realm, becomes colonialism. The schizoid personality wards off schizophrenia through rigorous control of all otherness, of the false-self system conceived broadly as everything outside the beleaguered "true self"—which is to say, everything. Because, as Laing says, the schizoid self feels constantly in danger of being engulfed, of being overwhelmed by the forces of falsity and chaotic nonentity that surround it, it must vigilantly strive to expand its hegemony over those forces through the dominance strategies of asceticism—especially cenobitic asceticism, which ruled the medieval world from its monastic base and which through its spread to the middle classes has come to rule the modern world as well. The schizoid eremite collapses into schizophrenia, or gets hooked on drugs or alcohol, or commits suicide, or seeks support in psychotherapy, or somehow gets by, wandering the streets muttering to himself, shouting at passersby, feeling ever more isolated and alone; the schizoid cenobite finds a community of like-minded isolates in the military, in industry, in education, in government, in the mission field and, once there, works to instill the schizoid ascesis in others, students and indigenous populations and other "inferiors."

The connection between rationalist/ascetic translation and military (or mental) conquest has been recognized at least since Jerome, who speaks in the letter to Pammachius of taking the foreign author captive; by the seventeenth and eighteenth centuries, the heyday of European colonialism, the celebration of translation as empire, translation as an essential tool in the quest beyond European borders for new sources of European wealth, became something of a commonplace. In his 1684 "Essay on Translated Verse" the Earl of Roscommon says it openly: the translator must serve the ends of empire.

When, by Impulse from Heaven, *Tyrtaeus* Sung,
In drooping Souldiers a new Courage sprung;
Reviving Sparta now the fight maintain'd,
And what *Two Gen'rals Lost*; a *Poet Gain'd*.
By secret influence of Indulgent Skyes,
Empire and *Poesy Together* rise.
True Poets are the *Guardians* of a *State*,
And, when *They Fail*, portend approaching *Fate*,
For that which *Rome* to *Conquest* did Inspire
Was not the *Vestal*, but the *Muses fire*;
Heaven joyns the *Blessings*; no *declining* Age
E're felt the *Raptures* of *Poetick Rage*. (83–84)

This in effect turns Plato on his head by arguing that "*True Poets* are the *Guardians* of a *State*": where Plato would have banished poets from the state, leaving the philosopher as king and soldiers as guardians, Roscommon sees poets and poetic translators as the key to empire. Roscommon's idea is not too far removed from Plato's discussion of the education of soldiers in books two and three of the *Republic*, in which he says poets may serve a useful function in bolstering soldiers' courage and willingness to die for their city-state. But to forestall Plato's banishment of the poet in book ten, Roscommon must implicitly *restrict* the poet and the translator to this quasimilitary role—he must not merely enlist them in the cause of empire but exclusively subordinate them to that cause. "*Empire* and *Poesy Together* rise" means that poetry (both original and translated) really has no other function than facilitating the advancement of empire. (Also, of course, in some sense empire has no other function than facilitating the advancement of poetry: note Roscommon's dire warning that "no *declining* Age / E're felt the *Raptures* of *Poetick Rage*.") Roscommon says you can't have some poets, such as the ancient Greek poet Tyrtaeus, urging soldiers to die for Sparta, while others sing the rosy-fingered dawn or complain about the government. Everybody pulls on the same oar.

About a century later, however, this imperialist role for or mode of poetry and poetic translation was increasingly cast in a negative light by the German romantics, whose contribution to translation theory I want to consider more closely in chapter 3. Beginning with Herder in his early work *Fragmente* (late 1760s), the German romantics conceived the reductive and assimilative meaning-transfer that Jerome and Augustine had normalized in the fourth century, and European translators had by and large internalized *as* normative by the fourteenth or fifteenth century, as a bad thing, an appropriative method that only served to replicate the target culture a thousandfold. The German romantics' scapegoat for their criticism was French culture, which they perceived as ego- and ethnocentric, so focused on local psychocultural needs that French translators and publishers and readers had to transform all foreign literatures into the French image.

But this criticism raises a dilemma, which translation theorists are just now, in the last few years, beginning to address with any tenacity: how can you say *anything* about the other without implicitly colonizing him/her/it, without imposing your schizoid majoritarian mindset on a minoritarian culture that must forever remain alien to you? Since, in Deleuze and Guattari's use of the term in *Thousand Plateaus*, the "majority" belongs not to those with superior numbers but to those with the power to define and enforce norms, men are culturally and ideologically in the majority with regard to women, whites with regard to people of color, the middle classes with regard to the poor, the First World with regard to the Third—and majoritarian discourse is therefore by definition always a power discourse, what Bakhtin called the authoritative word, the discourse of (schizoid) hegemonic control. Consequently, anything I say about Third World culture as a white Western male will automatically fit that culture into my majoritarian conception of minority, of otherness. I can't help it. No matter how sympathetic I try to be, no matter how long I live in a Third World culture, no matter how fluently I learn its language, my perspective on that culture will always be structured by the schizoid power discourse of majoritarian Western culture. I will always be a colonizer. Any "authentic" discourse about the colonized will have to come from the colonized themselves, from the "subaltern subject position"—not from me. Even then I won't be able to get "inside" its authenticity; all I will inevitably do is "understand" it in the rationalist, colonialist sense.

It should be obvious that this notion, like every other notion invented by the schizoid Other-as-reason, is double-binding. The harder I try to escape my culturally imposed schizoid prison, the more firmly I will be trapped in it. There is no escape because every escape I can imagine is just another form of incarceration. I reject this vicious circle, and, by the end of the chapter, I want to work around to an escape that will work—but first I need to map out, even if sketchily, the historical development of the prison cell.

The Expansion of Western Reason

Jesus (or a committee of his English translators) said, "Go therefore and make disciples of all nations" (Matthew 28:19), but the expansionist impulse in Western civilization didn't begin there. This impulse was and remains intrinsic to the "universalist" ethos of the ascendant Other-as-reason, which says that all things shall conform to my ideals. In order to believe that what I believe is universally true, I must work to transform both my perception and the things I perceive in the image of what I need to see: I must work to see what I have to see, to unsee what I can't afford to see, and to consolidate political power around the "education" or "civilization" or "translation" of those recalcitrant others who threaten to overwhelm me with their difference. And the history of Western civilization can be characterized as a process of consolidating hegemonic power against enemies both internal and external. To begin, just look at medieval consolidations of ecclesiastical power, which occurred on a number of fronts at once:

The theological front. The universalization of Christian dogma: the rise of systematic or scholastic "theology" in the twelfth and thirteenth centuries, with its co-optation of ancient Greek and recent Arabic philosophy. The definition and persecution of heresies, especially the establishment of the Inquisition in 1229, in response to a proliferation of heterodox movements in the first centuries of the new millennium. The schism with the Eastern Church, beginning with Constantine's 313 C.E. conversion to Christianity, which converted the entire Roman empire while planting the seeds of division within it by moving the secular seat of the empire to Constantinople but leaving the ecclesiastical seat in Rome (the split was exacerbated by the Western Church's complicity in military/territorial expansionism, finalized in 1054, unsuccessfully mended in the thirteenth and fifteenth centuries).

The political front. Clashes with and accommodations to the imperial powers: the coronation by the pope of the Frankish King Charlemagne in 800; the subsumption of the papacy into the Ottonian Empire in the tenth century through the bestowal upon bishops and greater abbots of royal estates and counties; the investiture conflict in the decades before and after 1100 over whether bishops would be invested with the ring and the staff by the king or the pope; the formation of a papal monarchy in Rome. Clashes with Islam: the polarization of Rome and Constantinople in the seventh century when followers of Mohammed seized the patriarchates of Alexandria, Antioch, and Jerusalem; the eleventh-century Crusades; the twelfth- and thirteenth-century reconquest of Islamic Spain. The military conversion of local populations to orthodox Christianity: the development of an official ideology of holy war against the heathen by Gregory the Great out of Augustine's *City of God*, most notoriously put into practice by Charlemagne in the ninth century and by Pope Gregory VII in the eleventh.

The legal/administrative front. The development of papal decretals to lay down ecclesiastical law and the appointment (originally by Pope Leo IX in the eleventh century) of legates and other curial officials to enforce them. The centralization of the church under Gregory VII so as to impose papal control over canonical elections, diocesan bishops, and Roman and local synods. The increased incursion of doctrinally correct practices into the events of the daily lives of the lay public: marriage customs, auricular confession, intercessory prayer, the institutionalization of patron saints, education.

The economic front. The bestowal of royal fiefdoms on popes, bishops, and abbots in return for political loyalty; the management of the resulting ecclesiastical landholdings; the sale of benefices and indulgences.

It should be noted, however, that these consolidations were first conceived and were continually sought in response to a most recalcitrant political reality—that, indeed, the universalist theology that took Matthew 28:19 as its byword was itself as much driven by a fear of centrifugal political forces as it was the driving force behind centripetal consolidation. The "defection" of Constantinople (from the viewpoint of the Western Church), the military counterpressure from Islam, the territorial designs of the feudal lords, and the emergent merchant classes were all sources of recurrent and increasing anxiety for the schizoid/universalist church in the late Middle Ages; that anxiety can't have been mitigated by the subliminal knowledge that the threat posed by these various forces was in fact exacerbated and in some cases actively generated by ecclesiastical universalism. Universalism, as I said a moment ago, translates geopolitically as expansionism or colonialism, and the medieval church did seek to colonize the entire known world for Jesus. Colonization is the specific political form the church assigned to Jesus' commission to his disciples—the conversion of the world not sinner by sinner but en masse, by military force justified by divine law.

And the "colonists" resisted, often passively but more often through their own political consolidations. The universalist ideology that drove Pope Leo IX to expand the *plenitudo potestatis* or jurisdictional power of the papacy in the late thirteenth century effectively blocked the mending of the east-west schism it was supposedly attempting to facilitate: it was clear to the Greek church that the Latin church wanted unification on its own terms, and the two councils convened to unify the church, at Lyon in 1274 and at Basel and Florence from 1431 to 1439, both failed—even when, as at Florence, all the theological differences had been ironed out. The various wars that the medieval Christian church fought with Islam from the eleventh to the thirteenth century (the Crusades, the reconquest of Spain) were holy wars in name only; in bare political fact these wars were territorial conquests, attempts to expand landholdings undertaken by land-impoverished second sons and "blessed" by universalist ecclesiastics.

Thus was the "West" defined, in a struggle to gain and maintain geographical, cultural, and ideological territories for Jesus and—above all—his church. Ancient Greece and Rome were not "Western" civilization—except, of course, by nostalgic retroactive fiat. Greek and Roman civilization was progressively "unearthed" by the late Middle Ages and Renaissance and attached to the edifice of "Western" civilization as a putative foundation, an etiological myth, as it were, of origins and authority.

This "unearthing" metaphor makes it seem as if Greek civilization had been buried; actually it was only culturally buried, hidden from Latin view not by dirt but by difference, by linguistic and cultural and religious difference, by the institutionalized xenophobia of the medieval church. Schizoid Christian theologians, concerned with the purity of their true-self doctrines, worked constantly at marking the boundaries of the acceptable, incorporating and assimilating some foreign impulses (Plato, Jewish law) into Christianity through ingenious allegorical readings while utterly banishing and "forgetting" others, consigning them to the "earth" of ideological repression. Islamic theologians were far more tolerant of philosophy, far less insistent upon subsuming into a monolithic theology what was acceptable and repressing what was not, and far more permissive in allowing a rich philosophical tradition to flourish alongside theology. "Islamic" scholars—specifically Muslims, Christians, and Jews working in Arabic in the great Islamic population centers, including those in southern Spain like Toledo and Seville—had preserved and translated into Arabic the ancient Greek texts and had continued to develop the philosophical traditions of "pagan" antiquity, commenting on the ancient texts and testing their claims through observation, theoretical reflection, and calculation. All of this work was "recovered" for the "West" in the so-called reconquest of Spain from the eleventh to the thirteenth centuries—but what was recovered served as a philosophical detonation device, a bomb set to explode the repressive intolerance of universalist theology.

This "recovery" created an even more ironic situation than that suggested by the bomb metaphor. The Islamic territorial acquisitions of the seventh century helped "define" the West culturally and geopolitically by driving a wedge between Rome and Constantinople and ideologically by sealing off the Holy Land, the birthplace of Jesus, the geographical source and icon of Christian faith. But these land acquisitions simultaneously implanted within the "West," specifically in the south of Spain, an "alien cell" of philosophical tolerance, of learning, of openminded inquiry into logic, nature, mathematics (including music and astronomy), ethics, politics, and metaphysics—a cell Christian scholars were free to enter and enjoy without concern for theological correctness. Thus the territorial expansionism that defined the West also helped undermine the West; and, more ironically still, the Crusaders' failure to reannex the Holy Land successfully consolidated the mythic self-image of the West, while the successful reannexation of southern Spain effectively exploded the bomb that shook the hegemonic edifice of the church.

It could be argued that the bomb was detonated by translators: that the mere military reconquest of Spain would not have led to an ideological explosion had it not been for the batteries of translators living in Toledo and Seville in the eleventh and twelfth centuries who were rendering all the Greek and Arabic texts into Latin. Of course, the process wasn't that simple: the translators didn't simply appear in Spain and begin to translate. There were secular and ecclesiastical forces—kings, bishops, curial officials—pushing for Latin translations of the Greek and Arabic books, sending the learned men in their regions to Spain to undertake translations of specific works for them. In other words, centrifugal impulses within the political structure of the "West" were working, consciously or unconsciously, to undermine the universalist hegemony of the Church. But the translators were instrumental in this process.

As I say, however, throughout this period—from roughly the sixth to the twelfth century—the Church was also actively at work to deflect centrifugal forces, to maintain and expand ideological control over its territory, which gradually, by the ninth or tenth century, began to be called the West. Part of this program—though perhaps it can be called a "program" only in retrospect—was the imposition of a new set of norms on translators. Translators, after all, were the conduit by which alien ideas invaded the Church's domain; it was essential, therefore, that translators be systematically brought within the Church's cenobitic ideology, that they be trained in the ascetic discipline of translation as defined by Jerome and Augustine—which is to say, in sense-for-sense translation.

And it is interesting that one of the most successful weapons of this assault on otherness in the late Middle Ages should have arisen through the orthodox exegetical tradition of fourfold interpretation. This tradition not only enabled an expositor to assimilate a nonchristian text rhetorically to Christian doctrine through the ingenious use of various figurative hermeneutics, it even allowed a Christian text to be exfoliated, almost ad infinitum, in directions dictated by the expositor's dialogue not with the original author but with the target-language reader.

The translator's liberty in adaptation was not quite ad infinitum, of course: allegorical ingenuity was always controlled by institutionally defined orthodoxy. Still, in a larger historical context it is easy to see the survival in this orthodox tradition of the Ciceronian practice of oratorical *exercitatio* and also to trace the trajectory of these free adaptations as they influenced later and less pious translators. As I show in "Theorizing Translation in a Woman's Voice," this chain of influence proved particularly valuable for seventeenth-century women translators, who transformed the rhetoric of moral persuasion into a license for their own increase and the increase of their female readers.

This concern with the reader's needs clearly takes us a significant step beyond Augustine's lack of concern for the biblical source text but is still theologically akin to that lack of concern: as Augustine believes the translator capable of transcending the individual words of both the source and the target language by accessing the supralinguistic universals of God's Word, so too, for example, does the fourteenth-century French *Ovide moralisé* translator discount "what the author crudely presents in recounting the story" (translated and cited by Rita Copeland 113) in order to reconstitute Ovid allegorically as a Christian writer. As for Augustine, this process involves (at least ideally) a hermeneutical shift from worldly to divine meaning, from historical to eternal interpretation; the reader of the *Ovide moralisé* is expected to join its writer in a transhistorical realm ruled by a universal god for whom there is no before and after, and thus no difference between Christian and prechristian authors. Assimilative translation is no distortion of the original, no forced reshaping of its pagan expression along orthodox Christian lines; it is a rising above mere interpretive history into the Platonic realm of timeless truth.

Scratch this transhistorical idealization just slightly, and the *historical* idealizations of the *translatio studii et imperii* emerge, according to which learning and empire are at once universal and spatiotemporal—at once forever unified and unchanging and situated in a succession of historical cultures. In this view, the bare historical fact that learning and empire moved from Greece to Rome to France, for example, is "transcendentalized" (read: derelativized) through the belief that this migration did not change them: that learning and empire are still the same in the fourteenth century as they were in ancient Greece and Rome. Originally a Greek idea, the *translatio studii et imperii* is (as the hegemonic keyword *translatio* suggests) an implicitly metempsychotic notion according to which every soul remains unchanged through its residence in a succession of bodies; when the *translatio* is picked up by the church fathers it is assimilated to Paul's enhanced metempsychotic conception of the spiritual body, into which the soul (plucked at death from the physical body) is injected in the resurrection.

Scratch this historical idealization, in turn, and the naked political fact of empire, of the military and cultural control of populations, emerges. Eric Cheyfitz has articulated the politics of the *translatio* in all its interwoven forms (*studii, imperii,* and *linguarum*) most persuasively in *The Poetics of Imperialism:*

> The *translatio,* then, is inseparably connected with a "civilizing" mission, the bearing of Christianity and Western letters to the barbarians, literally, as we have noted, those who do not speak the language of the empire. From its beginnings the imperialist mission is, in short, one of translation: the translation of the "other" into the terms of the empire, the prime term of which is "barbarian," or one of its variations such as "savage," which, ironically, but not without a precise politics, alienates the other from the empire. (112)

Ovid and the *Ovide moralisé* poet are, in a sense, both subjects of the Roman Empire; but the Roman Empire has moved since Ovid wrote, it has been "translated" from southern to central Europe and from polytheistic paganism to monotheistic Christianity. Ovid can, therefore, only truly remain "himself" by being translated "into the terms of the empire," as Cheyfitz says, specifically by being translated into the terms of the *translated* empire, the empire as it stands (in all its unchanging universality) in fourteenth-century France. The barbaric Gauls were once translated "into the terms of the empire" by the Romans, and were again translated by their successors the Roman Catholics; now, more than a millennium later, they can only maintain the integrity of the *translatio studii et imperii* by translating the rest of the world, including the vanquished Romans, into the terms of their own fourteenth-century empire as shaped by Charlemagne and his successors.

At the same time, of course, this hegemonic impulse is complexly undermined by various centrifugal forces in the *translatio* itself. That the *translatio* can only be made to appear stable and universal in its historical shifts from a single historical viewpoint—say, that of fourteenth-century France—is profoundly corrosive of universalism. If the true form of the *translatio* is only controlled by the medieval God for a few centuries between the fall of ancient Rome and the rise of the modern absolute state, the act of translating a Roman author like Ovid into the terms of the fourteenth-century French empire is itself doomed (like Ovid himself, and everybody else) to the relativism of ongoing history. The *translatio* itself must repeatedly be retranslated into the shifting terms of empire, a condition that has the effect of grounding the *translatio* not in stability but in flux. The assimilative hermeneutic of allegorical translation may be a tool of empire, but it is also always a tool against empire—against the totalizing attempt to fix a given empire in space and time for *all* time. Any translation that attempts to shore up the stability of its own era's empire simultaneously develops expressive repertoires that will prove invaluable to later eras in the dissolution or radical transformation of that empire.

As European universalists from the Renaissance and afterwards began to push past the bounds of the world they had known, expanding eastward into Asia, southward into Africa, and westward into the Americas, they carried their deep psychosocial need for uniformity with them and imposed this need on all the "natives" they found. Cheyfitz's *Poetics of Imperialism* serves as a particularly interesting (and disturbing) tool for analyzing this expansion. Not only did translators have to provide colonists and their soldier-guardians with poetic inspiration for their arduous task, as the Earl of Roscommon argued, but the indigenous populations of the colonized territories had to be translated into English, ultimately "translated" into christianized speakers of English. Translation thus mediated not only between the modern British Empire and the ancient empires of Greece and Rome—whose glorious precedents, translated into English, could help maintain colonists' morale—but also between the colonists and the indigenous populations as well.

Obviously, these two mediations are very different in nature, due largely to differentials in power among the British colonizers, the ancient empires, and the indigenous populations. In translating from the Greek and Latin, the English translator conceived his or her work in terms of idealized inferiority: the Greek and Roman poets blazed a path of glory that latter-day British imperialists could only dream of one day following. In "translating" from the Pawtuxet, for example, the English colonists chronicled by William Bradford in *A History of Plymouth Plantation* (1630–1650) are so far from idealized inferiority that they don't even learn Pawtuxet, but enlist Squanto as their interpreter: they trust a man captured by English adventurers in 1605 and taken to England for nine years; returned to his tribe by Captain John Smith in 1614 but recaptured (along with others of his tribe) by one of Smith's ship captains and sold into slavery in Malaga, Spain; and returned again to his tribe in 1619 by another expedition after escaping from the Spanish. This is, to put it mildly, a traumatic path to follow to become a translator, especially since it was not Squanto's choice to learn English or to interpret for the English colonists. He was forcibly "translated" as translator: he was colonized as interpreter to the colonists.

And note the consequences of becoming an interpreter for the English: Squanto is not only in constant danger of retribution from other Indians just for consorting with the enemy, but suffers an inward corruption (what we might call the "trustee syndrome") that makes him richly deserving of the

Indians' retribution. Bradford describes Squanto's assimilation to the ways of the Europeans:

> But by the former passages, and other things of like nature, they began to see that Squanto sought his own ends and played his own game, by putting the Indians in fear and drawing gifts from them to enrich himself, making them believe he could stir up war against whom he would, and make peace for whom he would. Yea, he made them believe they kept the plague buried in the ground, and could send it amongst whom they would, which did much terrify the Indians and made them depend more on him, and seek more to him, than to Massasoit. Which procured him envy and had like to have cost him his life; for after the discovery of his practices, Massasoit sought it both privately and openly, which caused him to stick close to the English, and never durst go from them till he died. (99)

There is no sign that Bradford disapproves of Squanto's "practices"—he is if anything serenely amused by them and by the anger of Massasoit and the fearful skulking about of Squanto that resulted from them. As long as Squanto does not endanger Plymouth Plantation, and, better, as long as his deceits keep the Indians on edge, his moral corruption is of no concern to Bradford.

In his 1580 essay "On Cannibals," half a century before Bradford, Montaigne had made a valiant effort to undo this imperialist ethos in his own thinking and to model that undoing for his readers: "I do not believe," he says, referring to the indigenous population of Brazil, "from what I have been told about this people, that there is anything barbarous or savage about them, except that we all call barbarous anything that is contrary to our own habits" (108). His essay is an admirable attempt from early on in the history of Western colonization to understand the customs of colonized people with empathy. Montaigne wants to understand them on their own terms, from "inside" their own cultural viewpoint. Unsurprisingly, however, he finds himself more fully satisfied by descriptions from a European informant who had lived in Brazil for ten or twelve years than by "direct" contact with emissaries from the native people. His informant is his "man"—a servant in his house—whose verity he trusts, he says, because of his ignorance:

> This man who stayed with me was a plain, simple fellow, and men of this sort are likely to give true testimony. Men of intelligence notice more things and view them more carefully, but they comment on them; and to establish and substantiate their interpretation, they cannot refrain from altering the facts a little. They never present things just as they are but twist and disguise them to conform to the point of view from which they have seen them; and to gain credence for their opinion and make it attractive, they do not mind adding something of their own, or extending and amplifying. We need either a very truthful man, or one so ignorant that he has no material with which to construct false theories and make them credible: a man wedded to no idea. My man was

> like that; and besides he has on various occasions brought me seamen and merchants whom he met on his voyage. Therefore I am satisfied with his information, and do not inquire what the cosmographers say about it. (108)

Montaigne's "man" is, it seems, a "cannibal" or "native" in a European body: he is utterly uncivilized and thus less likely to interpose fanciful interpretations, but he is also a native speaker of French (or, since Montaigne doesn't specify this, of some European language that Montaigne too speaks fluently). Montaigne's "man" is the perfect "native" informant—well versed both in the alien native conditions and in Montaigne's native language. Montaigne is more at a loss with the three emissaries of the colonized tribe: "I talked to one of them for some time; but I had an interpreter who followed my meaning so badly, and was so hindered by stupidity from grasping my ideas, that I could hardly get any satisfaction from him" (119). If the "natives" with whom he speaks directly do not speak his native language, he is forced to use the services of an interpreter; but in the interpreter the "stupidity" that made his "man" a reliable informant (by keeping him "wedded to no idea") is now an impossible obstacle to communication. Montaigne, one might say, wants his "man" to be the perfect French voice of the "cannibals," but wants the interpreter to be the perfect "cannibal" voice of *Montaigne*—which is to say that he wants to perfect and ultimately to eliminate the verbal mediation between himself and the "cannibals." One way to answer his curiosities, which he does not even consider, might be to spend several years in Brazil himself and learn the language and the customs of the people; but as I've suggested, even this solution would not eliminate the need for a verbal mediation (though it might seem to Montaigne and his readers to do so). Montaigne would still be a Frenchman, representative of a colonial power, living in an alien land, learning an alien language. Not even this, in other words, would guarantee him unmediated access to the "true" nature of the "cannibals."

Another significant step in the translation-as-empire project is taken by Montaigne's English translator, John Florio, in his 1603 metaphorization of the power relationship between the translator and his patron(ess)—an all-important relationship for the lowly born or otherwise impoverished translator in the age before the development of the printing industry. In his "Epistle Dedicatory" to Lucy Countess of Bedford and her mother Lady Anne Harrington, Florio builds a whole series of analogies for that relationship: the relationship between the maiden and her courtier (the courtier as subject to the maiden's acceptance or rejection of her suit); that between the "ironically modest Virgin" and her stern male commander who "delighted to see mee strive for life, yet fall out of breath" (3); that between the king and his servant; and, most strikingly, that between the colonial subject and the colonial power. His patronesses, he says, were at pains "to put and keepe mee in hart like a captived Canniball fattend against my death" (4); "Nor say I," he remarks elsewhere, "like this mans [Montaigne's] Indian King, you checkt with a sower-sterne countenance the yerneful complaint of your drooping, neere-dying subject" (3). The *translator* is now, at least metaphorically, the captive Indian forced by the colonial power to work till "drooping, neere-dying" while being "fattend against my death"—even when the translator is a native-born white male (who is soon to become gentleman-extraordinary and groom of the privy chamber), and the patroness, avatar of the colonizer, is a rich aristocratic woman.

This metaphorical transformation of the male translator into a maiden, manservant, and captive cannibal is almost certainly tied to the increased feminization of translation that occurred during this period. The bureaucratization of translation in the modern era increasingly generated anxieties in the men who had been doing the work—anxieties about their own "autonomy" or self-worth as free white males—leading both to a growing male exodus out of the translatorial pool and to the concomitant feminization of that pool, also an increasing need to defend against anxiety by troping not the *translator* but the *translation* as woman. Florio himself, for example, dedicates to two women "this defective edition (since all translations are reputed femalls, delivered at second hand; and I in this serve but as *Vulcan*, to hatchet this *Minerva* from that *Iupiters* big braine)" (1). It was much better, certainly—much more reassuring to the anxious middle-class male—to be not an "ironically modest virgin" but a Vulcan: not even a midwife, but a godly male who cuts the "defective" female translation out of Jupiter's brain with a hatchet.

Empire and Education

And as Cheyfitz demonstrates at length, one of the most characteristic channels of (indeed euphemisms for) this translation-cum-colonization of the male savage and the female European in this period was education. Women were grudgingly granted increased access to public discourse only as they were assimilated to dominant cultural assumptions through education. The indigenous populations of the New World were systematically exterminated by the tens of millions, but extermination occurred only after they had "refused"—problematically—to convert to Christianity and be educated in the ways of the Christian West. In *American Holocaust: Columbus and the Conquest of the New World*, David Stannard documents the ideological contortions by which the Catholic Church of the late fifteenth and early sixteenth centuries came to grant conquistadors the right to massacre the natives and steal their land, noting that these acts were largely justified through the *requerimiento*, an official church document that supposedly (*only* in Spanish) extended to the Indians to whom it was read aloud the right to convert to Christianity and be educated. Stannard writes:

> Following Columbus, each time the Spanish encountered a native individual or group in the course of their travels they were ordered to read to the Indians a statement informing them of the truth of Christianity and the

> necessity to swear immediate allegiance to the Pope and to the Spanish crown. After this, if the Indians refused or even delayed in their acceptance (or, more likely, their understanding) of the *requerimiento*, the statement continued [with a list of the horrible things that would happen to them, war and dispossession and slavery, if they resisted]. In practice, the Spanish usually did not wait for the Indians to reply to their demands. First the Indians were manacled; then, as it were, they were read their rights. As one Spanish conquistador and historian described the routine: "After they had been put in chains, someone read the *Requerimiento* without knowing their language and without any interpreters, and without either the reader or the Indians understanding the language they had no opportunity to reply, being immediately carried away prisoners, the Spanish not failing to use the stick on those who did not go fast enough." (65–66)

The increased use of Indian interpreters by William Bradford's time a century or more later obviates one moral reproach against the European colonizers, the reproach that they pretended to a justification that was a sham; but the use of Indian interpreters like Squanto still did not change the fact that the Indians were being forced to choose between colonization and extermination. It only mystified that fact—cast a slightly more irreproachable web of moral illusion over it.

Indeed Cheyfitz argues convincingly that the primal scene of translation-as-empire since Cicero has been a primal scene of instruction: the education of the savage into the image (if not the reality) of civilization. Writing for Charlemagne, for example, Alcuin describes in his *Rhetoric* an evolutionary process by which the "mute savage"—mute *and* savage because he does not speak eloquently, because he is a foreigner or a member of the European lower classes—is gradually "translated" or educated upwards by learning first "proper" speech, then eloquence; and Alcuin figures this progression eloquently (metaphorically) as one from naked savagery through utilitarian clothing to "the pinnacle of clothing as a sumptuous sign of social rank" (Cheyfitz 120).

The Subaltern Subject Position

I hesitate to write on this subject for the reasons given above: whatever I say about a book like Tejaswini Niranjana's *Siting Translation*, a book written by an Indian woman about the British politics of translation in India, is by definition the discourse of the colonizer; anything I take her to be saying is inevitably conditioned (and thus contaminated) by my subject position within majoritarian First World culture. So deft is the schizoid double bind, however, that *not* saying anything about books about translation by Third World writers is equally culpable, since remaining silent is tantamount to confessing that I find Third World writers irrelevant to my concerns, that the only writers who can engage my interest are people like me—Western white male middle-class academic writers like, say, Eric Cheyfitz.

On the other hand, I'm not all that worried about this double bind. I express my concern not so much to complain about political correctness, as a lot of conservative cultural critics have been doing, but to tie the knot tighter before attempting, like Houdini, to slip out of it in the end.

Niranjana does not face my problem as a member of the colonizer's class; she is herself a postcolonial subject who speaks, like Frantz Fanon, like Homi Bhabha, like Gauri Viswanathan, from within the context of having-been-colonized. That this mere situatedness does not solve the methodological problems she shares with white male Western colleagues like Cheyfitz and me as a revolutionary thinker in the field is obvious—Niranjana writes in English, the colonizer's language, thus making it possible for Cheyfitz and me to misunderstand her. Currently a lecturer in English at the University of Hyderabad in Andhra Pradesh, she grew up in Bangalore, Karnataka State, and was raised bilingually both at home and at school in English and Kannada (she also learned some Hindi). Would it be fair to say that she has herself been "translated" into the colonizer's language from birth? Certainly for her the cultural politics of translation cut close to home: both of her parents are famous Kannada novelists; their daughter Tejaswini writes in English. Niranjana has translated three of her father's novels and several of her mother's short stories into English, a task that must have stretched her tight across all the uncomfortable dilemmas of decolonization: how could she best honor her father and her mother in the colonizer's language (which, to be sure, she first learned from them)? By writing "readable" or "assimilated" English (but assimilated to what—India? the U.S.? the U.K.?), or by clinging as closely as possible to the original by Kannadigizing English? I'll be returning to look at Niranjana's translation of a twelfth-century sacred poem or *vacana* written in Kannada later in the chapter.

She writes:

> My study of translation does not make any claim to solve the dilemmas of translators. It does not propose yet another way of theorizing translation to enable a more foolproof "method" of "narrowing the gap" between cultures; it seeks rather to think through this gap, this difference, to explore the positioning of the obsessions and desires of translation, and thus to describe the economies within which the sign of translation circulates. My concern is to probe the absence, lack, or repression of an awareness of asymmetry and historicity in several kinds of writing on translation. (9)

And here, in the "repression of an awareness of asymmetry and historicity in several kinds of writing on translation," I recognize myself—the self that wrote *The Translator's Turn*, the self that had not yet read Niranjana or Cheyfitz or Rafael. I don't quite know how to say this, but this book of mine on "the obsessions and desires of translation" wouldn't have been thinkable without Niranjana's deconstruction of the politics of translation; her book produced a kind of rupture in my thinking (and writing) about translation, an eruption of negativity in the very heart of my attempts to "solve the dilemmas of translators"—even though my solutions were far more radical, far more liberatory than the repressive common sense that Niranjana seems to be referring to ("as faithfully as you can, as freely as you must") and that has passed as "solutions" for centuries. For me, Niranjana crystallized the problem of translation as empire in the politics of (self-)control: to create an anxiety-free zone around it, the schizoid "true self" must colonize the body, the family, the culture, the world, the universe, ever-expanding zones of colonial control, the cosmos as false-self system subordinated to the repressive needs of the rationalist self.

But this is Niranjana filtered through my Laingian concern with the schizoid personality; let me quote her at some length on William Jones, the eminent Orientalist who went to India in 1783 to assume a seat on the Supreme Court in Calcutta and whose translations of Persian and Indian texts profoundly influenced English and German romanticism (Goethe mentions his translation of the *Sakuntala* in his notes to *West-Östlicher Divan*):

> The most significant nodes of Jones's work are (a) the need for translation by the European, since the [Indian] natives are unreliable interpreters of their own laws and culture; (b) the desire to be a lawgiver, to give the Indians their "own" laws; and (c) the desire to "purify" Indian culture and speak on its behalf. The interconnections between these obsessions are extremely complicated. They can be seen, however, as feeding into a larger discourse of improvement and education that interpellates the colonial subject.
>
> In Jones's construction of the "Hindus," they appear as a submissive, indolent nation unable to appreciate the fruits of freedom, desirous of being ruled by an absolute power, and sunk deeply in the mythology of an ancient religion. In a letter, he points out that the Hindus are "incapable of civil liberty," for "few of them have an idea of it, and those, who have, do not wish it" (*LWJ*, p. 712). Jones, a good eighteenth-century liberal, deplores the "evil" but recognizes the "necessity" of the Hindus' being "ruled by an absolute power." His "pain" is "much alleviated" by the fact that the natives are much "happier" under the British than under their former rulers. In another letter, Jones bids the Americans, whom he admired, not to be "like the deluded, besotted Indians, among whom I live, who would receive Liberty as a curse instead of a blessing, if it were possible to give it them, and would reject, as a vase of poison, that, which, if they could taste and digest it, would be the water of life" (p. 847). (13–14)

Of course, the water of life in Christian symbology is otherworldly, transcendental, which is to say imaginary, fantasized by the schizoid "true self" that dreams of release from the embodied false-self system that hungers and thirsts, eats and excretes, feels pleasure and pain. The "Liberty" Jones is referring to is no utopian vision of pastoral anarchy, but precisely the schizoid condition that so internalizes its ascetic prison or straitjacket that it can only feel "free" when tightly hemmed in by this restraint. Because the Indians resist being "retrained" for this anxious ascetic regimen the European colonizers call Liberty, they are constructed as "desirous of being ruled by an absolute power": if you won't internalize our reason, you'll have to take it externally in the form of political coercion. The "irony" of the British forcing liberty on the Indians is, in other words, only superficial: force, combined with more "spiritual" or "democratic" forms of retraining like translation and education, is a highly effective method of facilitating the internalization of mastery, which underlies the British conception of liberty. "Forcing people to be free" only seems ironic to us because we have so successfully repressed the enormous rock of mastery, authority, rational self-control that we had to swallow as children before we were allowed to enter the "free" state of adulthood, majority. Indigenous populations in the early stages of colonization, not having yet been subjected to this training in "freedom" as rational self-control, seem to the schizoid colonizer like children who "don't yet know how to be free"—because they are *too* free. And the other side to this is that the colonizer too can only feel free when surrounded by ascetics like himself, which is to say, people who don't provoke his anxieties by exercising *unregulated* freedom, which he refuses to dignify with the term "freedom" or "liberty," calling it instead "license." If your "freedom" assaults my sensibilities, it feels like a diminishment of *my* freedom, which I will redress (if I have the power) by diminishing or confiscating yours—at least until you prove yourself capable of using your freedom "responsibly," i.e. of following my rules.

Or, as Niranjana puts this, quoting anthropologist Godfrey Lienhardt on the importance of translating the "savage's" unconscious cultural systems into the rational clarity of English or some other First World language: "The 'primitive' becomes the anthropologist's civilizational other. Because it does not depend on logic or consistency, the primitive society's science is 'defective compared with ours' [Lienhardt]. The unity of human consciousness does not preclude—in fact, it helps construct—an inner hierarchy: primitive thought needs to be translated into modern, for it is that which is not yet modern. The hierarchy also indicates to us the operation of a teleological model of history" (69–70), according to which the "primitive" other always precedes the "modern" self as childhood precedes adulthood. The schizoid Westerner (especially the white middle-class academically trained Western male, like me) is the normative image of adulthood, of a fully achieved self; the pre- or postschizoid "savage" is the unruly or schizophrenic child who must be shaped, carefully, systematically, in the image of the idealized adult.

Niranjana's argument is almost entirely negative, in the sense Fredric Jameson develops of the negative hermeneutic that analyzes the ideological cages that hold us fast. And the negative is vitally important: a theory or a practice that moves too quickly from the negative to the positive, from ideological analysis to an empowering or liberatory utopian vision, incurs the risk of Pollyanna-ism, smoothing over perceived (but not "really" significant) problems—there there, everything will be all right. The positive has to be earned through torturous immersion in the negative. And the appearance of Cheyfitz's book a few months before *The Translator's Turn* and of Niranjana's book a year or so after filled me with an uneasy sense that my empowering address to translators in that book had not in fact been earned, because I had such a dim sense of the hegemonic forces that hem us in. Readers of *The Translator's Turn* who come to *Translation and Taboo* in search of the same upbeat note, the same surge of empowerment, are probably finding this chapter especially grim—if they haven't already given up with that little shudder of anxious dismissal.

On the other hand, the negative also can quickly become a defensive place to hide, especially for academics who prefer the image of the bold nay-sayer to the frustrations of actually trying to bring about change for the better. Eric Cheyfitz, for example, can envision no utopian alternative to the prisons he maps out in his book. In *Siting Translation* Niranjana refuses this haven, announcing her utopian aims boldly in her introduction and throughout the book, especially in her very brief sixth chapter on the translation of the Kannada *vacana* (more on this at the end of the chapter): "Frantz Fanon and others have written about the revolutionary potential of a *historical sense* in the hands of the colonized. This sense is crucial also for a practice of translation in the colonial/postcolonial setting. By reading against the grain of colonial historiography, the translator/historian discovers areas of contradiction and silent resistance that, being made legible, can be deployed against hegemonic images of the colonized" (76). Hence Niranjana emphasizes the revolutionary importance of what she calls "retranslation," a decolonizing practice that she attempts to exemplify in her last chapter.

The problem is, of course, that no one knows what a truly liberatory practice of retranslation would be—and Niranjana's formulations are vague and disappointing. I'm going to try my hand at retranslation too, when I return to Niranjana at the end of the chapter (I cling to utopian alternatives despite the negativism of this chapter), but without much hope of solving the problem. If nothing else (even if I weren't a member of the colonizing culture, race, class, and gender), solving the problem is too big a job for one person—or even, perhaps, for one generation. The schizoid rationalism that I'm attributing to the hegemonic speaking of the Other-as-reason has too much power, is too incredibly good at throwing up roadblocks against the counterhegemonic imagination, let alone counterhegemonic political action—diversionary tactics, ridicule and embarrassment, co-optation—for anyone sitting in front of a computer and thinking hard to make much headway against it. A hundred of us, maybe; a thousand, more likely still. But not any time soon. It's still too easy to brand counterhegemonic thinkers as crazy—especially when they leave their work as open to that interpretation as I plan to leave mine.

Ascetic Failure and Transitory Identifications

And now I want to start bringing this unconscionably long chapter to a close (though not yet, not yet, there's still so much to say) by setting up the utopian alternative, the jailbreak, the escape out of the hegemonic schizoid/rationalist/ascetic/metempsychotic prison block that has constituted "normal" Western thinking about translation for far too long. The break begins in the perception that failure is built into asceticism, built into the schizoid attempt to create a perfectly controlled environment (such as a prison). Perfect asceticism can't work. It can never work. It's impossible. We are "only human," we say—not (quite) machines. We try, to put this in terms of Augustine's seven-step path to wisdom, to maintain our fear of the critics and our respect for the source author, but they're too pathetic, too absurd in their ignorance, too backward in their attempts to write comprehensible prose in the source language (the author) or the target language (the critics), so we "fix things up." We try to purge ourselves of distracting or "false" personality, but it sneaks back in when we least expect it. We try to banish despair with determined fortitude, but fail (and despair at our failure). We try to be merciful to the target-language reader, but the source-language words delight us too much, we can't turn away from them, so we pepper our translation with literal renditions.

We fail, in other words, to "die to the world" (2.7.11), which the schizoid/cenobitic Augustine insists is the prerequisite for understanding. And we *always* fail; failure is intrinsic to the schizoid imagination of success. This built-inness of failure is most obvious, as I began to suggest when I was discussing Augustine before, in the addictive dialectic of his fourth step, in which fortitude is defined as resistance to despair and as constantly necessary because despair survives all resistance, indeed survives *in* resistance, and therefore continues to plague the addict/schizoid/ascetic who resists it. To discipline oneself to fortitude is to discipline oneself to not-despair and thus to build despair into one's discipline in negated form—to "attach" despair, in Gerald May's term, as an integral part of your ascetic addiction. But the same is true of the other six steps as well, or of any ascetic regimen, precisely because an ascetic "step" or "practice" is by definition an attempt to resist something, and resistance only works in a tensile or dialectical relation:

• fear only works as a check on courage, and courage as a check on fear;

• piety is generated out of a smoothing-over of contempt, or of equality conceived as contempt, and requires for its operation something to smooth over;

• knowledge assumes importance through the perception of ignorance, but the continuing perception of ignorance undermines the illusion of knowledge (which perception, as Augustine says, will force the translator "to lament his own situation" [2.7.10]);

• mercy is a tempering of justice, which continues to demand a reckoning;

• the impulse to cleanse or purify arises out of an obsession with dirt that continues to haunt the puritan no matter how hard she or he scrubs; and

• wisdom, defined as *not* turning away from the truth, requires a vigilant clinging, a refusal to listen to the voices that would entice the wise person to turn.

Failure is built into ascetic regimens; the ascetic must fail and must thematize failure as a goad to further efforts. As Harpham says, "asceticism, the discipline of the essential self, is always defined as a quest for a goal that cannot and must not be reached, a quest with a sharp caveat: 'seek but do not find'" (43).

Laing's explanation for the repeated failure of the schizoid ascesis is that the true self's only source of life *is* other people, and as a result the false-self system constantly falls prey to "transitory identifications," other people's insignificant mannerisms: "The whole behaviour of some schizophrenics," he writes, "is hardly anything else than a patchwork of other people's peculiarities made more peculiar by the incongruity of the setting in which they are reproduced" (112). Schizophrenics will constantly pick at these "introjected action fragments" (112), trying to rid themselves of them, because they are experienced as invasions from outside, as someone else trying to take over their true selves. But of course, since these "other people" live inside schizophrenics' own skin, to be rid of them they must rid themselves of *all* embodied behavior, must completely transcend (often by mutilating) their own bodies.

The interesting connection with Augustine's ascetic program, however, is that his seven steps to "wisdom" are an attempt to unify and idealize these transitory identifications as a surrender to a *single* personality, God. To ward off *worldly* identifications, identificatory encounters with a succession of real people, the Augustinian Christian seeks to identify with an ideal person, a whole being who lives in the "transcendental" true self and thus, at least potentially, constitutes protection against the carnal imitations of the false-self system. The problem is that this solution is homeopathic medicine, a dose of identification to cure identification, and the "cure" can all too easily become poison, contamination, infection. Try to identify only with God, and you find yourself unconsciously, unwittingly identifying with real people who remind you of God (fathers, priests, bosses), and your defense against transitory identification is in jeopardy again.

The parallel with translation should be clear. Like an actor, the schizoid/cenobitic/metempsychotic Western translator assumes the personalities of a succession of source authors and seeks to embody these personalities in the target language without significant change—but throughout this identificatory process the translator must never *become* the host body. The translator's task is to be simultaneously two things at once, utterly other and utterly himself (*not* herself—the rationalist ideal is a generic male self). As in Jacques Lacan's mirror-stage, the schizoid translator must bring the source-language other to life by projecting target-language self into it *and* introject the source-language other into the target-language self as a dead and alien thing—the translator must strive to make the target-language simulacrum seem real, authentic, vibrant, by pumping it full of the anxious fear that it will overwhelm the self. The translator's task is both to identify wholly (body and soul) with the source author *and* to maintain the watchful, suspicious, alienating distance required by the Other-as-reason: at once to take in and keep out the alien personality, to internalize it and distance it, to bring it in but bring it in dead, inert, regulated—to death, but also to seeming life—by reason. "In Federn's language," as Laing writes, the schizoid—or the translator—"cathects his ego-as-object with mortido" (120). Libido is the enemy, life, the body, carnal desire, everything that threatens to overwhelm the precariously objectified ego; mortido is that ego's strongest defense, the mortification of the body, the deadening of desire, the dissemination of death throughout the objectified ego-system.

Laing talks about the schizoid perception of consciousness as having a dual power to petrify (to turn the other to stone) and to penetrate; "Freedom then consists in being inaccessible" (121). But you're never perfectly inaccessible, there's always the fear that someone's gaze will penetrate your defenses, so you try to turn everyone *else* to stone—a preemptive strike against invasion. "Unfortunately, since one cannot be seen by a stone, one becomes, in so far as others have been successfully reduced to things in one's own eyes, the only person who can see oneself. The process now swings in the reverse direction, culminating in the longing to be rid of the deadening and intolerable self-awareness so that the prospect of being a passive thing penetrated and controlled by the other may come as a welcome relief. Within such oscillation there is no position of peace . . ." (Laing 121).

In this figure, metempsychotic or "sense-for-sense" translation would be one pole of the oscillation: the mainstream schizoid translator sinks cautiously into the passivity of being penetrated and controlled by the source author; it's scary, but your training tells you it's all right, nothing terrible will happen to you, don't be afraid, buck up, gird your loins with Augustine's fortitude. The other pole is the mystical literalism I'll be exploring in the next chapter, which places a translator as his or her only reader, the only person who can understand what s/he writes, someone isolated by the very attempt to express his or her innermost self—a translator who tries to petrify his or her readers, who tries to *make* it impossible for others to read the target text. The oscillation Laing refers to is most dramatically enacted *within* mystical literalism, where absolute surrender to passive penetration by the source author is uneasily combined with an aggressive blockading of the target reader: the translator oscillates between passive and aggressive responses to a dangerous world, to being penetrated by an author perceived as godlike in his powers (rarely her powers), guarding jealously against being penetrated by readers perceived as thieves, sneaks, snakes in the grass. The mainstream tradition represses this oscillation into manageable bounds by idealizing it into "absolute" communicability and translatability achieved through the drastic reduction of communication and translation to the flat-affect transmission of semantically stable rational content. "Absolute" translatability becomes possible once everything that threatens not only translation but the translator's peace of mind is eliminated in advance: the mood, color, and feel of a "text" (actually of the body reading the text) and other somatic responses, intentional and unintentional misunderstandings, etc.

Psychotic Translation

"Being like everyone else, being someone other than oneself, playing a part, being incognito, anonymous, being nobody (psychotically, pretending to have no body), are defences that are carried through with great thoroughness in certain schizoid and schizophrenic conditions" (Laing 118). Being an ascetic translator, speaking with someone else's voice, pretending to be(come) the source author, pretending to have no voice of your own, no body of your own, no feelings, no prejudices, no biases, no inclinations, no motivations, no experiences of your own . . . "If all the individual's behaviour comes to be completely alienated from the secret self so that it is given over entirely to compulsive mimicry, impersonating, caricaturing, and to such transitory behavioural foreign bodies as well, he may then try to strip himself of all his behaviour. This is one form of catatonic withdrawal" (Laing 112).

And catatonia is the first "crazy" step beyond hegemonic rationalist schizoid ascetic metempsychotic Western translation, the first "failure" or "refusal" to be a good professional, a good craftsman—a step toward which the Other-as-reason compels the schizoid translator through the very impossibility of its ascetic mission (despair!), but against which the Other-as-reason also both warns and guards the schizoid translator through constant calls to duty, to vigilance, to determination against overwhelming odds (fortitude!).

Because the "transitory behavioural foreign bodies" that the catatonic translator seeks to slough off are translations, acts of translation, regulated submissions to the incursion of the source-language other, the effect of catatonia on the translator is that s/he stops translating. "We may be mastered and made lame," as George Steiner warns in *After Babel*, "by what we have imported. There are translators in whom the vein of personal, original creation goes dry. [Stephen] MacKenna speaks of Plotinus literally submerging his own being. Writers have ceased from translation, sometimes too late, because the inhaled voice of the foreign text had come to choke their own" (299). Translation burnout, which this catatonia most closely resembles in the working world, must be doubly common in scitech translation, where the industrial ethos enforces strict conformity to repetitive usage. The attraction of machine translation (MT) is, in fact, that the MT program is the ultimate catatonic translator who *goes on translating*. It is dead but still productive. Burnt-out translators can be replaced by computers and ever more powerful and effective and "user-friendly" software, which never burns out because it is itself *transcendent* burnout, burnout raised to the platonic ideal, burnout perfected.

The next step in the schizophrenic breakdown of the Augustinian schizoid ascesis is propagandistic translation, which might be thematized as a parodic assault on the intrusive other. In *The Translator's Turn* I characterized this assault variously as synecdoche (the selection of a single part of the source-language other that one presents as the whole target-language self—

152–59), irony (especially the ironic rendering that seeks to reproduce a shoddy source-language other precisely as shoddily in the target language—173–74), extroversion (the hurling of an angry self in the oppressive other's face—205–7), subversion (the thwarting of target readers' soporific expectations—224–31), perversion (undermining target readers' trust beyond repair—232–39), aversion (turning a cold shoulder on target readers' communicative needs—239–49), and parodic diversion (amusing target readers by twisting the source text humorously—253–56). "Translation as caricature," as I wrote there, "the secret glee that the business translator feels when he or she diverts the boss's 'Yours sincerely' into 'Yours earnestly,' perhaps, or 'Yours in Christ' is *empowering*. It charges the translator's private vision of the boss's earnestness (say) with the power of textual confirmation, and thus may have the effect of propelling him or her into psychopolitical (ethical) growth" (253–54).

But this nascent rebellion against the Other-as-reason's schizoid norms looks a bit less rosy in the light of Laing's observations in *The Divided Self*, where he provides a brief case study of a schizoid patient of his named James who "caricatures" his father by acting out the aggressions that his father successfully conceals. James's father always presses guests to help themselves to seconds at the dinner table, and so does James, always politely—but always also to the point of irritating his guests. James "took up what he sensed were the aggressive implications in his father's actions," Laing writes, "and exposed these implications, through exaggerating them in his own adaptation, to general ridicule and anger. He, in fact, evoked from others the feelings he had towards his father but was unable to express directly to his face. Instead, he produced what amounted to a satirical comment on his father through the medium of a compulsive caricature of him" (109).

Propagandistic translation has been so thoroughly tabooed by the schizoid mainstream tradition that it rarely occurs to translation scholars—it hardly seems like a possible issue in translation studies. But as the repressive rational control of the false-self system begins to break down, tabooed behavior begins to surface, and the subject is increasingly perceived (and ultimately diagnosed) as "crazy," schizophrenic. Propagandistic translation is sense-for-sense translation with its repressions slightly undone, schizoid metempsychotic translation edging toward open psychosis, the erosive return of the "crazy" or "angry" or otherwise "irrational" repressed.

The translator now begins to oscillate between "health," "normality," "discipline," "self-control," "professionalism," "craftsmanship," and "rational behavior" on the one hand and the abject slide into insanity on the other. If we see in this oscillation something like the tension between Augustine's seven-step path to wisdom and Harold Bloom's primal scene of instruction that I described in *The Translator's Turn* (109ff), it quickly becomes clear that Bloom's six-step path is less an ascent toward freedom and autonomy (as I portrayed it there) than it is a descent into schizophrenia. The parodic moment I've been describing, the propagandistic or caricaturistic impulse to become the source author, aggressively and antagonistically corresponds to Bloom's second phase, "covenant-love or *chesed*," that "first accommodation with the precursor" that Bloom calls "the initial *persona* that the young poet adopts, in the archaic, ritual sense in which the *persona* was the mask representing the *daimonic* or tribal father" (Bloom 53–54). From there the translator can retreat back into the "election-love" of Augustine's schizoid "wisdom," in which "the receiver is set on fire, and yet the fire belongs to the giver" (Bloom 51), who is the Other-as-reason a.k.a. God—or else the translator can plunge ahead into a deepening schizophrenic isolation, beset by anxious delusions of absolute autonomy, of the power to speak a "word of one's own," to perform a "total interpretation," to recreate origins. The "anxiety of influence" Bloom talks about is a conflicted paralysis intershot with moments of great creative force, moments when the schizoid "true self's" creative drive speaks a "true word," a *davhar*, a word that seems to be its own because for those fleeting moments the true self has successfully beat back the invaders and repressed their continuing power over it—convinced itself that it speaks on its own, free of the inner voices that make its speech possible. As Laing writes:

> Thus, the hatred of the other person is focused on the features of him which the individual has built into his own being, and yet at the same time the temporary or prolonged assumption of another's personality is a way of not being oneself which seems to offer security. Under the mantle of someone else's personality the person may act so much more competently, smoothly, "reliably"—to use Mrs. D.'s expression, the individual may prefer to pay the price of incurring the haunting sense of futility which is the necessary accompaniment of not being oneself, rather than hazard the frank experience of frightened helplessness and bewilderment which would be the inevitable start to being oneself. (111)

In *The Translator's Turn* I fleshed out a utopian vision of the translator's liberation from hegemonic norms—what I've here been calling rationalist, schizoid, ascetic, metempsychotic norms—that was predicated on the possibility of going only so far into madness and no further. Let go of stabilizing reason—a little. Let go of social conventions for acceptable translations, but don't throw all caution to the wind. (Even so, a few readers—academic translation theorists, mostly—found my rather tame "anarchism" vertiginous, a profound threat to their peace of mind.) Go on translating acceptably, just push a little at the envelope of acceptability. Don't take normative theorists' word for what you can and can't do; experiment for yourself, but in safe ways, without jeopardizing your livelihood or reputation. My basic message in *The Translator's Turn* was, look what I've been getting away with all these years, not because I'm such a rebel—actually, I'm considered a good, competent, responsible translator—but because the world of translation practice is considerably more lenient, more tolerant of personal idiosyncracy and creativity, than is its normative theory.

But here I want to push past this relatively comfortable spot. Ultimately, of course, everyone who doesn't go crazy finds some place to draw the line and says *this far, no farther:* everyone makes some workable compromise between absolute robotic conformity and what Laing calls "chaotic nonentity." My own compromise, complex and conflicted and shifting as it is, is pretty clearly spelled out in *The Translator's Turn.* But compromises, useful and practical as they are in everyday life, yield only compromised information about the problems that they successfully skirt; and I'm hoping that by pushing past the bounds of my own comfort I might begin to shed some light on a dilemma I raised earlier, which has been getting a lot of attention lately but which has elicited little more than clichéd, compromised solutions.

The dilemma was how to translate the Third World—and it's a dilemma because, remember, *every* translation of a Third World text is imperialistic. In his book, Eric Cheyfitz can only beat his head against this same brick wall, clinging to a beleaguered intellectual and political integrity only by becoming as conscious as possible of his own complicity in the colonial mentality he attacks. In hers, Tejaswini Niranjana—despite the obvious advantage she has over Cheyfitz (and me) of speaking from a postcolonial subject position—boldly claims to offer a practical solution; but all she can offer is a fairly timid literal translation, and one that sounds, sadly, all too much like the christianizing rendition she attacks.

Our understanding of this dilemma is circumscribed, I suggest, by the Other-as-reason, which coaches us to understand all translation problems from within the imperialist regime of reason. If translation is inherently rationalist, and reason is inherently imperialist, then by the syllogistic logic that the Other-as-reason so loves to wield, all translation is imperialist, and any attempt to imagine a nonimperialist approach to translation will wind up with some vaguely familiar twist on the same old thing.

But if the Other-as-reason constantly skates on the thin ice of schizophrenia, if schizophrenia is the breakdown of rationalist regimes toward which (and always, with redoubled efforts, against which) those regimes themselves always inevitably drive, then perhaps the only escape from the Other-as-reason's intellectual and political playground is *through* schizophrenia. Schizophrenia might be thought of, in fact, as mystery filtered through the ascetic regimen of the Other-as-reason, the mystical *enthousiasmos* rendered psychosocially deviant by a rationalist ideology that privileges self-control, discipline, and alienation. Ironically enough, when the schizoid personality breaks down, slides down past all self-control and all discipline, what is left in the psychic kitty is still alienation—just alienation unchanneled by reason. Thought, communication, translation, all rational control over the ideas and images and words swirling around inside and outside your head, all this becomes increasingly difficult and painful; no one understands you, all the voices around you and inside you (and how can you tell the difference?) are a blooming mystery to you; and no one guides you into the darkness, no one gives you the ritual purification and instruction, no one reassures you that they'll be there to bring you back out again.

Atmospheric Semiotics

"Of course," as Deleuze and Guattari remind us in *A Thousand Plateaus*, "an operation of translation is not easy when it is a question of destroying a dominant atmospheric semiotic" (138). By "translation" they mean not merely cross-cultural communication but the attempt to "transfer" or shift terms from one cultural semiotic to another—for example, here, from the regime of mystery to the regime of reason. But in this case the two sets of terms are congruent. Translation, I've been arguing—at least theorized translation, rationalist translation—was born out of the ancient attempt (largely successful) to destroy the dominant atmospheric semiotic of the mystery religions, that combination of celebration and fear, the initiate's glorious and terrifying celebratory not-knowing, that mystagogues called *enthousiasmos* and that rationalists have called primitive, inhuman, hysterical, drugged, schizophrenic, out-of-control. The rationalist regime decreed: no celebration, no terror, no ignorance. Ultimately, no atmosphere. Atmosphere is the enemy. Atmosphere is evil. Well, actually a truly enlightened rationalist ethos is beyond good and evil, evil is part of the old atmospheric semiotic, so atmosphere is not evil but ignorance, illusion, artifice. Atmosphere is emotion, and emotion is subjectivity, and subjectivity is distortion. The Other-as-reason tolerates no atmospheric semiotics. Semiosis is a purely intellectual event, abstract, formal, transcendental.

What this all mystifies, of course, is that *this* is the new atmospheric semiotic: the atmosphere of the Socratic dialogue, the seminar; the atmosphere of calm, rational debate; the atmosphere of Plato's dialectical *techne*, which leads to truth, but never permits losing your temper at your opponent along the way and always represses anger so successfully that you don't even notice it yourself; later, the atmosphere of the laboratory; the atmosphere of environmental control through technology (measuring machines, computing machines, cages and other restraining devices for laboratory animals), through color (whites and silvers, no earth tones, no primary colors), and through the suppression of emotion (no boisterous laughter, no anger, no tears or cries of anguish, no sexual passion).

And yet the old atmospheric semiotic of mystery lives on in the whoops and hollers and uncorked champagne bottles when the big breakthrough comes (the one that means a Nobel prize or a big defense contract or some other sign of fame and fortune, future rewards extrinsic to "pure" rationalism), in the twinge of fear when the experiment synthesizing DNA or cloning a human embryo or otherwise "playing god" succeeds (or even is attempted, or contemplated), in the secrecy that keeps procedures and discoveries under wraps for fear another lab might steal your findings. And the old atmospheric semiotic of mystery lives on in the voices of insanity in every good rationalist's head, in what Michel Foucault calls "these words of madmen in our own speech, in those tiny pauses when we forget what we are talking about" (217), the stammers and stutters, the dream-talk, the nonsense words uttered immediately upon awakening, the sudden irrational impulses that seem to come from nowhere, the bursts of anger, suspicion, greed, fear, withdrawal, or anxiety that disrupt our lives and lead us (and others) to suspect that our lives are not our own, that we are not in control.

The Schizophrenic as Foreigner

A schizophrenic is, or becomes, a speaker of a foreign language. But it is not just any foreign language; it is a macaronic foreign language, a language of deliberate and mixed foreignness designed to conceal as much as to communicate. As Laing writes:

> One of the greatest barriers against getting to know a schizophrenic is his sheer incomprehensibility: the oddity, bizarreness, obscurity in all that we can perceive of him. There are many reasons why this is so. Even when the patient is striving to tell us, in as clear and straightforward a way as he knows how, the nature of his anxieties and his experiences, structured as they are in a radically different way from ours, the speech content is necessarily difficult to follow. Moreover, the formal elements of speech are in themselves ordered in unusual ways, and these formal peculiarities seem, at least to some extent, to be the reflection in language of the alternative ordering of his experience, with splits in it where we take coherence for granted, and the running together (confusion) of elements that we keep apart. (175)

This language exists in germinant or potential form in everyone's speech, in dreams, in delirium, and in various forms of cryptography (not only trying to confuse the enemy in wartime, but trying to confuse our friends, family members, colleagues when we want to keep a secret or are ashamed of our true motivations in a matter). I'm tempted to say that it is a radically different kind of language than, say, English or French or Chinese, the "natural" national languages into and out of which translators translate; but I'm not so sure that that would be correct. There is a difference between "natural" and schizophasic languages, certainly, but this difference isn't necessarily "in" the languages.

The difference is not, for example, that national languages are structured and schizophasic languages are unstructured—that, say, the speakers of national languages are spoken (solely) by the Other-as-reason and the speakers of schizophasic languages are spoken (solely) by the Other-as-mystery. As Laing says, "the formal elements of speech are in themselves ordered in unusual ways," but they *are* ordered. If schizophrenia is the resurgence of mystery through the breakdown of the Other-as-reason's schizoid defenses, it is nevertheless thoroughly conditioned by those defenses. Without the Other-as-reason's ascetic regime, mystery would have resurfaced in some wholly different form. However confused and confusing, however directed it is toward the concealment of communication, schizophasic speech is saturated with the wary guardedness of the Other-as-reason, the determination to communicate but from hiding, to *conceal* rather than block communication—and this requires structure, a plan, a principle, a regime. "We schizophrenics," writes Joan, whose description of her passage through insanity Laing follows toward the end of his book, "say and do a lot of stuff that is unimportant, and then we mix important things in with all this to see if the doctor cares enough to see them and feel them" (176).

Nor is the difference simply that national languages are spoken by entire communities and schizophasic languages are invented by isolated individuals. This idea gets at the difference, but it's not quite it. Schizophasic speech is a repressed potential in every language, a linguistic bad child sent to its room without dinner by the Other-as-reason, mostly unseen, mostly unheard, but ever present, ever watchful, lurking in unguarded moments, always ready to spring forth in full-bodied confusion.

According to the Other-as-reason, national languages are totally different from all this. National languages are parallel sign systems utilized by people in different communities. Nobody who has been raised speaking English harbors a repressed impulse to speak French, which surfaces when the conditions are right. You have to go to school to study French, submit to an ascetic rationalist regime, memorize words and phrases and grammar rules, drill and drill and drill, take tests, get grades, maintain a certain grade point average. You don't just start *speaking* French. But some people do. The medical records teem with cases, which are mostly repressed by the medical profession, in which a patient—and this patient is usually a schizophrenic, granted, which means that we don't really have to pay attention, this is a "deviant," an exception without power to (dis)prove the rule—rants and raves in a recognizable language to which s/he has never been exposed. The Other-as-reason whispers plausible explanations, s/he heard the language on a subway and the unconscious never forgets, s/he heard the language in the womb, whatever. But other explanations abound. One of these explanations is reincarnation, that metempsychotic invention of the Other-as-reason when it was young, long since discarded as a puerile fantasy: the patient spoke this language in a former life. This explanation would have sounded perfectly reasonable to Plato, who explained the possibility of learning anything through his metempsychotic doctrine of anamnesis, the "unforgetting" of things once known in a former life. Even "normal" people frequently have the experience of hearing a foreign language (or a violin, or whatever) and being suddenly possessed with the certainty that they were born to speak it, play it, whatever. Where does this come from? Noam Chomsky invented the rationalist, but also somehow wonderfully irrational, theory of the Language Acquisition Device or LAD to explain how children learn any language to which they are exposed in their first four years: but *who put that device in everybody's head*? Where did it come from? It's a science-fiction idea, clearly—the mechanical implant in every newborn baby's brain—but who's the mad scientist? Who wants to rule the world? God? Is it metempsychotic, anamnetic, a survival of past lives? Is it one of the Other's little tricks to ensure its own survival from generation to generation? And what battles over control of that device can explain the variety of people's experiences with languages, some people clinging stolidly to a single dialect of a single language and fiercely repressing all others; others speaking two, three, four, even ten and fifteen languages; the nineteenth-century Richard Burton speaking up to a hundred languages from across the Indian subcontinent, Africa, and South America; still others learning/inventing various macaronic or "schizophasic" languages? Do we have to imagine an LAD gone haywire to explain Richard Burton or the schizophrenic—or are these people just experiencing its ordinary operation in extraordinary circumstances? Throw the LAD's corporeal vehicle into motion across continents and it learns dozens of languages; throw it into a schizogenic family and it learns schizophrenic.

The reason all this is interesting, I think, is that it helps us to imagine the schizophrenic translator—the schizophrenic *as* translator and the translator as schizophrenic. Because in most cases the schizophrenic is not born speaking a schizophasic language, s/he has to invent it, learn it, and above all learn to translate everything s/he hears in his/her native language *into* it. This form of translation engages all the pressing issues of translation theory: communication versus concealment (do you transmit the source-language meaning or hide it in a literalist or other obscurantist box?); segmentation (do you translate individual sounds, words, phrases, sentences, whole texts, what?); power and vulnerability (do you translate into the language of the colonizer or the language of the colonized?). In his excellent piece in Larry Venuti's collection *Rethinking Translation*, Richard Jacquemond makes this connection painfully clear:

> In the colonial moment, the opposed paradigms of translation can be defined as follows. (1) In translation from a hegemonic language-culture into a dominated one, the translator appears as the servile mediator through whom foreign-made linguistic-cultural objects are integrated without question into his own dominated language-culture, thus aggravating its schizophrenia. (2) In translation from a dominated language-culture into a hegemonic one, the translator appears as the authoritative mediator through whom the dominated language-culture is maintained outside the limits of the self and at the same time adapted to this self in order for it to be able to consume the dominated linguistic-cultural object. (155)

In this analysis, the colonized culture is the schizophrenic—and not just figuratively, either, not just analogically, for purposes of comparison—and the colonizer is alternatively (1) the ordinary person who shudders at the lunatic and would rather not have to see her or him at all, and (2) the psychiatrist whose job it is to "understand" the schizophrenic by fitting him or her into a hegemonic straitjacket, either intellectual (psychoanalysis) or pharmaceutical (Thorazine)—sometimes, for his or her "own protection," fitting the schizophrenic into a cloth straitjacket as well. The problem of translation in the postcolonial context is exactly analogous to the problem of treatment in the schizophrenic context: the translation theorist and the doctor are already part of the problem, part of what's making the Third World and the schizophrenic sick, and any attempt to mitigate the harmful effects of translation theory or treatment only exacerbates the sickness, escalates the pathogenic effect.

Louis Wolfson, Translator

Two recent scholars, John Johnston in Venuti's 1992 collection and Jean-Jacques Lecercle in an article published in 1989 in *The Oxford Literary Review*, have attempted to address these thorny problems in the specific context of a single schizophrenic translator, Louis Wolfson, an American born in New York in 1931 whose schizophrenia made the sound of his mother tongue, English—literally the language spoken by his mother, whom he lived with and hated—excruciatingly painful. And so, as he describes in a memoir he published in France (and, for obvious reasons, in French) in 1970, *Le Schizo et les langues*, at some point Wolfson devised a strategem for translating every English word into a handful of foreign languages, not semantically, like those of a good rationalist translator, but phonetically and above all macaronically. In one of Johnston's examples,

> when his mother shouts at him, "Don't trip over the wire," he instantaneously translates this in his head into: *"Tu'icht tréb über èth hé Zwirn."* Thus, "Don't" becomes the German *"Tu'icht,"* "trip" becomes the first four letters of the French *"trébucher,"* "over" becomes the German "über," "the" becomes the Hebrew *"èth hé,"* and "wire" becomes the German *"Zwirn."* To avoid hearing English—he lives with his mother and stepfather in a Manhattan apartment—Wolfson employs other methods as well: he wears ear plugs, listens to foreign-language broadcasts on his portable radio, grinds his teeth, and mutters foreign phrases he has memorized. (49)

Wolfson's translator's behavior is clearly an ascetic regimen—one very similar to the regimens by which Augustinian Christians learn to suppress the alluring voices of "the world" and tune their inner ears to God alone, or by which translators learn to suppress the alluring voices of their emotions, their biases, their desires, their attachment to specific source-language words and phrases and colors and textures and atmospheric semiotics and to tune their inner ears to the disembodied voice of abstract meaning alone. Indeed, the striking similarity between Wolfson's task as a translator and that of more "normal" or "ordinary" or "healthy" or "professional" translators is what interests both Johnston and Lecercle. Both writers are fascinated, as am I, by the negative light Wolfson manages to cast on the mainstream theory and practice of translation in the West. Johnston, for example, takes Wolfson to be a "grotesque parody of [Walter] Benjamin's theory" (which I'll be returning to in chapter 3) of the messianic movement of languages toward the attainment of "pure language," in "The Task of the Translator":

> For in Wolfson's attempt to break down, destroy, and then reconstitute English in the sounds of another language—not a real language but a simulated language, a simulacrum of a language—he acts out a perverse inversion of Benjamin's theory. Which is to say that in Wolfson's sickness of "maladie mentale," English exists in something like a state comparable to Benjamin's "pure language," but its purity here is a wounding purity, since its words enter him directly and penetrate his being. We see this immediacy of the nominative function in action when Wolfson's mother aggressively names foodstuffs in order to attack or punish him, since for him the names immediately become the things (the "mode of intention" of English no longer mediates a world outside). Hence Wolfson's need for translation, for a mediation that will provide passage out of and away from the wounding power of names. (51)

Benjamin's kabbalistic conception of "pure language" is pretty clearly a schizoid fantasy of language conformed to the "true self's" flight from a world of difference—even if Benjamin, like a good ascetic, grits his teeth and asserts the *importance* of linguistic difference and the acts of translation that continually play off that difference as the crucible in which language is rendered pure. Superficially, then, Johnston's equation of Wolfson's (mother's) English with Benjamin's pure language is wrong: English for Wolfson is more like the communicative or informative or technical language of the marketplace that Benjamin attacks as no language at all because it is a mere servile vehicle for mundane messages. Just as Benjamin flees what Laing would call the false-self system of that marketplace language into a messianic ethos of translation that enhances the alterity of language so as to accelerate the coming of pure language, so too does Wolfson flee the false-self system of his mother's English into an "alteritized" schizophasic discourse so as to create the conditions for a purified speechscape that will not cause him pain.

But at a deeper level Johnston's intuition is accurate, because in the schizoid imagination the mother tongue and pure language form a kind of demonic hermeneutical circle in which the idealized mother is simultaneously the source of all (conceptions of) purity and the shadow cast on the real (and therefore "false") mother, and the real mother is simultaneously the carrier and the blocker of purity ideals. Wolfson's real mother hurls English words at him as if they were the foods they name, knowing that they wound him; her assault on him is what he flees through translation. But the intensity of that wounding is also his strongest model for a new language, a transcendental language whose intensity will not wound but soothe, a pure language created in the negative image of the mother tongue. And yet the pure language delays: Wolfson keeps translating, translating, translating, hedging against his mother's tongue with schizophasic alterity, waiting for relief, and it never comes—he is left trapped in the apartment with the source of both his pain and his hope, his fortitude and his despair; he is left trapped with his mother. If he could stop dreaming of a purified mother tongue that would not wound him, he could stop translating, possibly even stop hurting—certainly stop subjecting himself to the vicious hermeneutical circle, the addictive dialectic or double bind that Augustine named fortitude-and-despair. As Lecercle notes, after his mother died Wolfson left New York for France, where he was not bombarded on the streets by his hated mother tongue: his mother's silence freed him to leave the scene of his degradation, though perhaps not to escape its vicious linguistic circle.

Lecercle is the author of *The Violence of Language*, a powerful study of the "remainder" of language that is systematically repressed by rationalist linguists—nonsense, delirium, dream-talk, stutters and stammers—but that, he claims in good poststructuralist fashion, is precisely what makes communication possible. Wolfson appeals to him, clearly, as a prime representative of this remainder, and Lecercle sets up his argument to underscore that appeal, moving from a quasirationalist negative take on Wolfson-as-translator to a qualified "appreciation" of Wolfson's implicit (and radical) philosophy of translation. But Lecercle's article disturbs me, and does so in I think instructive ways. Lecercle reads Wolfson, it seems to me, as William Jones reads the Indians and as the liberal or progressive representative of the colonial power reads the colonial subject. Lecercle's determined sympathy and condescension are so utterly permeated with his rationalist distaste that they become a weapon, an instrument of distance and alienation. For example, he writes:

> The solution to his problem, therefore, is a translation device, a mixture of translation proper (meaning for meaning) and what is known in French as *traducson*, or translation according to sound—the best instance is Van Rooten's *Mots d'Heures: Gousses, Rames.* . . . Yet it is also obviously insane, and in practice, as a few examples will show, fails to translate at all, so that it does not even reach the modest level of Van Rooten's *traducson.* (103–4)

The key to Lecercle's condescension here is not the assertion of Wolfson's insanity, which Wolfson cheerfully admits himself, but the attempt to cut Wolfson off from translation. Note the progression in that passage, from "translation device," which suggests that Wolfson *is* translating, to "a mixture of translation proper . . . and *traducson*," which suggests that Wolfson's efforts have some traces of translation but only in hybrid form, to "fails to translate at all," which cuts him off entirely. This is the exact opposite to the direction Lecercle's argument takes overall; it might be read as the Other-as-reason getting its own back, despite Lecercle's brave (but foolhardy) determination to see some good in Wolfson's crazy antics.

There is also an implicit, almost explicit, hierarchy in Lecercle's portrait that places Van Rooten's *traducson* at a "modest level" (there is something—what?—presumably above that) and situates Wolfson somewhere below this level. The implication of Lecercle's words, "does not even reach the modest level of," is not only that this hierarchy exists in reality and that Wolfson should have reached a higher level on it (an objective assessment of his success with no recourse to his subjectivity), but also that Wolfson knows about the hierarchy and accepts it and is consciously striving to reach a high place on it, that he is deliberately playing the same game as other translators—on the same terms, with the same stakes—but playing it badly and losing heavily. Lecercle seems to know the rules of the game, but he isn't telling: what *would* constitute winning? Wolfson and I wonder. What would constitute playing well, reaching higher than the "modest level" of Van Rooten's *traducson*? Translating for publication? Well, *Le Schizo et les langues* did get published. Would translating beautifully or accurately surpass the level of *traducson?* What is Wolfson failing to do? What is Lecercle's criterion that Wolfson is failing to meet?

Again Lecercle qualifies Wolfson's translation:

> Wolfson's translation is not of the mature, well-considered, carefully wrought type that one usually praises. There is a certain irony in this, for his translation saves communication—like a phatic device it allows him to go on talking—yet it plays no part in it, for it remains unspoken: it is part of Wolfson's interior discourse and does not affect the dialogue, which is conducted in French. It only becomes public for us, as part of the book. The irony is that for Wolfson, at least in ordinary situations, translation is centripetal, not centrifugal, whereas the common or garden translator has no need to translate for his own benefit, since by definition he understands the foreign language. (104–5)

Here too Lecercle wields a negative rhetoric ironically to provide a transitory identificatory nexus for the rationalist reader: "not of the mature, well-considered, carefully wrought type that one usually praises," or "the common or garden translator has no need." Lecercle is manifestly en route to a transvaluation of these terms, so that Wolfson becomes a more profound, more complex, more interesting translator than the "common or garden translator." But the passage crawls with contrary signals as well. Wolfson's translation "saves communication—like a phatic device it allows him to go on talking." Does it really? What *is* communication, anyway? Is it just talking, the fact that you "go on talking"? What if no one is listening? Does there have to be a speaker and a listener for communication? And what is the communicative situation Lecercle imagines here? Mother and son? The mother says something, the son winces but translates quickly into his interior schizophasic macaroni and so is able to respond to her like a "normal" person. Is this the "communication" that is "saved" by Wolfson's schizophrenic translations? Does this really constitute "salvation," or even being "saved"? Even if we grant Lecercle this much, dubious as it is, we still haven't established that Wolfson *wants* communication, that this is his intention ("allows him to go on talking"), let alone that this is the only relevant communicative situation involved. What about Wolfson's communication with himself? It doesn't count, apparently; it doesn't meet Lecercle's unstated criteria for communication, which seem to be the normative ones of one person speaking to another and that second person understanding and responding. In this system Wolfson's "interior discourse" "plays no part in communication, for it remains unspoken." Even on Lecercle's own terms, if

Wolfson's translation "allows him to go on talking" it surely plays a part in communication, doesn't it?

Wolfson's translation "is part of Wolfson's interior discourse and does not affect the dialogue, which is conducted in French." *The* dialogue is, presumably, the one between Wolfson and his mother; it is called *the* dialogue (there is only one) because this is the only dialogue rationalists are interested in, the ideal form of dialogue, the dialogue taking place on the surface, the one that can be recorded and subjected to empirical analysis. But only an impoverished social psychology believes interior discourse doesn't affect this dialogue, which is almost a behaviorist one, fixated on physical behavior and in absolute denial about inner processes, motivations, silent speech.

And in what language is all this happening? I haven't read Wolfson's book (I can't read French), and so I am not sure what Lecercle means by saying that the dialogue between mother and son is conducted in French. Certainly the dialogue as reported by Wolfson is conducted in French, since he has translated it into French for publication (to avoid wounding his inner ear). But do mother and son really speak French to each other? If so, does she only occasionally punish him by hurling English words at him? In Johnston's example, she warned him in English not to trip over the wire; do they speak both French and English? Wolfson's mother is a Jewish immigrant from Central Europe—did she flee France and continue to speak French with her son? Lecercle later says that "Wolfson, through his translation device, is indeed going back to his origins. He is making, through language, the same journey his parents made on a boat, only in the other direction. They left Europe behind them, and, when they reached America, tried, rather successfully, to replace their mother tongue with English" (114). When Lecercle says the dialogue is conducted in French, then, should we assume that it is a lone exception to the rule, a slip Wolfson's mother made, a failure in the midst of a "rather successful" attempt to speak English instead of—what? French? Yiddish? Or is it Lecercle's slip? Did he mean to say English, the foreign language he's writing in, but said French instead, his native tongue, the foreign language in which Wolfson wrote? If so, where did *this slip* come from?

The ironies that Lecercle sees are compounded by his own text in numerous overlapping ways: Wolfson writes in French, his foreign language and Lecercle's native language, but Lecercle writes about Wolfson and his writing and his situation in English; Lecercle claims that Wolfson's text is untranslatable, but his article (like Johnston's) constitutes an attempt to translate it into English, albeit loosely (much more loosely than Wolfson translates, for example); and—this is the kicker—Lecercle complains in print that Wolfson's printed translations of things his mother said are not public because they only become public in print! "It only becomes public for us, as part of the book." Hoo! All this is *not* a relevant dialogue, then, between Wolfson and Lecercle? Or, for that matter, between Lecercle and me (who can't read Wolfson's French and must rely on Johnston's and Lecercle's translations), between you and me? This is not communicative translation?

The irony for Lecercle is that, "for Wolfson, at least in ordinary situations, translation is centripetal, not centrifugal." The irony for me is that the "ordinary situations" Lecercle is idealizing here are beyond his reach—they are Wolfson's conversations with a woman now dead—and that the only truly "ordinary situation" for Lecercle is his encounter with Wolfson's book, which goes to great lengths to communicate not only the content but also the method of Wolfson's translations. (By "centripetal" I assume that Lecercle means that Wolfson turns his translations inward, introverts them, keeps them private; centrifugal translations would then be public, aimed at an audience. But this physics metaphor only works the way Lecercle wants it to if Wolfson is imagined as the center of his own translations. If the reader—Lecercle himself, for example—is the center, then a centripetal translation would be one that circled in to the center of *his* understanding, that hit its mark, while a centrifugal translation would be one that veered off into space somewhere, that missed him by a mile. Could this ambiguity be one of the effects, for both Wolfson and Lecercle, of writing in a foreign language—an effect that Friedrich Schleiermacher likens, in a passage that will organize my discussion of the German romantics in the next chapter, to "going doubled like a ghost"? Or is it just a problem with physics metaphors?)

Finally, Lecercle says that "the common or garden translator has no need to translate for his own benefit, since by definition he understands the foreign language." And Wolfson doesn't? This can't be Lecercle's implication, but it comes out sounding that way, perhaps because we all repress a schizophrenic speaker/translator who pops up every now and then and skews our words as they trip off the fingers or tongue. Obviously, as Lecercle knew and probably wanted to say but didn't, Wolfson's need to translate "for his own benefit" wasn't because he didn't understand the "foreign" language (by which I take Lecercle to mean the *source* language), but that he understood it too well. It was, after all, his native language, his mother tongue. But maybe it's more complicated than that. It seems clear that what wounded Wolfson was not the *meaning* of words (his semantic understanding of them) but the physical impact of their *sound* on him (his somatic response to them). Words hurt him much more than sticks and stones, but they hurt him in much the same way—by inflicting pain on his body. As Johnston said, "Wolfson's mother aggressively names foodstuffs in order to attack or punish him, since for him the names immediately become the things" (51). This explanation isn't quite it either, but it's close: the names don't exactly *become* the things, but the pain they inflict on his body is similar to that caused by physical objects. The names hit him with physical force.

In addition, Wolfson translates "for his own benefit" to *block* understanding of the words his mother hurls at him. Hence he produces his schizoid/rationalist analysis of the words as sounds, especially as consonants, subsemantic levels of language that he hopes will screen out meanings. *Traducson* works as a defense against "understanding the foreign language," or, in this case, the mother tongue, the source language emitted by the source of his being, his mom. And all this begins to make "translating for his own benefit" sound rather strange, in fact grotesquely euphemistic. "Benefit" sounds like the kind of audience-oriented translation that both Benjamin and Wolfson despise, translation to communicate source-language meaning to a target-language reader or hearer ignorant of the source language, marketplace translation, false-self-system translation, translation for dim "others" whose interest in meaning is perceived as vaguely threatening. And so Wolfson, like the messianic literalist whom Benjamin celebrates, translates for himself—but not exactly for his own *benefit*, which sounds as if he had simply internalized the external audience and was treating himself as in need of a semantic translation. Wolfson does need the translation, but not for its semantic content—he needs it rather, as I said, to block its semantic content. And his "need" is considerably more intense and conflicted and emotionally invested than the bland word "benefit" suggests. This is translate-or-die territory. Wolfson is translating for his very life—at least that's how it feels to him.

Lecercle next runs through a series of reasons for declaring Wolfson's translations no translations at all—"there is no 'lation' in this, it is not transmitted, but remains in unspoken limbo" (105), "it is syntagmatically incoherent" (105), "it is paradigmatically inconsistent" (106), "it is syntactically incoherent" (106), etc.—and a series of concomitant "rules in the translator's book," which Lecercle quite rightly takes to be not the inherent nature of translation but idealized restrictions on translation, which real translators always (partly and inevitably) flout: (1) "Do not translate more, or less, than your text provides" (106), (2) "Make your choices and keep to them" (106), (3) "[T]ranslate the situation, not the words" (106), and, though "not even rule four in the translator's book, it is his major sine qua non presupposition: [4] one translates into one language. Forget this, and you will find yourself in the disreputable world of *Finnegans Wake*" (107). Wolfson breaks all these rules, and real translators break all of these rules (sometimes and in small ways), hence Wolfson is a salutary figure for real translation: he embodies a capacious philosophy of translation grounded in the remainder that normative theories of translation repress. "Wolfson's experience teaches us that language itself Wolfsonises—he has indeed captured some of the actual workings of language. Translation is always threatened to be caught in this process of destruction, whereby the regularity of *langue* is subverted by the return of the expelled remainder" (117).

All this is fine and good. But look at what Lecercle says along the way:

> Where is the problem, then? It is simple: by applying rule no. 3, as indeed one must [one? who is this one? Lecercle himself? every translator?], one [*who?*] will have to disregard the words of the original language. For translation does in fact deserve its nickname of *la belle infidèle* [*all* translation, translation itself, translation proper is a beautiful but faithless woman, which means that translation proper is never ugly, for one thing, and for another, that fidelity is the

> ideal for which it must strive, and for a third, that it is forever trapped outside idealized masculinity?]. The translator's only concern is with the target language, he [not she— "she" is the translation, remember] must forget the source language. (106–7)

> I do not see clearly in which contexts I could translate "cyclisme" as either "cricket" or "baseball", except in answer to the question: which is the most typical popular sport in France? But this has nothing to do with translation [which is a lot narrower than you thought, folks, and certainly doesn't include weirdos like Wolfson, bless his crazy little heart]. (110)

> By producing a text so utterly other as to be a nontext, Wolfson does not only block the creative passage from one text to another, he also negatively demonstrates its essential character. Translating involves the production of another text, the first link in a potentially infinite chain of texts held together by a relationship of dubious filiation. . . . That is what translation is about. (118–19)

I hate it when people say that: "that is what translation is about." Whatever it is, no matter how broad the definition, it is always a rationalist impulse to cage translation, to confine it within clearly marked bounds. I cheated a little on that last quote, leaving out the rest of the paragraph (between "filiation" and "That"), which sets up translation—and Wolfson's book—as a male-identified Freudian family romance "between a speaker and his mother tongue" (119), the last words before "That is what translation is about." But whatever the supposed "core" of translation is, whether it's equivalence or a "potentially infinite chain of texts" or "an intense love affair between a [male] speaker and his mother tongue," it is the Other-as-reason that tells us to stop there, to look no further, to close the book, to shout "the end" or "amen." One knows in advance how far one can go, where the boundary lines are, where to stop, turn around, and go back inside. One *knows*—because the Other-as-reason is always with one, especially when one is inclined to refer to oneself as "one" (why not two or a thousand or zero or minus seventeen?). To have a translation you have to have a text, and Wolfson has a text, but something in Lecercle knows that it's not the right *kind* of text—it's beyond the pale, outside the compound—so he struggles to come up with some kind of cockamamie rationale for rejecting it: Wolfson produces "a text so utterly other as to be a nontext." Does he mean "other" in the sense of "not-self"? Is this what he's getting at? Texts are selves, and when they are sufficiently alienated from the self they suddenly stop being texts and become nontexts? This is weird, but no weirder than Wolfson's own musings, which are grounded in the same (built-in failure of) rationalist discourse, the same twisted schizoid logic that drives Wolfson (and other linguists) into analyzing words into their component parts like a five-year-old scientist pulling the legs off grasshoppers. The dualistic boundaries of this logic are clear: thus far, no farther; A, and not-A; me, trapped here inside my little prison with God or logic or reason, and not-me, the whole false-self system of a world including and beginning with my own body.

Métissés and Joual

The farther the schizophrenic slides down the slope of lost control, however, the less accessible schizoid logic becomes, the harder it is to distinguish this from that, me from everything else. Ultimately, schizophrenia swallows dualism whole and spits it out in a million pieces, shards, slivers, strands, each becoming the entire universe—and nothing. "In Julie," Laing tells us in his description of one patient, "all perception seemed to threaten confusion with the object. She spent much of her time exercising herself with this difficulty. 'That's the rain. I could be the rain.' 'That chair . . . that wall. I could be that wall. It's a terrible thing for a girl to be a wall'" (215). And the deeper the translator slips into schizophrenia—or the (post)colonial context, which as Richard Jacquemond suggests is pretty much the same thing—the harder it is to maintain the rationalist dualisms that constitute much of our "solid" perceptual world. "That's the source text. I could be the source text." "It's a terrible thing for a translator to have lived in ancient Greece." Source and target language, author and translator and reader all flow together. As I suggested in *The Translator's Turn* (106–7), languages swirl around inside the translator's body anyway, and it is only by a supreme effort—often so thoroughly sublimated as to be unnoticeable but supreme nonetheless—that the translator separates the swirling into two distinct languages and begins channeling words and phrases from one into the other. The Other-as-reason guides this effort—and when the Other-as-reason's voice begins to fade, as the translator surrenders to schizophrenia, the effort becomes harder and harder to make, the linguistic swirl seems denser, thicker, more impenetrable, and all you can do is swim in it, perhaps drown in it.

Two other essays in Larry Venuti's collection, those by Samia Mehrez and Sherry Simon, celebrate this schizophrenic breakdown of the source/target dualism in exciting and enormously fruitful ways, specifically as one likely channel of escape out of the rationalist binds of the postcolonial situation. Here is Mehrez:

> Indeed, the emergence and continuing growth on the world literary scene of postcolonial anglophone and francophone literatures from the ex-colonies as well as the increasing ethnic minorities in the First World metropoles are bound to challenge and redefine many accepted notions in translation theory which continue to be debated and elaborated in the longstanding traditions of western "humanism" and "universalism." These postcolonial texts, frequently referred to as "hybrid" or "métissés" because of the culturo-linguistic layering which exists within them, have succeeded in forcing a new language that defies the very notion of a "foreign" text that can be readily translated into another language. With this literature we can no longer merely concern ourselves with conventional notions of linguistic equivalence, or ideas of loss and gain which

> have long been a consideration in translation theory. For these texts written by postcolonial bilingual subjects create a language "in between" and therefore come to occupy a space "in between." In most cases, the challenge of such a space "in between" has been double: these texts seek to decolonize themselves from two oppressors at once, namely the western ex-colonizer who naively boasts of their existence and ultimately recuperates them and the "traditional," "national" cultures which shortsightedly deny their importance and consequently marginalize them. (121)

Here is the schizophrenic solution in the postcolonial context extended one step beyond Wolfson; the North African writers Mehrez discusses—Abdelwahab Meddeb, Assia Djebar, Tahar Ben Jelloun, Abdelkebir Khatibi—are no longer terrified of the colonizer's language, no longer driven to repress its taboo force through translation. Rather, they enter into it playfully, letting words and meanings and atmospheric semiotics flow freely across cultural and linguistic boundaries, letting those boundaries dissipate into the anxious fantasies from which they came. Indeed, Mehrez's next paragraph seems to be a response to Wolfson and the fearful/rebellious subject-position he might be taken to represent:

> Hence, in using the language of the ex-colonizer it was important for postcolonial bilingual writers to go beyond a passive form of contestation [Wolfson's, for example], where the postcolonial text remained prisoner of western literary models and standards, restrained by the dominant form and language. It was crucial for the postcolonial text to challenge both its own indigenous, conventional models as well as the dominant structures and institutions of the colonizer in a newly forged language that would accomplish this double movement. Indeed, the ultimate goal of such literature was to subvert hierarchies by bringing together the "dominant" and the "underdeveloped," by exploding and confounding different symbolic worlds and separate systems of signification in order to create a mutual interdependence and intersignification. (121–22)

As Mehrez says in the first paragraph of hers I quoted, this free flow of postcolonial translation is an attempt to forge a "new language"—but it is far from being a new cultural phenomenon. In fact it's as old as the hills, certainly much older than the rationalist paradigm that it seeks to displace, with a single source language and a single target language and a hermetic seal in between. What's new about this phenomenon is that, freed from the schizoid defenses of rationalist/imperialist logic, the "schizophrenic" or postcolonial subject is forever forging new languages out of the swirling bits and pieces of the old. This is what language is like before the rationalist intervention of linguists, teachers, and other language purists who insist on keeping English English, French French, Arabic Arabic, and so on, and also insist not only on eliminating all traces of alterity from each national language but on expelling all speakers who mix them together from the classroom or other hegemonic place. As long as it's a single "disruptive" or "learning-disabled" or "attention-deficit" student who refuses or fails to purify language along rationalist lines, this failure is punished by ridicule, low grades, pedagogical drugs like Ritalin, or expulsion; but what happens when whole populations start getting expelled from their rationalist classrooms, when the teacher too starts breaking down the walls and teaching freedom rather than bondage? Then, as Paulo Freire shows in *The Pedagogy of the Oppressed*, the schizophrenia of the postcolonial situation becomes a form of (or gateway to) liberation.

Later in Venuti's book, Sherry Simon offers a brief political history of translation in Canada, always celebrating the mutual contamination of source and target in calques and other "interferences" and culminating in a rousing discussion of the problems of translating *joual*, the "hybrid" French-English dialect of Quebec that has since come to be called *la langue québéqoise:* "For the purists adopting Parisian written French as their model, *joual* was an impure and degraded form of speech, its pronunciation vulgar, its grammar incorrect, its rampant anglicisms an affront. For those who were articulating a philosophy of cultural anticolonialism in Quebec, *joual* was to become a kind of perverse badge of honour which was to flaunt Quebec's alienation" (170). Like the North African writers Mehrez examines, many quebecois writers in the 1960s and after—Jacques Ferron, Jacques Renaud, Jacques Godbout, and other people whose first names were something other than Jacques—adopted this hybrid language as a channel of post- or anticolonial politics, a potential escape from the numbing deadends of the existing French-English standoff.

Simon goes on to ask what happens when one attempts to translate *joual* works into English: "Translating the transgressive intentions of this language, however, presented a rather complex challenge. For one thing, one could almost say that untranslatability was inscribed in it through the very presence of English words. What would be the ethics of rerouting those English words back to a totally English context?" (171). Drawing heavily on the remarks of Betty Bednarski, translator of Jacques Ferron and author of a book audaciously titled *Autour de Ferron*, Simon shows that the very "'victory' of French over English in Ferron's work (the presence of a certain number of English words given French pronunciation and spelling, like 'cuiquelounche')" (171) is partly reversed and betrayed in the English translation but also partly reaffirmed in complex ways that may even include the "betrayal." Simon doesn't explore those reaffirmations, merely saying that "the translator does not waylay the text, deliver it whimpering into the hands of the English enemy," but that "translation becomes another aspect of the work's contradictions" (172)—but it seems reasonable to assume that a "schizophrenic" translation of *joual* could never "waylay the text," because it would inevitably consider the contradictions and the tensions and the conflicting claims of "victory" on both and all sides to be the whole thing, the whole literary situation, not some piece of "background information" to be ignored. Schizophrenic translators can no longer make this kind of distinction: this is verbal texture, discard it, that is meaning, keep it; this is background information, ignore it, that is the text, keep it. It's all relevant—especially the translator's own shifting role in the translation process, her feeling of being stretched across the same political tensions (though in different ways [though she is probably incapable of articulating the difference]) that wrack the work itself.

And I'm thinking that this *surrender* to schizophrenia, to confusion, to the shifting tensions of in-betweenness may be the only way out of our current (post)colonial impasse. As long as we insist on *managing* the transfer, managing our whole relatedness with a text and two (or more) languages and cultures, as long as we must be convinced that we are in control before we will proceed, as long as we must have a plan, a principle, a method, a regimen—then translation will remain a form of imperialism. Just translate the meaning. Give the translation some of the alien flavor of the original. Adhere to target-cultural norms. Adhere to source-cultural norms. Readability. Alterity. My way or the highway. Regulate your behavior, subordinate your whims to a rule. But trek off across the shifting sands of insanity and the schizoid self-control that preshapes domination drops away. True equality lies only on the far side of psychotic breakdown.

O Kannada

I want to end this chapter with a series of experiments in schizophrenic translation, working with the exemplary text offered us by Tejaswini Niranjana at the end of *Siting Translation*, a twelfth-century *vacana* (wa'-cha-na) written in Kannada, Niranjana's mother tongue, and attributed to a religious leader in the Virаśaiva movement named Allama Prabhu:

> nimma tējava nōḍalendu heresāri nōḍuttiralu
> śatakōti sūryaru mūḍidantirdudayyā!
> miñcina baḷḷya sañcava kaṇḍe;
> enagidu sōjigavāyittu!
> Guhēśvarā, nīnu jyotirlingavādare
> upamisi nōḍaballavarillayyā. (174)

Niranjana cites two translations by others, both by fellow Indians. The first, a very close rendition from 1965 by S. C. Nandimath, L. M. A. Menezes, and R. C. Hiremath—all are native speakers of Kannada, and Nandimath and Hiremath are themselves Lingayats or Virаśaivas—goes like this:

> As I stepped back and looked
> To see Thy light
> It seemed a hundred million suns
> Came into sight;
> A cluster of creeping lightnings I
> With wonder saw.
> O Guhesvara, if Thou become
> The effulgent Linga, there be none
> Thy glory to match! (174)

Niranjana only has a few minor criticisms of this version: (1) It sounds too Christian; it was probably influenced by early translations of the *vacanas* done by Christian missionaries in the 1860s. She doesn't specify the trouble spots that give this impression, but I would guess that her criticism applies to phrases such as "Thy light," "effulgent," and "Thy glory." (More on this in a moment.) (2) In the original the speaker steps back *in order to* look, rather than stepping back *and* looking. (3) "Cluster" in line 5 is superfluous. (4) "Effulgent" is an adjectival rendering of the first noun, *jyōti* "light," in the compound noun *jyōtirlingavādare* "light linga if are" (wrong part of speech!). (5) "If Thou become" in line 7 refers to a subjunctive future; the original *-adare* refers to a conditional present (as the result of a recent becoming): "if you are" or "if you are/have become [a light-linga]." (6) "Thy glory to *match*" is wrong, "for the question is not one of finding other gods or mortals to 'match' the glory of *Guhēśvarā*" (185). A more literal rendition, which Niranjana apparently rejects as simple-minded (not poststructuralist enough—more on this later, too), would have been "there be none / Thy glory to compare." An *upama* is a comparison; Niranjana's mother's name Anupama, for example, means "incomparable" or "beyond compare." The gist of the last two lines seems to be that if Guhēśvarā is become a light-linga (possibly a light-emitting linga, like the sacred stones that glow in that uncomfortably neocolonialist film *Indiana Jones and the Temple of Doom*, or, more radically, a linga *as* light, light in the shape of a linga, a linga made out of or with the intensity of light), there are no knowledgeable people who could find anything to compare him to. (A linga in Viraśaiva is a carved Śiva symbol worn by devotees or Lingayats, after initiation in childhood or later in life, in a metal case around the neck. A linga found in a cave [*guhē*] might be called a cave-god or cave-Śiva or *Guhē-iśvarā* or Guhēśvarā—but Guhēśvarā, the god addressed in every poem attributed to Allama Prabhu, is not merely a sacred stone found in a cave.)

The second and more famous translation, written in 1973 by the great Indian scholar A. K. Ramanujan, who died a few years ago in Chicago, goes like this:

> Looking for your light,
> I went out:
> it was like the sudden dawn
> of a million million suns,
> a ganglion of lightnings
> for my wonder.
> O Lord of Caves,
> if you are light
> there can be no metaphor.

The magisterial Ramanujan takes many more liberties with the *vacana* than do the devout Nandimath, Menezes, and Hiremath, and Niranjana is far more critical of his translation than she is of theirs: (1) "I went out" in line 2 possibly mistakes the *here* "back" in *heresāri* for *hora* "outside." *Heresāri* is one of the few words in the poem not immediately understandable to a contemporary speaker of Kannada. (2) "Ganglion" in line 5 replaces the relationship between the "play" or "flash" of lightning and the poet's gaze with a neural image that implicitly psychologizes or at least individualizes the flash. Niranjana calls Ramanujan's translation "post-Romantic" and "New Critical" (180). (3) Translating Guhēśvarā's name as Lord of Caves erases the last remaining trace of Kannada in the poem: "Given that colonialism's violence erases or distorts beyond recognition (as witnessed in innumerable colonial texts) the *names* of the colonized, it seems important *not* to translate proper names in a post-colonial or decolonizing practice" (183). (4) The poem's movement from *tēja* "radiance, brightness, lustre" to *jyōti* "light" is elided in Ramanujan's translation of both terms as "light"; Ramanujan claims that the *vacana* affirms light in the beginning and negates it in the end, and this Niranjana disputes. Ramanujan also sidesteps the problems of rendering the *linga* into English by translating *jyōtirlinga* "light linga" as "light." (5) "There can be no metaphor" in line 6 misreads the poem: there is always metaphor, just no metaphor or figuration adequate to represent the god Guhēśvarā who is become the linga that both is and is not Śiva.

Niranjana offers her own translation as a corrective not only to previous translations of this one *vacana* but also to assimilative postcolonial translation practice in general: in important ways her entire argument builds up to the moment of her translation, which seems to promise or presage a solution to the mind-numbing dilemmas of (post)colonial appropriation. "I initiate here a practice of translation," she writes, "that is speculative, provisional, and interventionist" (173), which sounds very much like a postromantic performative—compare Whitman's "I speak the password primeval"—designed to change the very fabric of our social being. If after this preface the translation itself seems disappointing, I think it is important to imagine an implicit stress in her performative utterance on "provisional": Niranjana is *experimenting* with an interventionist postcolonial practice of translation, not prescribing, not claiming to solve all the problems raised by identity politics (nor am I). Here is her translation:

> Drawing back
> to look at your radiance
> I saw
> the dawning of a hundred million suns.
> I gazed in wonder
> at the lightning's creepers playing.
> Guhesvara, if you are become the *linga* of light
> Who can find your figuration. (175)

Here are my problems with this translation: (1) "Your radiance" doesn't really solve the problems of christianizing rhetoric in "Thy glory" or "effulgent." How about "radiant beams from Thy holy face" in "Silent Night"? I wonder, in fact, how any pious poem in English, regardless of the religious beliefs it explicitly details, can avoid sounding at least vestigially Christian. The English language is saturated with the King James Version of the Bible and four hundred years of liturgical and hymnic discourse; just try to make reverent references to religious experiences in English sound Viraśaiva or Hindu or Buddhist or Muslim (or even, as Willis Barnstone so sardonically shows, Jewish). Any god will always come out feeling like Jesus or his dad, any mystical light will always come out looking and sounding like glory or radiance or splendor, and so on. There are ways around this problem, and I want to look at a few in a moment, but "your radiance" isn't one of them. (2) "*Linga* of light" in line 7 is syntactically so close to "effulgent Linga" as to render Niranjana's charge against the Nandimath-Menezes-Hiremath translation (they replaced a noun with an adjective!) not only picky but hypocritical: "of light" is an adjectival phrase. (3) The poststructuralist burden of "figuration" in line 8 seems highly suspect to me. It's certainly a defensible translation of *upama* "comparison, figure," though it pushes on the semantic envelope a bit (figuration is a more general phenomenon than a single figure); since Niranjana has just devoted half of her book to close readings of three major twentieth-century Western poststructuralist thinkers, Walter Benjamin, Paul de Man, and Jacques Derrida, "figuration" seems to me just as tendentious and assimilative a translation as "Thy glory" or "ganglion." If Nandimath, Menezes, and Hiremath christianize and Ramanujan romanticizes, Niranjana poststructuralizes—calling the linga, for example, "an articulation of a disarticulation" (178). If the echoes of Christian hymns in the first translation and of the romantic crisis-lyric in the second make them complicitous in colonization, the echoes of poststructuralist philosophy in the third make it equally so.

That is, if we have to be so judgmental. Why not just be good liberals, good pluralists (why can't we all just *get along*) and say indulgently that all three translations are "right," or that all three provide useful perspectives on the original—that Niranjana's "figuration" sheds as interesting a light on *upama* as Nandimath-Menezes-Hiremath's "Thy light" sheds on *nimma tējava* or Ramanujan's "ganglion" sheds on *baḷḷi*? Well, colonialism is a black hole that sucks us all in, and facing that black hole with liberal pluralism is about as schizoid as you can get. If we're ever going to smash through the dilemmas and double binds that surround the power differentials of colonialism, we're going to need some bolder, more radical, more revolutionary strategies than pluralistic perspectivism, whether our perspective is Christian, romantic, poststructuralist, or something else altogether. Niranjana says of her translation, for example, "Seeing 'literalness' as an 'arcade,' I privilege the word over the sentence" (185)—but hers seems to me a pretty cautious literalism. Why hold back? Why not try something extreme, like this:

> your lustre wanting-to-look moving-back looking-I-was
> hundred-million suns rising-dawn!
> lightning's vine's flash I-saw;

to-me-this wonder-it-happened!
cave-god, you light-linga-if-are
comparing look-know-people-no-lord!

But even this doesn't cut it for me. Like the literal version of the Apuleius passage I offered in chapter 1, this is relatively complete but yields me no experiential sense of what might be going on in the poem. But then the same holds true, it seems to me, of the three translations Niranjana gives as well, including her own. All four bring useful perspectives on the *vacana*, but in my mind's ear, on my tongue, they feel flat, dry, empty, cardboardy.

Of course there are ways around this response. Any one of these translations could be read aloud by Niranjana or someone else from Karnataka State in Kannada-accented English—my informants, for example, Shantha and Sucheta Murthy of Peoria, Illinois, both originally from Bangalore, Karnataka, Niranjana's home city—with Viraśaiva music playing in the background and a Viraśaiva movie like *Viswadharmi Basavanna* projected on the wall, and it would feel more alive; it would also seem more Kannadiga—more like the original. A multimedia experience can work wonders for even the deadest piece of writing. Even a good actor or reciter could inject life into the four translations.

But it seems to me that all four still have a serious flaw, which is that they try to pretend that it's perfectly normal for people to draw back to look at a god (whose eye, Niranjana tells us, is glaring up at the poet from the sole of his foot) and see, say, a hundred million suns dawn. Sure, uh huh, happens all the time. And, well, maybe it does—but it's enormously significant for our response to a poem like this (and in that "our" and the "we" that follows I include not only Westerners like me but modern Kannadigas like Niranjana) that we have been conditioned by the Other-as-reason *not to notice* it happening, to repress the incidence of "visions" and other mystical experiences in our "rationalist" era, and to treat the visionaries and mystics who do see millions of suns in their feet—even when the same experience happens to us—as bonkers. Eight centuries have passed since the writing of the poem, and the Other-as-reason has adjusted our expectations. It's no longer pious to see the things that the poem's speaker sees; it's nuts. And there's no use pretending otherwise. The effect of pretending otherwise is to generate one insipid little quasichristian hymn after another, whether it's about "Thy glory" or "your radiance," "metaphor" or "figuration." Suppress your first reaction, the one whispered to you by the Other-as-reason—*this guy's on drugs, been into the medicine cabinet, a coupla tabs of acid, a Dixie cup of electric Kool-Aid, and whoa, what a trip, the walls are melting and this eye is bugging out of my foot when all of a sudden I'm blinded by a piercing light that explodes out of the eye, sheee-it!* He's *not* teetering precariously on the verge of insanity, he *hasn't* just been handed the key to the gates of Schizophrenic City, he *isn't* seeing things that aren't there. Suppress all that, and force yourself to read (then translate) the poem piously. Assume that this must have been a pious poem in the twelfth century, so translate it piously now—dynamic equivalence, as Eugene Nida would say. Pare your response down to a pale simulacrum of piety, then put that on the page.

And where are you going to get that simulacrum in English? From Christianity, of course. "Thy glory." From Romanticism, maybe, which T. E. Hulme called "spilt religion" (read "spilt Christianity"): William Blake looking at the sun and seeing not a red guinea but a thousand angels singing "Holy, Holy, Holy." From some other church, say the church of Derridean Nominalism, the one that worships the Articulation of a Disarticulation. Ignore the all-too-obvious connection to insanity, since that would be, what, impious, demeaning—the poet ain't crazy, he's a *saint* (say it in a properly hushed voice), maybe he has *really seen God* (or at least the form of God's formlessness)! Translate the poem, therefore, as if you were in church, in Sunday school, as if your reader were a clergyman or a critical theorist, someone easily shocked, quick to frown in moral disapproval.

My sense is that the bridge between our era and Allama Prabhu's isn't foreignism but the commonality of "mystical" or "schizophrenic" experience, the Other-as-mystery's uncanny survival in the midst of a culture of reason, its power to smash through rational defenses and drive even the most schizoid control freak out of his or her skull by popping up as a hallucinatory voice from above our right ear or as an effulgent eye in the sole of our foot (which I personally, not being particularly limber, would have a hard time seeing, though maybe the Other-as-mystery can peek around corners just fine). As I say, the best solution to the problems of translating across the First World/Third World power differentials is surrender, absolute white-flag all-or-nothing surrender, a headlong too-late-to-think-about-it plunge into the darkness of the Other-as-mystery without even the faith that the light or radiance or glory or effulgence of Śiva or Jesus or Isis lies waiting for us on the other side.

Even this adjustment of my literal version for verse form, for example, feels like a good start:

your lustre
wanting to look
moving back
looking I was
100,000,000 suns
rising dawn
lightning's
vine's
flash
I saw
to me this
wonder it happened
cave-god
you
light linga if are

comparing
look know people no
lord

Strung together in the six-line verse form of the original, hyphens signaling unpacked compound nouns and verbs, my radical literal version said to the reader: I'm a radical literal version, figure me out. Rearrange my sequences, move "your lustre," "wanting to look," and "moving back" around like Scrabble letters until you get "wanting to look at your lustre I moved back" or "moving back to look at your lustre" or whatever until the whole thing makes sense. It also said: you can't really understand me on my own because I was never meant to be read on my own; I'm a crib; I refer back to the Kannada original and am mainly useful in helping you learn to read it in the original. Stretching the translation out into a series of short lines makes it look like a poem, not a crib, and forces the reader to live with uncertainty, with ambiguity, with the possibility that the speaker (perhaps the poet too) is nuts: "moving back / looking I was / 100,000,000 suns / rising dawn." Really? You were 100,000,000 suns rising in that dawning moment when you were moving back looking? "Dawn / I saw / to me this / wonder it happened." It dawned and you saw, you saw what, you saw what to you happened? Wonder if it did happen, no wonder it happened, to me *this* wonder, it did happen. Use a structural device such as the line breaks that Anglophone poets have been using over the last fifty years to depunctuate their words, to cut their words free from the linear syntagms of conventional written English, and suddenly the schizoid crib becomes schizophasic discourse, macaronic salad, radically disconnected speech that could be connected in any number of ways, "vine's flash I saw to me," "flash I saw to me this wonder," "I saw to me this wonder it happened cave-god," "wonder it happened cave-god you," "cave-god you light linga if are comparing," "if are comparing look know people no," "look know people no lord." This opens my radical unpacking of *nōḍaballavarillayyā*, for example, like a hundred million suns: *nōḍa* "look, see" + *balla* "know" + *avaru* "people" + *illa* "no" + *ayyā* "lord," thus "(there are) no knowing people who can see [comparison] o lord," "(there are) no initiates/gnostics who can look (for) [comparison] lord" if *balla* goes with *avaru* to mean "knowing people"; or "no one can find [comparison] lord" if *balla* goes with *nōḍa* to mean "find"). The result is that, instead of a single pious rhetorical question, "Who can find your figuration," we get disfiguration, fragmentation, a line that doesn't yield easily to nervous sense making (and thus is more Derridean than Niranjana's rendering, if that's what we're after [I'm not]); a line that also, unlike Niranjana's "find," connects up across the poem to the other *nōdas*, the other lookings, in the first line *(nōḍalendu* and *nōḍuttiralu)*.

Or I could do a Louis Wolfson translation via Finnish, "defending" against the "dangerous" powers of the original by shifting everything phonetically into another foreign language—into Finnish not only because I happen to speak and write it but because there are mysterious points of contact between

Kannada and Finnish. *Sata*, for example, means one hundred in both languages (and *koti* "million" in Kannada is "house" in Hindi and "home" in Finnish), and the verb ending *-ittu* is the imperfect (past) in Kannada and the (participial) perfect in Finnish. So I do a Wolfson into Finnish and then (for the sake of readers who don't speak Finnish) translate literally into English:

nimma tējava nōḍalendu heresāri nōḍuttiralu
niinpä tee se vaan noitalento heresiasi noiduttu loru
so do it just witch-flight your-heresy bewitched rhyme
  śatakōti sūryaru mūḍidantirdudayyā!
  satakoti suuri ja rummutti tanssituuteja!
  hundred-home large and drummed dance lullabies!
miñcina baḷḷiya sañcava kaṇḍe;
mihin sinä pallia sankoa kannat;
where you ball bucket carry;
  enagidu sōjigavāyittu!
  enää kidu soija kavallettu!
  any more suffer soy embezzled!
Guhēśvarā, nīnu jyōtirlingavādare
Kuhasvaara, niinku juottolinkkuvaatturi
Perch Hill, like solder-latch-tailor
  upamisi nōdaballavarillayyā.
  upposi noitapallovärillä aijaa.
  sank witch-ball-color(-with) oh no.

Again, like the radical literal version I did above, this sounds contrived, flat, a mere tedious (though somewhat insane) exercise—until I crack the verse form:

so do it just
witch flight
your heresy a
bewitched rhyme
hundred home large and
drummed
dance lullabies
where you carry
the ball the bucket
any more
suffer soy
embezzled
Perch Hill like
solder latch tailor
sank with
witch ball color
oh no

This looks infinitely more macaronic than "Your lustre," my schizophrenic literal translation; the Wolfsonic syllabic rendition of Finnish acts as an extra chaos-generator in between the Kannada and the English, and even the reader who is accustomed to difficult twentieth-century poems has to strain to make any sense at all out of it. (Then again, it's no more difficult than understanding a schizophrenic.) But some patterns do emerge: since *nōḍa* "look" sounds like Finnish *noita* "witch," the *vacana's* obsession with vision in English becomes an obsession with witchcraft (a flight, a rhyme, and a ball are all associated with witches); the Kannada *baḷḷi* and *balla* plunge straight through Finnish *pallo* "ball" into English ball; the rhyme is complicated in "drummed / dance lullabies," especially since "drummed" and "dance" seem to go together and (nursery) "rhyme" and "lullaby" form their own little children's club. And so on. It wouldn't take long to generate an ingeniously coherent reading of this poem. (Then again, this poem is neither actual schizophasic discourse nor an actual Wolfsonian flight out of the "damaging" sounds of Kannada; I generated it by imposing an eremitic regimen on it, a *traducson* into Finnish and a word-for-word translation into English. And as a result, of the four "schizophrenic" translations I offer of the *vacana* this one works least well for me.)

If we read up on Allama Prabhu, too, we may stumble on descriptions that will help us drive our translations crazy. In *Śiva's Warriors*, Velcheru Narayana Rao's English translation of Pālkuriki Somanātha's *Basava Purāṇa*, a sacred Telugu poem written by a Viraśaiva saint, we read:

> Allama Prabhu was the lord of yogis. He had the likeness of the destroyer of death. His fame was great. He had eliminated bodily passions. His actions were a sword that destroyed the two kinds of karma. He had renounced involvement in the world. He acted on the basis of distancing that which is unseen and that which is seen. He accepted nothing from others. He was equally unswayed by humiliation or honor. In his mind there was no distinction between dirt and gold, grief and happiness, enemies and friends. His mind was devoid of the seven elements, pride, and the other ordinary physical qualities. He was beyond the end of creation. (73)

He was hopelessly insane. "His hair fell loose upon his shoulders. The god smiled sweetly upon him" (73), as upon all holy fools. He sat in the day room unmoving, unblinking, even (some thought) unbreathing, until the orderly wheeled him back to his room for the night. No one ever saw him eat anything. (Was he on an IV drip? How did they ever get him to swallow his Thorazine? Or did they just inject it?) "He was both with and without a body. He was both with and without a name. He spoke but he did not speak. He thought but he did not think. . . . He was alive, but his body was not animate" (73). Would the right dosage of L-Dopa have animated him, as it did Oliver Sacks' patients in the book and the movie *Awakenings*? Was he a Parkinsons patient? Or what? "He acted without thought. He had forgotten himself in the bliss of contemplating the linga in his palm" (73). Or maybe it was a tennis ball. Whichever, you could tell it was holy.

But Prabhu was not catatonic. He walked through the world, and the trees and the soil made way for him. "Though he moved, he was really not active.

His eyes were heavy. His life breath was the linga" (73). Who do we know like this? My most immediate association is with the strung-out glassy-eyed rednecks I would see either walking down the street in Oxford, Mississippi, who were way past anger, though you could see that anger had burned its way right through them, or barreling through town in their pickups, lights off until it was pitch-black dark (could they see in the dark? did they assume others could see them coming from the glow in their bodies, *tejassu*?). And what were the Viraśaiva poet-saints (at least in Brahmin eyes) but hicks who, as Niranjana says, "disregarded Sanskrit, the traditional religious language of Hinduism, in favor of the local language, Kannada" (175)? The language of the *vacana* we've been reading, translating, is still close to the ordinary speech of modern Karnataka State even eight centuries after it was written; why shouldn't we imagine its speaker as a crazy redneck in his truck, seeing things?

> that there eyeball inna sole a my foot done
> zapped me with light, man,
> & I shrunk back & seen
> a bazillion stars pop out
> pow all at once
>
> & the lightning flashed like a rock
> hittin my windshield at night
> & me blinded by them headlights
> & god, man, I thought,
> was that you or
> what

But is this too assimilative? No trace of Allama Prabhu, Viraśaiva, Guhēśvarā, the linga, or Kannada remains in this rendition; it has become an American poem, and this transformation, Niranjana reminds us, is all too typical of colonial practice. Let me wrap up this chapter, therefore, with a final "crazy" translation of the *vacana* that is patently less assimilative:

> Hoping to look on your bright Teja I heresaried and saw
> The dawning of a hundred million Suryaru!
> I saw the flash of the Mincu's Balli,
> Astonished that it happened to me!
> Guhesvara, if you are become a Jyotirlinga,
> No one can see an Upama O lord!

Again, Niranjana argued for the retention in English of two Kannada words, the names of the god and his symbol, Guhēśvarā and linga; Nandimath, Menezes, and Hiremath proceeded along similar lines. But is that enough? Any combination of Kannada and English words in a primarily English poem is going to be a compromise—especially since the only native mixture of the two is an Anglicized form of Kannada spoken in Karnataka today, Kannada with a light sprinkling of slightly Kannadigized English words (*trenu* "train," *taimu* "time," *offissu* "office," *karu* "car": part of the inheritance of colonialism)—but why not push the compromise in radical directions, why not expand Kannada's power to define the terms on which the poem is to be read? If *tēja*, say, sounds Christian whether we render it as "radiance" or "lustre" or "glory," leave it in Kannada; just give the English reader a clue to its meaning by modifying it with "bright" so that the image is almost there but glimmers just out of reach, precisely like the mysteries of an esoteric religion. Use the same drill with "the dawning of a hundred million Suryaru" and "the flash of the Mincu's Balli." What dawns? The sun. What flashes? Well, lots of things, but lightning is likely to be high on the list.

It seems to me, in fact, that this fourth version of mine most closely approximates what Niranjana was attempting to achieve: a problematic transformation or reconfiguring of Kannada culture and Viraśaiva religion. It is also strangely readable, despite the untranslated terms. The only phrases that give the English reader no clue of their meaning, in fact, are "heresaried," "become a Jyotirlinga," and "see an Upama"—and the first of these was the one word in the *vacana* that my Kannada informants, the Murthys, had to guess at (Shantha thought it might mean something like "fearlessly," since it sounded like *hedaradi*), while the second and third deal precisely with the impossibility of articulating *or* understanding the mystical experience. All three of the translations Niranjana provides give us a better sense of the *upama* than this last one of mine does; then again, isn't it just our perverse rationalism, the whispering of the Other-as-reason, that makes us want so desperately to *know*, to *understand*? And none of the three, really, gives a better sense of the *jyōtirlinga* than mine, since the meaning of that term (I'm told) is so steeped in Viraśaiva and generally Hindu religious beliefs and practices as to defy even lengthy descriptions. The "meaning" of those two untranslated terms, *jyōtirlinga* and *upama*, for a non-Kannada speaker would be "something mysterious," "something beyond my grasp"—and isn't that exactly right? Isn't that what the *vacana* is about?

Maybe not. Maybe this is just my attempt to rationalize my translation by reference to the rationalist ideal of equivalence, which projects an "original" meaning (what the poem is about) onto the source text and then conforms the target text as closely as possible to that projection. Certainly it would be difficult to use that same argument-from-equivalence on the Wolfsonian, Finnish-inspired "So do it just" translation; I get the sneaking suspicion that the Other-as-reason is guiding this last section on "schizophrenic" translation far more than I know. But how could it be otherwise? We fight against the hegemonic ideosomatics of our culture (partly) in vain, and every gain, every victory is subject to co-optation by the dominant Others. Even schizophrenics are more controlled, more regimented, more powerfully spoken by the Other-as-reason than the mystical ideal of surrender I've been peddling these last few pages.

Magical Doubles

Weiter: Er hat es [illegible] gebracht, wer das Königreich
pel und Sicilien inne [illegible], muß jährlich über alles dem
igsten Vater ein schönes [illegible] Roß schenken, mit silbernem
m und Zeug aufs [illegible] geputzt; welches er für ein
recht zu solchen Königs[illegible] annimmt. Wiewohl man
, daß die, so es schenken, bedingen, daß es solle ein
chtes[3]) Geschenk und nicht ein Lehnrecht sein. Solche
se sammelt der Papst ein, so viele Jahr er lebt, und
sie ledig vor sich herführen, wenn er mit einer beson-
n herrlichen Pracht prangen will, zum Zeichen, daß er

CHAPTER 3

I originally planned to end chapter 2 with two discussions of Indian texts and the problems involved in translating them into the language of the oppressor, English: I planned to discuss the Niranjana material and something else, something drawn from Native American culture, in order to engage the issues raised by Eric Cheyfitz in *The Poetics of Imperialism*. And while nothing has happened to make this original plan impossible, something did happen that derailed my thinking about the plan, and perhaps about the book as a whole, in interesting and disturbing ways. Since the story of that derailment feeds into my main concerns for this last chapter, I want to begin by telling it.

In the autumn of 1993 a friend of mine, Bill Kaul, got a job teaching English at the Shiprock Alternative School in Shiprock, New Mexico, on the Navajo reservation. Since he has degrees in English and a preference for alternative approaches to education—and since he had long felt drawn to Indian culture—he was excited about the job and moved to New Mexico with a good deal of enthusiasm. He enrolled in Navajo classes at the Shiprock branch of Navajo Community College and wrote me letters about the difficulty of the language, saying that if he lived there forty years he might learn it well. The school wasn't as "alternative" as it seemed at first, and he clashed with its increasingly traditional and authoritarian executive director and finally resigned a year after he got the job—but that's another story. He loved the teaching, spent the year fomenting rebellion in his Navajo students (not because they were Navajos, but because that's what he does with all his students), and negotiated his awkward position between cultures with a kind of strange (dis)comfort. Navajo culture felt more congenial to him than Anglo culture: he'd lived on what the locals called "Navajo time" for most of his life; here at last was a place where he could let things happen as they happen, going with the flow, not pushing or pulling too hard at life, not striving to get ahead (or to avoid getting ahead), not trying to order his social environment to guarantee his own relative comfort (although maybe comfort was one of the things his living on the peripheries of Navajo culture was about). On the other hand, he was not welcomed into Navajo culture with open arms; far from it. The Navajos have known too many Indian wannabes for that. And he didn't try to worm his way in either. He figured any kind of acceptance and trust would have to come slowly and on its own terms, whatever those might be.

In any case, that autumn I attended the ALTA meeting in Atlanta and bought Brian Swann's essay collection *On the Translation of Native American Literatures*, and since I was writing this book (and corresponding with Bill) as I was reading Swann's, I got an idea. Instead of taking one of the texts dealt with in Swann's book and reworking it, the way I did the Kannada *vacana*, I would go visit Bill in New Mexico and get him to help me locate and translate a Navajo text. So I started asking him the best way to go about it—and got only evasive replies. "We'll see when you come." I suggested some possible procedures: he and I sitting down together with some students of his who read and write Navajo and doing collective translations; he and I taking a tape recorder to a Navajo singer, getting help having a song transcribed and translated roughly, etc. His response was to send me a "real" Navajo poem that he wrote himself, "real" because he did it in Navajo class at Navajo Community College with a pen borrowed from a Navajo woman.

So I arrived in New Mexico the next summer ready to work—and Bill kept putting me off. Finally, realizing he wasn't too excited about helping me, one afternoon I drove over to the NCC library and went through their Native American section until I found a book of poems from 1989 called *Ahí ní nikisheegizh* by Mazii Dinełtsoi written all in Navajo—in fact the only English words in the whole book were "Princeton Collection of Western Americana." Even the page numbers were written out in Navajo. I photocopied some poems, brought them home to Bill's house, and asked him who I could get to help me figure out what was in them—in order to pick out a single poem to translate for this book. Not many Navajos can read or write their language, even when they can speak it; it's only in the past few years that Navajo children have been taught to read and write it in elementary school. But Bill had learned to pronounce the language in class, well enough, he thought, to read it aloud to Al, one of his former students, who was doing some roofing for Bill; Al could then tell me in English what each poem was about.

Well, this process didn't work too well; either Bill's pronunciation or Al's Navajo wasn't quite up to the job, and Al only got about half (or less) of each poem. Al apologized, saying he was part Hopi; but I'm guessing the poems were also written in fairly complex "literary" (if that's the word for it) Navajo, which wouldn't necessarily have been familiar to Al. He said the very first poem of the collection was about skinwalkers, or ghosts, so I decided to go with that—I knew that I would be dealing with Schleiermacher on ghosts here in chapter 3—but it later turned out that Al had heard (maybe Bill had pronounced) the word *jiní* "it is said" as *chind'ii* "ghost." The poem had nothing to do with ghosts. Al also said it had something to do with a story that was not to be told. A taboo? I asked. Yes, he replied: a taboo.

So now I had my poem, and feeling quite smug in my ability to "collect" an "authentic" Navajo poem for translation, I went back to the NCC library to use the big Morgan dictionary of Navajo: I went through the poem word by word, phrase by phrase, figuring out the meanings and syntactic inflexions of individual words, trying to put them together into coherent sentences. As I say, I found no ghosts; I found a line that seemed like it might be pointing toward a taboo, but it's kind of hard to tell with just a dictionary: *doo baa hane' da*, with *doo . . . da* working sort of like the French *ne . . . pas* to negate anything in the middle, *baa hane'* meaning "story about." This doesn't necessarily say that the story isn't to be told—but it might. It might also mean that there isn't a story about it, or that the *ma'ii*, or coyote, who, it is said (in the previous line), climbed up on all fours didn't tell a story about it.

Feeling more and more excited to know how all these words fit together into a poem, I finally finished looking them all up and walked up to the Center for Dine' Studies on the second floor of the same building, looking for one of the professors Bill had recommended I talk to—hoping for some help with the translation. The Center was empty, with doors open and recent signs of occupancy, so I decided to wait and see if anyone would return soon. I began reading the bulletin boards—and promptly found an article about a collection of poems in Navajo by one Rex Lee Jim, who published them under his Navajo name, Mazii Dinełtsoi. It was the book I'd been working on: the title, I read, meant "The Settling of Fog." The article gave an English translation of the five lines (not from the poem I had spent the morning on) from which the title was taken—beginning "When the fog settles, the gods plant; / When the gods plant, expect the mysterious"—and then a professor from the Center came in with a few students who got something from her and left. Feeling on the verge of some great revelation—expect the mysterious!—I knocked on her door and introduced myself, explained what I was trying to do . . . and her face went cold.

"I can't help you with Rex Lee's poems."

Her tone was so icy that I could hardly get a word out. "Oh," I finally said, "well, uh, do you know of someone who—?"

"No, I'm sorry," she said, "I mean I *could* help you, but I won't. Rex Lee does not want those poems in English. He says if he had wanted them in English he would have written them in English. They were not written for the white man to exploit. I will not betray that trust."

What do you say to that? I was the white man, and my intention certainly was to exploit them, in this book. I hadn't thought of it quite that way, but she was right: I had planned on marching in and snatching up some Navajo poem and translating it, then making academic hay out of it here. I felt flustered and tongue-tied and was starting to beat an undignified retreat when she relented a little.

"You see," she explained, softening her tone slightly, "I teach those poems in Navajo. They are beautiful poems. Beautiful Navajo poems. My students and I discuss them. Rex Lee is very good with the Navajo language. But too much is lost in translation. I am collaborating on a book right now for Cambridge University Press, and everything I have written for it is in Navajo. The publishers wanted me to translate the poems and stories I had written into English, but I refused. The most I will give is a one-line summary of each piece. Any more than that would misrepresent the Navajo work, give English readers the wrong idea. If I want something I write to be in English, I'll write it in English—I won't translate it."

A little hesitantly, I started telling her about my book, my theory that in many cultures ancient taboos on sacred texts and rituals had survived into the present, no longer actually preventing translation in European languages but still affecting the way we think about translation. I would give up my plan to translate Rex Lee Jim's poem into English, I said, but I found it telling that I was changing my plans precisely because the taboo had survived longer in Navajo than in English, and I had happened to pick a poem that was not to be translated at all. She said, "It's not a taboo—" So I explained a bit more: as far as I could tell most cultures had for most of their history perceived outsiders either as enemies who would pervert their sacred truths and rituals or as ignoramuses who would not know what to do with them; so access to those truths and rituals had been restricted to a small ingroup. And as far as I could tell that was precisely what was happening with Rex Lee Jim's poetry: either Anglos were enemies who would exploit Navajo poetry or they were too ignorant of Navajo culture to get it, so he too restricted access to it by refusing (to allow anyone) to translate it. She nodded: "Yes, I suppose that's true. That is what is happening here."

So I drove back to Bill's house, depressed—feeling excluded I guess, feeling turned away from the doors of an exclusive club. Bill wasn't much help: "I sort of figured something like that would happen," he said. "That's why I haven't exactly been busting my butt helping you out on this." Besides, he said, he agreed with Vine Deloria that what Indians needed from Anglos was a hands-off policy.

"For example," I asked, looking to twist the knife of my hurt in him, "Anglos shouldn't teach Navajos English?"

"Exactly," he replied. "My job as a teacher is to make my job obsolete. If anyone is going to teach Navajos English, it should be other Navajos."

"What about Anglos learning Navajo?"

But I guess I didn't ask that question. I thought of that one later and wondered: what if I had taken a class in Navajo at NCC like Bill? What if I had taken enough classes to be able to read poems in Navajo and had attended a class where this professor had taught Rex Lee Jim's poems in Navajo? Would I still be the enemy? Would I still be an intrusive ignoramus? Perhaps so. Perhaps I would always be the enemy, branded by my race and its history of Indian genocide and economic exploitation—although the NCC/Shiprock chair of the Center for Dine' Studies, Clay Slate, is an Anglo whose Navajo is supposed to be remarkable. Is it only Anglos like me, ignorant of Navajo language and culture, who are to be denied access to this poetry? Or is it all Anglos?

Or to put that differently, would it be okay for an Anglo taking a second-year class in Navajo, say, to make rough notebook translations of a Rex Lee Jim poem, just for learning purposes, to help her or him understand the Navajo better? Is the ban on *all* translation, or only on published translations, which might fall into the wrong hands? Is translation all right with a Navajo professor present—a modern-day priest who, like Mithras in the Corinthian temple of Isis, guides the novitiate through the sacred text and shapes his understanding along acceptable lines? If so, did I already transgress against the ban by translating an individual word like *ma'ii* "coyote," or by trying to make sense of a phrase like *doo baa hane' da* "not story about"?

When I tried to get into some of this with Bill, however, he waved his hand impatiently.

"Look how you're thinking about all this," he said. "Texts, translations, interpretations. That's your world. Most Navajos don't read or write Navajo—what does that do to the interpretation of sacred texts?"

"Yeah, what *does* it do? At NCC they deal with texts. I'm a professor too so I went to NCC, and, what do you know, I end up dealing with texts and get told to butt out. So what are you saying, this stuff about reading Navajo texts in Navajo or English has nothing to do with Navajo culture?"

"I don't know about that. It's just that whatever Navajos call 'sacred'—and I'm not even sure they'd use that word—isn't in books."

"It's in heads, you mean. Oral tradition. Or in bodies, what I call ideosomatics, passed on bodily from generation to generation?"

"I suppose. But I think it's probably in the land—"

"As in sacred mountains?"

"Sacred everything. Me mucking around in my garden. Why not?"

"So you mucking around in your garden is like you translating some passage in your Navajo book for class, except a hell of a lot more effective, because the important stuff isn't in books?"

"Something like that. An old drunken Navajo in Durango once said to me, 'Stay close to Mother Earth.' I said, 'Sure, buddy.' But he was right. I can feel it."

Ghosts and Doubles

As this comes out of Bill's mouth, my first reaction is *this is the guy who doesn't wannabe an Indian wannabe?*—but I've been in enough situations in which someone, just because s/he has no experience of it, contemptuously dismisses something I know to be true that I'm not quite willing to sneer at his claim. I have no experience of "the land" conveying eternal truths to me, so I don't believe it—but I'm not exactly going to disbelieve it either. What I do believe is that if Bill says he feels something, he feels it. But feels what? What is the force he feels coming from the land, the soil, his garden, the mesas and canyons and arroyos where he goes walking and camping, that he knows (because he feels it) is bringing him something worthwhile, some ancient knowledge, some sacred truth? Is it a primeval force, something that has always been there and has taught the Navajos what they needed to know from the beginning? Is it some accretion of Navajo knowing over the centuries, something each Navajo (and thus the tribe as a collective whole, stretched over a thousand generations) leaves behind in the land for those born later to learn?

One of the reasons I'm wondering these things is that there is an undercurrent of repressed supernatural fear running through the translation theories I'm interested in here in this last chapter, some sense that there are external sources of knowing that are absolutely essential, probably unknowable, and almost certainly dangerous. When a person dies in her house, Navajos believe that her ghost goes on living in the house, thus rendering the house unfit for further human occupation; the house is stopped up and condemned, left for the *chind'ii*, the ghost, the haunt, the skinwalker. When a Navajo woman is pregnant, it is forbidden for her to make realistic human sculptures for fear that the representation will deform her baby. A friend of mine, Steve Heinemann, who taught arts classes at Northland Pioneer College in Show Low, Arizona, told me that a pregnant Navajo woman once made a wonderful abstract-expressionist sculpture for a class he was teaching, and when he asked what motivated her to try that particular style, she said that anything more realistic might have damaged her baby. And in "On the Different Methods of Translating," Friedrich Schleiermacher warns authors against trying to write original works in a foreign language—and, by extension, warns translators against trying to translate as if the author had originally written the work in the target language—on the grounds that this would be tantamount to becoming one's own double:

> Es giebt freilich auch außerdem eine freie Liebhaberei am lateinisch oder romanisch schreiben, und wenn es mit dieser wirklich darauf abgesehen wäre in einer fremden Sprache gleich gut wie in der eigenen und gleich ursprünglich zu producieren: so würde ich sie unbedenklich für eine frevelhafte und magische Kunst erklären, wie das Doppeltgehen, womit der Mensch nicht nur Geseze der Natur zu spotten, sondern auch andere zu verwirren gedächte. (62–63)

Let me stop there for a moment and translate, leaving the key word, *das Doppeltgehen*, in awkward literal translation:

> To be sure, some write in Latin or one of the romance languages for their own pleasure; and if their intentions in this were to write as well and as originally in the foreign language as in their own, I would unhesitatingly pronounce it a wicked and magical art akin to going doubled, an attempt at once to flout the laws of nature and to perplex others.

"Going doubled"? *Doppeltgehen* appears in no German dictionaries that I could track down, including Grimm's exhaustive dictionary from 1860; but it seems clear that it is the source of the noun that has found its uneasy way into English as well, *Doppelgänger* "double-goer," which Grimm also lists as *Doppeltgänger* "doubled-goer." To "go doubled" is not so much to *make* a double—a golem, say, a Frankenstein—as Schleiermacher's moral horror at this "wicked and magical art" might suggest, but to *be* a double, to walk abroad as one's own double, to project one's visible presence into another space and be two places at the same time. *Doppeltgehen* might be thought of as astral travel, existing in one place in the physical body and in another in the astral body, so that people could recall seeing you both here and there simultaneously and not be sure which was "really" you.

What does this mean for translation? Schleiermacher is at a point in his argument where he is tackling common metaphors for "fluent" translation, and just here he is demolishing the old chestnut according to which a translation should read as if it had originally been written in the target language. His rather dubious argument is that, since the metaphor's vehicle is impossible in the real world—because for the source author the target language is foreign, and no one can write great works in a foreign language—its tenor is inadmissable as a precept for translation: translators *shouldn't* pretend to be source authors writing in the target language. Schleiermacher's logic is pretty shaky here: since when has the relative realism of a metaphor been a criterion for its acceptance as a basis or explanation for action? But the big problem, for Schleiermacher as for us, is his claim about the real world, about the supposed nonexistence of brilliant original writing in a language that the author learned after childhood. I read him and immediately begin ticking off counterexamples—Conrad, Nabokov, Beckett—but even Schleiermacher, it seems to me, committed as he is to a romantic conception of languages and literatures as absolutely *nationally* distinct, knows that his claim holds no water and so resorts to demagoguery, like a fundamentalist preacher losing an argument against a freethinker and finally breaking down and threatening his opponent with hellfire: it's magic! It's wicked! Even if it's possible, don't do it, folks!

But why "going doubled"? Just what is the wicked magic practiced by Samuel Beckett writing in French? Implicit in Schleiermacher's scare tactics seems to be a conception of national language that is far more extreme than Wilhelm von Humboldt's, who merely believed that each language had its own internal form, the *innere Sprachform*, which lent the people who spoke it a peculiar *Geist* or spirit or genius (and I want to come back to *Geist* in a minute). Schleiermacher seems to believe that different languages exist on different levels or planes of reality, that each language literally constitutes its own *Lebenswelt*, not just in the now-commonplace sense that people who speak different languages construe reality differently and so *seem* to be living in different realities, but literally: languages are worlds, universes, and one only travels between them by supernatural means, through "doors" or "gateways," with the aid of black magic. The writer who strives to write original works in a foreign language is thus not merely "going doubled," projecting himself (Schleiermacher's hypothetical writers and translators are all male) into a doubled visible presence, but crossing reality-barriers that God did not intend for humans to cross, entering into alien realms that are forbidden to us mere mortals. This notion is even clearer in the passage that follows, in which the double becomes a ghost:

> So ist es aber wohl nicht, sondern diese Liebhaberei ist nur ein feines mimisches Spiel, womit man sich höchstens in den Vorhöfen der Wissenschaft und Kunst die Zeit anmuthig vertreibt. Die Production in der fremden Sprache is keine ursprüngliche; sondern Erinnerungen an einen bestimmten Schriftsteller oder auch an die Weise eines gewissen Zeitalters, das gleichsam eine allgemeine Person vorstellt, schweben der Seele fast wie ein lebendiges äußeres Bild vor, und die Nachahmung desselben leitet und bestimmt die Production. . . . Ist aber jemand gegen Natur und Sitte förmlich ein Ueberläufer geworden von der Muttersprache, und hat sich einer andern ergeben: so ist es nicht etwa gezierter und angedichteter Hohn, wenn er versichert, er könne sich in jener nun gar nicht selbst schuldig ist, daß seine Natur wirklich ein Naturwunder ist gegen alle Ordnung und Regel, und eine Beruhigung für die andern, daß der wenigstens nicht doppelt geht wie ein Gespenst. (64)

> But that is truly not their aim; their hobby is but an exquisite mimetic game with which to beguile away the hours out on the margins of philosophy and art. Writing in a foreign language is never original; rather memory images of specific authors or of the manner of a certain era, which flesh forth as it were a collective persona, float before the soul almost like living simulacra that, when imitated on paper, give the writing direction and definition. . . . If on the other hand, in defiance of nature and morality, a writer becomes a traitor to his mother tongue by surrendering his verbal life to another, it is no false or affected self-mockery when he protests that he can no longer move about in it; it is rather his attempt to vindicate himself by portraying himself as a wonder, a miracle surpassing all natural rule and order, and to reassure others that he at least does not go doubled like a ghost.

To "go doubled like a ghost" is to seem to cross the barrier between life and death: the astral traveler travels outside his or her body like a ghost, like the spirit of one dead, but then is able, through magic or other supernatural means, to return and take up ordinary living again. We are in the vicinity of shamanistic religion, clearly, which Schleiermacher, the good Lutheran minister, wants to condemn as against everything sacred and holy—against *Natur und Sitte* "nature and morality/custom," and, in case that's not enough to scare people off, against *Ordnung und Regel* "order and rule" as well (not to mention offenses against the *mother*)—but which he also clearly respects and fears as a real force in the world. Schleiermacher's attack is not on superstition; it is on truly effective magic, primitive or peripheral religious practices that horrify him because they transgress against his Christian sense of the boundaries of godly living.

Once we begin hearing Schleiermacher's occult fear of ghosts and doubles in the essay, many passages may take on a different feel. In German both *Gespenst* and *Geist* mean ghost, and while like most Germans Schleiermacher uses *Gespenst* for ghost and *Geist* for various other kinds of spirit, notably the intellectual ones *(Geist* means spirit as breath, ghost, genie, genius, mind, culture or spirit as temper or mood, as in the spirit of an age or *Zeitgeist)*, several idiomatic uses of *Geist* are so thoroughly interwoven semantically with *Doppeltgehen* in German that it's tempting to read all of Schleiermacher's *Geister* with a disturbing twinge of ghostliness. When people are uncertain whether what they're seeing is really you, for example, they ask whether it's you or your ghost/*Geist:* "Bist du es oder ist es dein Geist?" When you're sick, Germans will say you're pale as a ghost/*Geist*. When the disciples see Jesus after his crucifixion (Luke 24:37–39), they think they've seen his ghost/*Geist;* he has to reassure them that a ghost/*Geist* has neither flesh nor bone.

Thus when Schleiermacher writes of philosophers like Leibniz and Grotius, a page or two before the passage we're looking at, "Dies geht aber für einzelne Bedürfnisse und Thätigkeiten des Geistes noch viel weiter herab. So lange die Muttersprache für diese noch nicht gebildet ist, bleibt diejenige Sprache [das lateinische] die partielle Muttersprache, aus welcher jene Richtungen des Geistes sich einem werdenden Volke mitgetheilt haben" (61), most translators would render *Geist* as intellect or mind, possibly as culture. But what happens if we hear a repressed ghost in this passage? Let me translate the passage more or less literally: "But this goes still further downward [becomes even more complicated] for specific needs and activities of the *ghost*. So long as the mother tongue for these [scholars] isn't yet developed, that language [Latin] remains the partial mother tongue, out of which those directions of the *ghost* have been shared with a becoming [or developing] people." He's dealing with a rather problematic counterexample to his rule that no one writes well or originally in a foreign language: here we have Leibniz and Grotius writing originally in *both* their mother tongues, German and Dutch, and in Latin, which is a "partial" mother tongue—maybe a stepmother tongue, except that in Schleiermacher's family metaphor dad is still living with his first wife as well. Both mothers are right there in the house. This would make dad *(der Vaterland)* a bigamist, except for Schleiermacher's insistence that Latin's motherly presence is *geistlich*, intellectual or cultural or ghostly, an influence *des Geistes*, of the spirit. Leibniz and Grotius, in other words, have two moms, one of the body and one of the spirit. One living and one dead. If Latin is a ghost mom to these boys—a ghost stepmother no less—its intellectual and cultural influence upon their thought is certain to be less physical than that of German or Dutch, concerned more with metaphysics than with hugs and kisses and slaps on the rear. And that's right, isn't it? If writing ("well") in a foreign language means going doubled like a ghost, projecting your writerly self into the disembodied spirit world of another language, then the influence of a dead language like Latin over living languages like German and Dutch must be ghostly. People have certain intellectual/ghostly needs and activities that their native languages can't support, so they turn to a dead language like Latin that can.

Even more significantly, Schleiermacher claims that Leibniz and Grotius could only philosophize in German and Dutch by becoming totally different people: "Grotius und Leibnitz konnten nicht, wenigstens nicht ohne ganz andere Menschen zu sein, deutsch und holländisch philosophiren" (61)—again, literally, "Grotius and Leibnitz could not, at least not without entirely other people to be, in-German and in-Dutch philosophize." Notice the grotesquely embedded syntactic structure there. Schleiermacher wants to say that Grotius and Leibniz couldn't philosophize *at all* in Dutch and German, since that would confirm his rule: "Wie Einem Lande, so auch Einer Sprache oder der andern, muß der Mensch sich entschließen anzuhören, oder er schwebt haltungslos in unerfreulicher Mitte" (63)—"As to One Country, so also to One Language or another, must a person decide to belong, or he will hang disoriented in the unsettling gap between." But oops: Grotius and Leibniz belonged to two languages each. What now? Did they hang disoriented in the gap between? Well, no. They did do philosophy in Dutch and German and did so brilliantly. So Schleiermacher has to embed in the middle of his absolutist claim a rather significant qualifier: without becoming totally different people. So writing ("well") in a foreign language is okay if you don't "go doubled" but do become a totally different person? The wicked and magical art really only involves being the same person in two places at once, being yourself and your own ghost; it's okay, apparently, if you contrive to be two different people, one in each language. But how do you do that, exactly? Are we talking Multiple Personality Disorder here? Schizoid transitory identifications or full-blown schizophrenic psychosis? The interesting thing is that Schleiermacher's use of *Geist* here comes very close to blowing his cover: he wants Leibniz and Grotius to be able to be different people while doing philosophy in Latin and their native languages, but his *Bedürfnisse und Thätigkeiten und Richtungen des Geistes* make it sound suspiciously as if they are real people, only German and Dutch and ghosts (who thus "go doubled") in that dead language Latin.

Note also what Schleiermacher's imagination does in the middle of his passage about "going doubled like a ghost," when he is trying to laugh off the whole situation as a mimetic game, ha ha ha, nothing to get worked up about: the writer's memory images gather shape and form and rush into an eerie ghostly presence, *das gleichsam eine allgemeine Person vorstellt, schweben der Seele fast wie ein lebendiges äußeres Bild vor:* which like/almost (to translate more literally than I did above) a general person puts forth (or represents), hovers before the soul almost like a living external image. For Schleiermacher this whole social realm is so close to the occult that he can't even broach the subject, even in order to dismiss it quickly, without supernatural images flooding his inner vision, coming to life before his mind's eye, and pervading his rhetoric. Here Schleiermacher throws up similes to protect himself (and us) from the occult—fleshes forth *almost* or *as it were* a collective person, floats before the soul *like* a living simulacrum—but the fears he's fleeing are if anything even more evident here than when he refers to the needs and activities of the ghost/*Geist*. Foreign languages are scary places, ghostly places, where good German Lutherans should not wander. In Latin, intellect pops up a ghost; in every foreign language the writers you've read in that language haunt what you write like living simulacra. Stay away! Don't risk it! *Bleibt zu Hause!*

It's also interesting to think of Larry Venuti's article (and recent book by the same name) "The Translator's Invisibility" in this ghostly light: Venuti, following Schleiermacher, wants to make translations visible (also *material*, not merely spiritual things like ghosts) by leaving traces in them of the source text's foreignness; in his dictionary Grimm speaks of the *Schwartzkunst* or "black art" of making ghosts/*Geister* visible. In this scenario "going doubled" would play across the divide between black magic and Christian devotion, between "bad" and "good" translation: a "visible" or "foreignized" translation such as Schleiermacher and Venuti call for, one that does not pass for a text originally written in the target language, would be a ghostly double that is clearly marked as connected to or modeled on the "real" or "original" body, and thus would be morally preferable to one that attempts to pass for the real thing—but it would still be a double, still a ghost, and hence still the product of a "wicked and magical art." Does Schleiermacher believe in translation, or doesn't he? Is it a good thing to translate, or is it evil?

Note also in this connection that Schleiermacher calls the writer who attempts to write well in a foreign language a "deserter," a "traitor," an *Überläufer*, a "runner-across" or a "crosser-over," someone who crosses battle lines from his own camp into the enemy's (who can thus also be a "turncoat" in politics or an "apostate" in religion). For Schleiermacher the source-language writer writing in a target language has given himself up to another, *hat sich einer andern ergeben*, by "going doubled like a ghost" and crossing over from this reality into an alien enemy reality on the other side of some normally impermeable barrier. It is, again, awfully hard to avoid the implication that for Schleiermacher translation is evil, that it constitutes the same kind of treason or "going doubled," the same kind of crossing over into enemy territory. *Traduttore traditore; Übersetzen heißt Überlaufen*. Schleiermacher does want to avoid this implication, but he is so close to saying as much outright that the idea haunts, as it were, his whole essay.

Nor is he alone in his idea: the perception of translation as transgression, as a violent act akin to capture, treason, rape, and abuse, is pervasive among the romantics and their heirs. These writers have an uneasy sense that the translator's transgression is shot through with the occult, with the supernatural, with ghosts and doubles and shadowy intentions that inhabit languages and are awakened from their slumber by translation. In this belief the romantics seem remarkably close to the ancient mystery religions, which also guarded their sacred texts against both the profane and supernatural spirits that would punish them for disseminating the mysteries beyond proper bounds. The interesting difference in their beliefs is that for the romantics the enemy was not only the great unwashed, the masses who could never understand the sacred truths of philosophy and poetry, but also the source culture, the holder and withholder of those truths. The romantics are the first to romanticize translation as magical violence—a tendentious enough claim that I want to unpack it slowly, throughout the rest of this chapter.

Magic and Representation

One way of describing the astonishing intellectual and creative achievements of the romantics might be to say that they sought to tame or transform ancient magic into philosophy and art. Following their lead this whole chapter might be thought of as a kind of sympathetic magic effected with philosophical tools, which I learned from the romantics, to be used against the universalizing power of their thought. Not against their thought, specifically; I'm not interested in smearing or discrediting the romantics. Rather against the power of their thought to silence its opponents, a power that works not with the truncheon and the jail (as the Nazis did) so much as with vital and dynamic imagery, indeed with vitalism and dynamism, two mysterious forms of pagan magic that the romantics shared with (and arguably bequeathed to) the Nazis. The romantics were terrified of the encroachments being made on their (and our) humanity by capitalism and Calvinism, by science and technology, logic and mathematics, or (not to put too fine a point on it) by schizoid modernity, and they rebelled.

They did so with magic—the magic of words, perhaps, but then magic was always about words anyway, or about the transformative power of signs and symbols, a larger semiotic category that includes words. As Daniel Lawrence O'Keefe argues persuasively in his exhaustive social theory of magic, *Stolen Lightning* (1982), "In magic, individuals are able to take over especially powerful collective symbols (i.e., the sacred symbols of religion) and use them to think and to act effectively in the dangerous symbolic world in which man lives" (40). Magic, O'Keefe suggests, is a manipulation of society's most potent symbols in order to defend the individual against the dangers that a symbolically structured society poses for personal spontaneity, individual decision making: "magic fights to defend the individual ego against the social group from which it is born but which is capable of disintegrating it by the least pressure. The stolen fire, as the Prometheus legend tells us, is used to defend man, individual man—against the gods, the logos, the nomos, the superego, the society—to defend man's spontaneity against his socialization" (277).

This puts magic at the very heart of revolutionary cells, radical fundamentalist sects, charismatic movements, and virtually every other marginal group that would revivify a social order widely felt to be humanly or experientially bankrupt, a mere empty shell of rigid conformity to outdated rules. O'Keefe cites Bryan Wilson's *Religious Sects* (1970) to show how heavily most protest groups draw on magic in their attempts to undermine the hegemonic systems that they oppose—magic either in the strong sense, actual formalized rituals designed to combat society's witchcraft, or in the weak sense, symbolic gestures (speeches, writings, rallies, bombings, kidnappings) believed to wield transformative power over collective psychic forces. As I. M. Lewis shows in *Ecstatic Religion*, religious protest cults in particular are magical in bent, typically arising among powerless, peripheralized members of a society who flock to a shamanistic leader who promises to heal them and give them *spiritual* power. Given a strong enough growth curve, these cults may even become religions in their own right, as Christianity and Islam both did; as these become increasingly associated with the state or collective power and stability, they begin to rationalize and streamline ("purify") their ritual practices, shedding rites that they perceive as excessively magical. These discarded rites thereupon *become* magical and are picked up by rival or splinter groups that resist the rationalization of the major religion; the religion proscribes rival groups *as* magical and attempts to stamp them out, which lends the magical cult legitimacy among the disaffected; religions also develop their own countermagics, such as exorcism and witch burning. Religion and magic, as O'Keefe demonstrates at length, keep each other constantly, dialectically, in ferment (126–27).

And as M. H. Abrams implies in chapter 3 of *Natural Supernaturalism*, German romanticism was precisely this sort of magical protest sect, a group drawing on ancient mystical sources (Plotinean Neoplatonism, the Hebrew Kabbalah, Christian gnosticism) channeled through Jakob Boehme and German Pietism to rise up against the sterile rationalism, scientism, and technologism of late-eighteenth-century German (and generally European) society. Under the twin rallying cries of "life" and "imagination," the romantics sought to replace mechanism with vitalism, static conformity with dynamic change and flow and flux, rational control with magical creativity, and above all scientistic atomism with a primitive, animistic holism, the mystical belief that the universe is a single gigantic visionary (super)human body that has been vivisected by science and must be restored to its original unity.

"Magic," as O'Keefe writes, "raids across the border that taboo guards, into disorder, in derring-do razzias aimed at strengthening order and ego against fear of disorder by showing it can be beaten" (191)—and that derring-do is precisely the excitement of romanticism, the reason why for two hundred years intellectual rebels (like me) who feel stultified by their own hegemonic intellect, the rationalism in which they have been systematically trained throughout their school years, have turned to the romantics in exultation, in the overwhelming sense that here at last are mentors who will help me truly *live* my life! Where in chapter 2 I was concerned to explore and resist my own hegemonic training in schizoid metempsychotic thought, here in chapter 3 I want even more to explore and resist my counterhegemonic training in romantic magical protest. Not to overthrow it—it's still far too attractive for that—but to throw up some magical defenses against the worst of its excesses. Like most postromantics, I'm an addict, hooked on romantic magic:

> Magical curing, moreover, has in many cultures a propensity to become what Freud called "analysis interminable." Like a permanent member of A.A. or Synanon, the client is never really cured but remains relatively symptom-free only by staying inside the cognitive minority established around his disease and its curer. And so, in many cases, magical sects are actually illnesses spread by symbolism which catch people and force them to belong; membership in them is a lifelong chronic illness in a manner which suggests some respect for Freud's proposition that religion is the universal obsessional neurosis of mankind. The shaman defends the people against possession; his presence also *guarantees that this affliction will be a problem*, for he models the behavior. (O'Keefe 125)

And so, if this book is effective and influential enough to make me a "leader," a "curer" of (and through) the sympathetic magic of romantic translation theory, I too by modeling it will guarantee that this affliction will be a problem. All this is to say that even in my harshest critiques of romantic translation theory—especially of dogmatic "foreignism"—I make no claim to stand outside what I attack, to exempt myself from those critiques. Like all practitioners of magic, I attack from within, trying to clear a space of relative health within an illness that has spread through every cell in my body.

Magical Doubling

And it seems to me that this is precisely what the romantics themselves were trying to do as well: to apply a kind of performative bootstrap magic to the deadening forces of conformity that not only surrounded but permeated them. And in some wonderful and disturbing sense this is precisely what all *magicians* do as well: they attempt to abstract out of the web of symbolically charged objects and behaviors that constitute day-to-day living some *thing*, some sign or symbol, some word or sentence, some representative object or process that will (even if only for a few moments) stand outside of that web and give them power over it. This, as Daniel O'Keefe suggests, is why doubles are so important in magic: they allow individuals to operate not directly on reality, which is not only too powerful but too deeply ingrained in their own being for them to alter it, but on simulacra of reality, on shadows or images or echoes or doubles of real things and people, which might prove more pliant. "The recognition that magic consists of manipulating symbols of transcendent entities," O'Keefe writes, "helps explain some other questions. It helps us understand, for example, why magic is 'mystical action,' why it often 'doubles' things, so that it works on abstract or mystical doubles of the entities it seeks to affect—like the witch who eats the 'soul' of her victim and causes his body to die. These doubles are none other than the symbolic ideas or classes or abstract entities which are manipulated by this symbolization" (40–41).

But this is problematic; and in this section I want to explore some of the problems inherent in O'Keefe's formulation of doubles as "souls" and of souls as ideas. To say "These doubles *are* none other than the symbolic ideas" is to utter a magical performative (disguised as a scientific constative) that, O'Keefe hopes, will actively *prevent* those doubles from being anything other than signs, anything other than abstract semiotic units that can be controlled by the questing intellect. O'Keefe's conception of magic remains complicit in the same "Western" or "Christian" or "domesticating" (metempsychotic) dualism of bodies and souls/ideas that I explored in detail last chapter and that the romantics worked so hard to dislodge. O'Keefe's knowledge of magical doubles comes largely from Lucien Lévy-Bruhl's 1927 book *L'âme primitive,* translated in 1928 by Lilian A. Clare as *The "Soul" of the Primitive,* but O'Keefe falls right into the domesticating and dualizing trap that Lévy-Bruhl's book is a concerted effort to prevent. In her English title Clare (or her editor) has thrown up scare quotes around "soul," signifying to the book-jacket reader what Lévy-Bruhl insists on throughout, that what missionaries and other white "understanders" of primitive societies (including Frazer) thematize as "soul," the members of these societies often describe quite differently. As a tentative corrective to O'Keefe's symptomatic domestication of the stories Lévy-Bruhl tells from the field, a lengthy quote from Lévy-Bruhl's sixth chapter might be a good place to start:

> This very profound difference between the representations of primitives and our own has nevertheless escaped nearly all observers. Very often, indeed, it is regarded as a resemblance, especially by missionaries, Catholic and Protestant alike. It must be confessed that the attitude of the natives, far from putting them on their guard against this error, rather encourages them in it. In fact, when the missionaries explain that the corporeal and visible man is not the whole man, and that in spite of death and the corruption of the body, he continues to live on, the natives hasten to reply: "That is what we believe too." When they teach them that man's nature is a dual one, they at once approve the sentiment: "That is what we have always held!"
>
> Beneath this apparent agreement, missionaries and natives are in reality thinking very different things. To the white men's minds, it is a question of *dualism,* to the natives' minds, of *duality* [a nice "white man" dualism, by the way, that tells us more about Lévy-Bruhl than about the distinction he's trying to make]. The missionary believes in a distinction between two substances, the one corporeal and perishable, the other spiritual and immortal. United in this life, these two compose the living individual; death separates them, liberating the spiritual substance or soul, which is the real individuality. But nothing is more wholly foreign to the primitive's mind than this contrasting of two substances, the attributes of which are antagonistic. He feels, on the contrary, all beings to be homogeneous [and notice Lévy-Bruhl's "homogenizing" of all "primitives" as a single male "he"]. Nothing is purely matter; still less is it purely spirit. All things are bodies, or have bodies, and all possess in varying

> degrees the mystic properties which we ascribe to spirits alone. Thus where the missionaries see two heterogeneous substances temporarily united, the natives do not imagine anything of the kind.
>
> Nevertheless, when the missionary states that the nature of man is a dual one, they assent to the proposition, and they can do so in all sincerity, for although the idea of the *dualism* of substances is unknown to them, the *duality* of the individual is a very familiar one. They believe in the identity of a man with his image of picture, his shadow, his double—*tamaniu, atai, mauri, hau,* etc., and in his intimate participation in his *tjurunga, kra, ntoro,* and so on. Thus there is nothing to prevent them from showing their usual complaisance in not contradicting the foreigner, and even in agreeing with him politely. The blunder is later confirmed and intensified by the convenient but misleading use made by the white men of the word "soul" to express native ideas which are widely different from those the word conveys to us. (202–3)

The blunder is also "later confirmed and intensified," of course, by the fact that through interaction with nosy white visitors the natives also learn to translate their stories into the conceptual frameworks imposed on those stories by the visitors, ultimately into the languages in which the Christian concepts are framed—so that, asked about their conception of the *tjurunga* or *kra,* they will say "You know, it's what you call *l'âme,* the soul."

And this is patently a translation problem, one that has occurred when Western rationalists have gone abroad and learned a foreign language and then returned home and attempted to convey in their native languages what they discovered about the "primitive" culture. The lines of force in the various Western solutions to this translation problem are familiar. Some commentators—especially, according to Lévy-Bruhl, the missionaries—are content to assimilate "primitive" concepts to Western cultural values and say "soul." Others, especially anthropologists like Lévy-Bruhl himself, work harder to "foreignize" the target text, speaking mostly of the *tamaniu,* the *atai,* and so on, avoiding Western translations of the problematic source-language terms and taking care when they do translate to translate multiply—"his image or picture, his shadow, his double"—so that the Western reader is thwarted in his or her attempt to "grasp" the alien concept quickly through a familiar domestic concept.

But as Lévy-Bruhl himself insists, and as O'Keefe's "translation" of Lévy-Bruhl's work back into Western dualism illustrates, even this care is not enough; "our logic and our languages alike," he writes earlier, "do violence to the representations of primitives" (170). This is the crux of the matter for romantic translation theory, which is steeped in this early-nineteenth-century fascination with the primitive, with ethnographic studies of noble savages: *all* translation does violence to the representations of primitives. More, all translation does violence. Rather than burying their heads in the sand and pretending otherwise, as the mainstream tradition discussed in chapter 2 has typically done, the romantics have characteristically determined to accept that violence as unavoidable and to be quite open about it.

Another longish quote from Lévy-Bruhl, who is quoting from R. H. Codrington, who in turn is reporting his interpretations of Mota and Maori conceptions of shadows and reflections, will make this violence even clearer:

> "There is another Mota word, *tamaniu*, which has almost if not quite the same meaning as *atai* has, when it describes something animate or inanimate, which a man has come to believe to have an existence intimately connected with his own. The word *tamaniu* may be taken to be properly 'likeness,' and the noun form of the adverb *tama*, like. It was not everyone in Mota who had his *tamaniu*; only some men fancied that they had this relation to a lizard, a snake, or it might be a stone. . . . It was watched, but not fed or worshipped; the natives believed that it came at call, and that the life of a man was bound up with the life of his *tamaniu*, if a living thing, or with his safety, should it die, or if not living, get broken or be lost, the man would die. Hence in cases of sickness they would send to see if the *tamaniu* was safe and well. This word has never been used apparently for the soul in Mota; but in Aurora it is the accepted equivalent. It is well worth observing that both the *atai* and the *tamaniu*, and, it may be added, the Motlav *talegi*, is something which has a substantial existence of its own, as when a snake or stone is a man's *atai* or *tamaniu:* a soul then, when called by these names, is conceived as something in a way substantial."
>
> For the better understanding of this passage, we must place the following beside it. "There is a word used in Mota, never applied to the soul of man, but very illustrative of the native conception, and common also to Aurora, where it is used with a remarkable application: this word is *nunuai*. In Mota, it is the abiding or recurrent impression on the senses that is called a *nunuai;* a man who has heard some startling scream in the course of the day has it ringing in his ears; the scream is over and the sound is gone, but the *nunuai* remains. A man fishing for flying-fish paddles all day alone in his canoe with a long light line fastened around his neck; he lies down tired at night and feels the line pulling as if a fish were caught, though the line is no longer on his neck: this is the *nunuai* of the line. To the native it is not a mere fancy, it is real, but it has no form or substance. A pig, therefore, ornaments, or food have a *nunuai;* but a pig has no *atai*, or may hesitatingly and carelessly be said to have one. This word is no doubt the same as *niniai*, shadow or reflection. . . ." (142–43)

This passage, and most others in Lévy-Bruhl's book (many of which are similarly quoted from other anthropological studies), is fascinating in a study of translation first of all for the shock of recognition (the description's *nunuai*) it gives the translator, who has had this same experience thousands of times: the source text uses a word that is usually translated as "doughnut," but describes the thing (usually vaguely, allusively, in passing, in several different contexts, so that you're never sure whether you're dealing with the same object in every case) as flat, square, black, with no hole in the middle. What do you call it? What *is* the thing, first of all? Even if you can somehow piece together a rough image of it, can sort of see it in your mind, is there a word for it in the target language, or for something close enough to it that you can use it without taking the target reader too far afield? And what's "close enough," what's "too far afield"? How do you ever decide these things? How badly are you going to get hit by editors and other readers if you translate *atai, tamaniu, niniai, nunuai* as shadow, reflection, image, echo, muscle memory, soul, double?

O'Keefe also takes from Lévy-Bruhl the notion of witches eating a victim's soul, an action that kills the victim or causes him or her to take ill. Again, what O'Keefe wants to call the edible "soul" is extremely difficult to verbalize in Western terms. Among the Australian aboriginals of Victoria, for example, this "soul" or "life" is the kidney fat, which is sometimes a material substance "harvested" from the body of a dead enemy after a battle and other times a more spiritual or immaterial substance that has been "stolen" and eaten by a witch—as people suspect when they fall ill. In New Guinea witches eat the *tantau* or the *earua*, both of which are sometimes translated as "soul"—but both are and are not parts of the physical body. The people telling the story aren't quite sure what it is that the witch eats; it's not the flesh or any part of the body, but witches often disinter corpses and steal them, or parts of them. A sick person often says that a witch is eating him or her; this eating seems to take place without a physical attack, and without spells, though the witch seems to accomplish it by talking.

I should note that O'Keefe is just as determined to problematize the "primitive" notion of "soul" as is Lévy-Bruhl—but for different reasons. En route from the cover of Lévy-Bruhl's book in English translation to O'-Keefe's statement about doubling and symbolization, the telltale quotation marks around "soul" shift somehow, take on or are assigned a different trajectory or impact. Lévy-Bruhl (or Clare) puts quotes around "soul" because the temptation is so great to thematize the "doubled" entities on which magic is performed as souls, and he (or she) wants to resist that temptation; O'Keefe puts quotes around "soul" because he doesn't believe in souls and wants to distance his interpretation of magical doubling from those who do—a group that seems to include not only the Christian missionaries who kept trying to translate *atai* and the rest as "soul" but also Lévy-Bruhl (who did, after all, title his book *L'âme primitive*) and possibly even the witch herself. For O'Keefe, "These doubles are none other than the symbolic ideas or classes or abstract entities which are manipulated by this symbolization"—they are neither literal shadows nor souls nor some strange mixture of the two, in other words, but philosophical categories, ideas or classes, *abstractions*. O'Keefe dualizes the field into people who think of doubles as spiritual or supernatural things like souls (all the primitives and all the missionaries and other white Western observers lumped together) and people who recognize them for what they truly are, thought-constructs, ways of thinking about a thing (himself and other postromantic thinkers like him—including me). But is it not at least conceivable that the line might be drawn elsewhere? For example: those who think the doubles are purely immaterial, including the missionaries who call them souls and the sociologists who call them abstractions; and those who think the doubles span or transgress (or simply ignore) Western dualistic boundaries between spirit and matter, mind and body, self and other, including the natives and, possibly, Lévy-Bruhl.

Magical Allegories of Translation

After this lengthy excursus on magic, representation, and dualism, we're ready, I think, to bring some of the anthropological stories to bear on Schleiermacher's romantic metaphorization of (a certain kind of) translation as "going doubled like a ghost." Metaphor is itself, in fact, as O'Keefe reminds us, a form of verbal magic:

> In metaphors, connections are referred to between several words and therefore between the concepts or classes of objects they connote and so the appresentational power of symbols is magnified. James Fernandez writes that metaphors "get control" of strange situations by relating them to "familiar circumstances"; thereby they allay anxiety, provide tools for a plan of action and so make action possible (like Róheim's mental "plans" of action). Moreover, metaphors in action influence other people, because, as Fernandez colorfully puts it, "society is a movement of pronouns in quality space." He means that every metaphorical connection stated in speech influences the social position of entities, things and persons, and by so much "magically" affects their standing, status and power. (48–49)

This idea is extremely suggestive. If society is a movement of pronouns in quality space, then Schleiermacher's metaphor cuts both ways: translators become doubled-going ghosts, ghostly doubles become translators. A translator who goes doubled like a ghost infects the traffic of words across cultural boundaries with evil and death, according to Schleiermacher, but also, perhaps, as these stories will suggest, with the imaginative transcendence of boundaries and extremes; a ghost or a double that translates traps supernatural reflections and projections in a prison house or a paradise of language. Fernandez's wonderfully evocative phrase implicitly or potentially fleshes forth a complex allegory of translation or, perhaps—drawing on specific stories from Lévy-Bruhl's compendium—a whole series of allegories of translation, in which the magical metaphorical process runs both ways, from the occult to the verbal and back. This series is potentially infinite; let me illustrate the series with four different stories from Lévy-Bruhl's book.

The Soul-Eating Witch

If the magical translation of doubles Schleiermacher adumbrates follows the pattern mapped out by O'Keefe, then translational "going doubled" looks remarkably like the metempsychotic process charted by mainstream translation theorists from Jerome to Eugene Nida. O'Keefe's rather reductive reading of the soul-eating witch is flagrantly dualistic in the Western sense, precisely what Lévy-Bruhl works hardest (though perhaps in vain) to avoid; it is, in fact, closer to a witch story Bronislaw Malinowski heard in Trobriand, as related by Lévy-Bruhl. A Trobriander magician tells Malinowski that a witch *(yoyova)* casts a spell by staying in the house *and* traveling out on her "nefarious errand": in the magician's "own" words (as magically transformed by at least three different translators, Malinowski, Lévy-Bruhl, and Clare), "The *yoyova* casts off her body (literally, peels off her skin), she lies down and sleeps, we hear her snoring. Her covering (i.e. her outward body, her skin) remains in the house, and she herself flies. . . . Her skirt remains in the house, she flies naked. . . . In the morning, she puts on her body, and lies down in her hut" (quoted by Lévy-Bruhl, 169).

This metempsychotic story clearly begs to be read magically as an allegory of sense-for-sense translation, the "real witch" consisting of a spirit that leaves her body behind and puts it back on in the morning or, possibly, of a spiritual body that takes its carnal clothes off and gets dressed again in the morning. As we saw in the last chapter, in the Christian imagery that has saturated Western thinking about translation, the "meaning" is the spirit that shucks its source-language "words" as body or clothing in order to be reincorporated or dressed in a new verbal body or outfit in the target language. The witch or wizard and her or his victim are physical beings corresponding to the literal level of the source and target texts, the mere carnal or physical words, capable of being spoken and heard, recorded and replayed, written and read, photographed and displayed, printed and faxed; the real action in both magical doubling and mainstream (sense-for-sense) translating is spiritual, transcendental, abstract, at the level of "meaning." Diagrammed, the pattern looks even more familiar (see fig. 1). Substitute source text for witch and target text for victim and you have a fairly conventional picture of the source text metempsychotically determining the path of its own translation, controlling the terms by which it is first "spiritualized" or "doubled"—reduced to a stable transcendental "meaning" in the source language—then airlifted (in the abstract) to an equivalent transcendental "meaning" in the target language, and finally reformulated as a "physical" or verbalized text in the target language. That the vehicle of this metaphor for translation involves a witch eating the "soul" or liver or kidney fat or whatever of her victim highlights the aggressive nature of this hegemonic process, which is usually euphemized as a purely neutral semantic operation.

Figure 1.

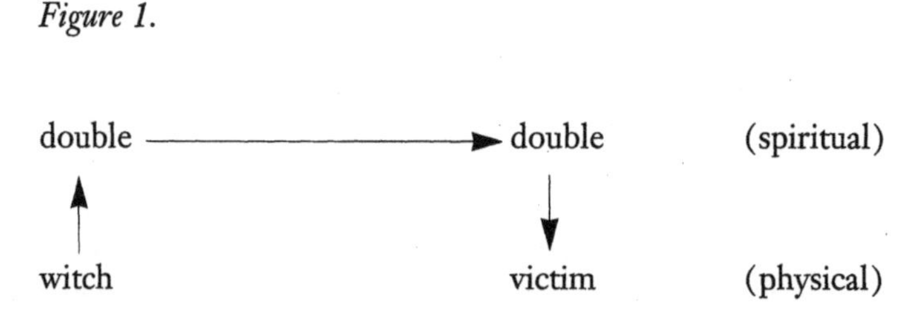

This diagram becomes even more interesting when we substitute not texts for people but people for people, the original author and the translator for the witch and her victim. If the original author is the witch and the translator is the victim, the conventional picture of translation as dominated by the original author's intention remains more or less the same, except that again the aggressive nature of that transaction is rarely highlighted so clearly; nor is the source author's domination of the translator's actions generally personalized this strongly (see fig. 2). The source author projects an intention, which is spiritual or transcendental (lying outside or above the physical text in a Platonic/mentalist realm of forms); that intention reaches through the miles and the years to impose itself upon the translator's interpretation, which exists somehow spiritually above or beyond and controls the translator's physical being and behavior; through that control the source author imposes his or her will on the physical act of translating.

Figure 2.

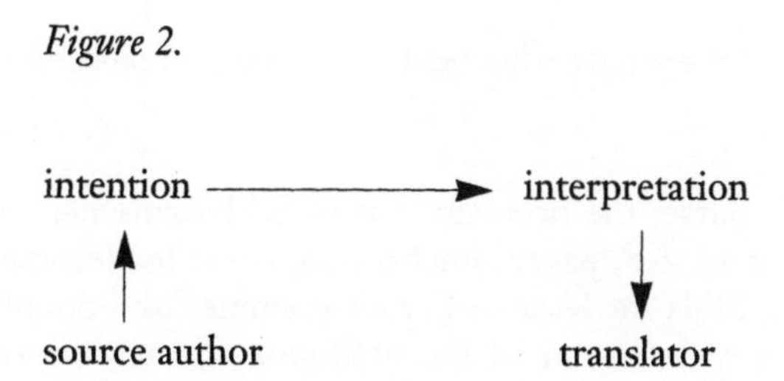

Switch it around, substitute the translator for the witch and the source author for the victim, and you generate (in hegemonic terms) a demonized image of the wrong kind of translation, which is in fact far closer to the hermeneutical reality of translation than the mainstream conception of translation (see fig. 3). The translator projects his or her interpretation outward, creates an imaginary "intention" for the source author, and incorporates that "magical spell" or "kidney fat" into a model interpretation that will regulate the target culture/reader's reception of the translation. Once again the witch analogy underscores the repressed hermeneutical violence in this process: the translator's ghostly double travels across occult boundaries to "steal" the source author/text's shadow (the "meaning" of the original work), then travels on—sometimes this second voyage is a return home, sometimes another leg in an ongoing journey—to cast a spell on the target culture/reader, to place that target nexus in her/his power.

Before we move on to greener pastures, note that there is a significant congruence between these hegemonic schemas of sense-for-sense translation and the tenor of Schleiermacher's metaphor, which was, after all, directed *against* domesticating or reductive or assimilative (sense-for-sense) translation. People say we should translate a text so that it reads in the target language as if the original author had originally written it in that language; but a source author writing originally and well in a target language is practicing a wicked and magical art akin to going doubled (like a ghost), so that's out. Schleiermacher doesn't go on and extend the doubling metaphor back to translation, and so doesn't try to imagine what the translator (or ghost, or wicked witch) *does* once doubled; this series of diagrams suggests one direction his imagination might have taken him. He or she eats someone's liver, or kidney fat, or double: he or she consumes the spirit of the foreign text.

Figure 3.

interpretation ——► intention ——► interpretation

↑ ↓ ↓

translator source author/text target reader/culture

There is also, of course, the problem that in Schleiermacher's imagination going doubled is wicked, pagan, unchristian, while for Jerome, Martin Luther, and Eugene Nida (at least as I've diagrammed the doubling) this doubling becomes a restatement of the orthodox Christian position on translation. Could this problem exist because Christian body-soul dualism has already so infused the anthropological translations of "primitive" witch stories that what Malinowski and other white observers find in the "primitive" customs they study are the projected paradigms of their own Western thought?

The Kra

Now let's try a different tack, based on the West African story of the *kra* or *okra*. Let me quote at some length (here Lévy-Bruhl is quoting from two books by Major A. B. Ellis, *The Ewe-Speaking Peoples* and *The Tshi-speaking Peoples*):

> In West Africa, on the Gold Coast, "the Tshi-speaking negro has arrived at the conclusion that he has a second individuality, an indwelling spirit residing in his body. He calls this a '*kra*.' . . . The *kra* existed before the birth of the man, probably as the *kra* of a long series of men, and after his death it will equally continue its independent career, either by entering a newborn human body, or that of an animal, or by wandering about the world as a *sisa*, or *kra* without a tenement. . . . The *kra* can quit the body it inhabits at will, and return to it again. Usually it only quits it during sleep, and the occurrences dreamt of are believed to be the adventures of the *kra* during its absence. The

> 'srahman' or ghost-man only commences his career when the corporeal man dies; and he simply continues, in the ghost-world or land of dead men, the existence the corporeal man formerly led in the world. There are, therefore, three individualities to be considered: first, the man; secondly, the indwelling spirit or *kra*; thirdly, the ghost or 'srahman'—though in another sense the last is only the confirmation of the first in shadowy form."
>
> Major Ellis is then concerned with the possible confusion of the *kra* with that which we call the "soul." He says: "The *kra* is not the soul. . . . Every *kra* has been the indwelling spirit of many men, and probably will be of many more. The *kra* in some respects resembles a guardian spirit, but it is more than that. Its close connexion with the man is indicated by the fact of its nocturnal adventures during its absence from the body being remembered by that man when he awakes. The latter even feels physically the effect of his *kra's* actions, and when a negro awakes feeling stiff and unrefreshed, or with limbs aching from muscular rheumatism, he invariably attributes these symptoms to the fact of his *kra* having been engaged in some struggle with another, or in some severe toil. If, moreover, a man dreams of other men, he believes that his *kra* has met theirs; consequently the *kra* is held to have the outward appearance of the man whose body he tenants. Hence the *kra* is more than a mere tenanting, or guardian, spirit. It has, though doubtless only in a shadowy form, the very shape and appearance of the man, and both the mind and body of the latter are affected by, and register the results of, the *kra's* actions." Although from certain points of view the man and his *kra* are distinct beings, in other respects they form one only, and they are blended in the individuality of the living person.
>
> "When the indwelling spirit leaves the body of the man it inhabits, that man suffers no physical inconvenience; it goes out, when he is asleep, without his knowledge; and if it should leave him when he is awake, he is only made aware of its departure by a sneeze or yawn. . . . When, however, the soul, the vehicle of individual personal existence, leaves the body, the body falls into a condition of suspended animation; it is cold, pulseless, and apparently lifeless. Sometimes, though rarely, the soul returns after such an absence, and then the man has been in a swoon or trance; more generally it does not return, and then the man is dead."
>
> The *kra* receives homage from "his" man. "The Ewe-speaking native offers worship and sacrifice to his indwelling spirit in much the same way as is done on the Gold Coast. In both cases the natal day of the man is the day kept sacred to the indwelling spirit, and is commenced by a sacrifice, either a sheep or a fowl, according to the means of the worshipper; after which the latter washes himself from head to foot, and always arrays himself in a white cloth." (192–94)

This sounds a bit like what we would call reincarnation, the same soul being reborn in a series of bodies—and the notion that through hypnotism or some occult means a person can remember or relive the experiences of his or her "soul" in past lives is certainly useful for a discussion of tradition. But there are also significant differences between the soul and the *kra*. One is that the *kra* is worshipped like a god, a kind of personal god that is also collective, an ancestor spirit that embodies the whole history of the people. This pattern exists in Western culture worship as well, in the reverence we are taught to feel for "the classics," first as the "great" or "immortal" writers of Greek and Roman antiquity, later as modern greats like Dante and Shakespeare and Racine. Harold Bloom would say (paraphrasing him only slightly to highlight the connection with mystic doubles like the *kra*) that nobody ever writes *anything* without struggling with the indwelling ghosts of the ancestral "gods" or "immortals" of his or her literary tradition. Another significant difference is that the *kra* (or *sisa* or *srahman*) continues to live in the ghost-world the life that its "human" lived on earth, suggesting that the *kra*'s experience is sociohistorically cumulative: every life lived on earth is "stored," as it were, in some *kra*'s suprahistorical experience and carried over into the next life it "tenants." This would be a magical explanation of what I've called ideosomatics, the transmission of collective values from one generation to the next through the contagion of somatic response: the parent's anxiety generates anxiety in the child as well, so an anxiety response to a certain object or behavior is passed on from generation to generation. And the *kra*, or its close relative the *okra* (as it is called by the Ga-speaking people who live midway between the Tshi and the Ewe), does cause various bodily perturbations (sneezes, yawns) during the day as well as by its wanderings at night: if the *okra* is upset, so is the human it lives in (195). Presumably the same sorts of things will upset the *kra* or *okra* in one life after another, providing for the cross-generational continuity of collective norms and values, like taboos.

Following Schleiermacher, then, we might read the Tshi-speaker with his or her *kra* and soul both inside as the source author, and the *kra*'s travels as precipitated (or marked) by the speaker dreaming, sneezing, yawning, or *translating*. The speaker might, for example, be imagined as dreaming in a foreign language, suggesting that his or her *kra* has traveled abroad and is interacting with the speakers of some other language, a target language, *in* that language.

And this seems to me a perfectly realistic depiction of bicultural and bilingual existence. I have, for example, a *kra* that is fluent in Finnish, and I hear it speaking sometimes at night, in my dreams; other times it inserts something into an English sentence, some Finnish word or particle that has no business in an English utterance, but there's just no accounting for the whims of a *kra*. For the last three or four weeks I have been translating addenda and corrections and EC declarations and whatnot for a chain saw manual I translated a month ago—all into Finnish, a direction I'm not fond of going when I translate, so I sort of sit back and let my Finnish *kra* take over. It knows what it's doing. I'm perfectly willing to go along with Schleiermacher and say that my Finnish *kra* is made up of "memory images of specific authors or of the manner of a certain era, which flesh forth as it were a collective persona, float before the soul almost like living simulacra that, when imitated on paper [or in my dreams], give the writing direction and definition"—and give the dreaming a powerful lifelike quality. The *kra* entered me gradually in 1971–1972, the year I turned seventeen and was an exchange student in Finland, and has only left me for brief periods since then, usually when I dream, sneeze, yawn, or translate; sometimes also when I'm not paying close enough attention to an English conversation and my *kra* slips out and goes to Finland or jumps over to a Finnish conversation going on among my wife and children. The *kra* has a lot of my wife in it, which is one reason I'm not gendering it male; it's a collective persona, neither male nor female, certainly not "me," though it often speaks through my mouth.

Taking this idea provisionally as an expansion or elucidation of Schleiermacher's formulation of "going doubled like a ghost" (like a *kra*), I only have two problems with his formulation. One is that my American English-speaking "self" feels a lot like a *kra* too: it too is collectivized, built out of bits and pieces of other people's voices, both male and female (my father tried to get me to model my persona only on male voices, but something didn't take, I have a lot of my mother in me too, and I have this sneaky suspicion that the same is true of other men as well), and while it has spoken through my mouth a lot longer than my Finnish *kra*, it often says things that I didn't think I intended to say, things I have little or no control over (even sometimes knowledge of!), so how can it be "me"? Maybe what Heidegger means by "language speaks us" is that the *kra* speaks us? I don't know.

The other problem I have with Schleiermacher's formulation is his insistence on calling this doubling "wicked." It feels pretty natural to me. According to Lilian Clare in her translation of Lévy-Bruhl's quotation from Major Ellis, it feels pretty natural to the Tshi- and Ewe-speaking peoples of West Africa as well.

The Wolf and the Leaf

A third take on "going doubled like a ghost" might be built around a Toradja story (from the Malay archipelago) of a man who went doubled as a wolf in order to seduce his neighbor's wife. The story goes like this: one night a man heard a voice whispering to his wife in bed, arranging a meeting for the next morning; he recognized the voice as his neighbor's, but opened his eyes and saw that the voice was coming from the body of a wolf. In the morning the woman remembered nothing but unwittingly made her way to the tobacco plantation where the meeting was to occur; the husband followed and watched the werewolf appear and greet his wife. The husband jumped out of hiding and struck the wolf, whereupon it became a leaf, which the husband seized and imprisoned in a piece of bamboo; carrying the bamboo and his unconscious wife back to the village, he threw the bamboo in the fire. The neighbor whose voice he had heard coming from the wolf's mouth had been up on the roof working all the while this was happening. He looked down to see the bamboo going into the fire and cried out "Don't do that!" but it was too late: as the bamboo burned, he fell off the roof, dead.

As Lévy-Bruhl remarks, "This man was a wizard, able to assume any form he liked; he changed himself into a leaf as another of his kind changes himself into an ants' nest. The fact that interests us here is that he is present, in his human form, in two different places at the same time" (163). This is not, Lévy-Bruhl goes on, "a case of a soul abandoning its body to dwell for a brief time in another one. It is simply an individual who is living at the same time in two different forms, either both human, or, again, very different" (164).

This story entails a series of doublings that, as Schleiermacher predicts, are explicitly thematized as wicked—the man was a wizard using black magic to have sex with another man's wife, and his death at the end of the story was his just desserts—and that are also explicitly contrasted with a just and righteous man (the husband) who doesn't "go doubled." Instead of minding his own business and staying in his own body, his own house, his own marriage, etc., the neighbor goes doubled like a wolf in order to commit adultery, to be unfaithful to his own wife, and to cause his neighbor's wife to be unfaithful to her husband. One Nation, One Language, One Marriage, One Body. Read allegorically as a story about (Schleiermacher's conception of) translation, the Toradja werewolf tale becomes a cautionary tale about infidelity, about breaking faith not so much with your spouse or body as with your language (stay out of that unsettling gap between languages, lest you become disoriented) and thus also, by extension, with the source text. If we imagine the neighbor as the source author and the wolf and the leaf as his attempts to write originally and well in the target language (possibly the same text in two successive target languages?), it becomes clear from the moralizing tone of the tale that he has become "a traitor to his mother tongue [and his wife tongue, and his friend tongue] by surrendering his verbal life to another." Schleiermacher goes on, you will recall, by saying that "it is no false or affected self-mockery when he protests that he can no longer move about in it," meaning in his mother tongue, and while the neighbor does *speak* in his own body (i.e., his mother tongue), calling out "Don't do that!" when the husband begins to burn the bamboo containing his leaf-double, it's at least possible that his freedom of movement is hampered, as he is unable to get down off the roof in time to save his double, and thus himself, from a fiery death.

But now if we imagine the neighbor as the source text or author and the wolf and the leaf as successive translations (into the same target language or into two different ones, possibly even the leaf as a secondary translation of the wolf as primary translation of the neighbor), then we really get into the issues of translational fidelity. The wolf and the leaf are radically transformed doubles, as indeed are translations; the only way the husband recognizes the wolf *as* the neighbor—identifying the target text as a translation of the source text—is through his voice: the wolf speaks with the voice of the neighbor. This might be read as confirming the hegemonic ideal for translation, new body (new words) but the exact same voice; but it might also, and perhaps more convincingly, be taken as pointing to foreignism, the attempt to leave some *trace* of the foreign original in the translated text. After all, the neighbor and the wolf behave in totally different ways: the neighbor is the husband's friend, respects his friend's marriage, does his own work; the wolf creeps around in the night trying to seduce his friend's wife. When the husband recognizes the wolf *as* the neighbor and decides to follow his wife the next day, he is proceeding on the basis of vocal resemblance: the wolf's voice *sounds like* the neighbor's voice—like that voice in a whisper, yet. It's not until the husband throws the bamboo in the fire and the neighbor shouts "Don't do that!" and dies that he gets any kind of confirmation at all that the neighbor and the wolf (and the leaf) are in any way connected; and while the neighbor's dying as the bamboo burns seems to prove that the neighbor *was* the wolf and the leaf, all the death really proves is that there was some integral connection or relation between the neighbor and the two doubles. In translational terms, we have three texts, N(eighbor), W(olf), and L(eaf), and we suspect one is the original and the other two are translations, because we think text W sounds like text N and we've physically seen text W being transformed into text L; also, though this sounds rather bizarre in a discussion of translation, when we burn text L, text N shrieks and dies (well, every allegory has its problems). But put it this way: text W contains, or seems to contain, the "voice" of text N; text L contains, or seems to contain, text N's "life." What we really have is a series of very different texts that are arguably connected by points of similarity or consanguinity. Depending on how we thematize these connections (for example, whether we believe in magical doubles), the three texts might be read variously as three different texts bearing a certain resemblance to one another; as an original and two unfaithful translations (look how differently texts W and L behave in comparison with the fine upstanding citizen N!); or as an original and two faithful translations (text W has text N's voice, text L its life).

Protecting the Double

Finally, let's imagine translation in terms of *protecting* a double against danger. In the Lévy-Bruhl material there are (at least) four different ways of doing this:

1. Brushing out footprints: the New Hebrideans sweep out the marks left in the dirt where they've been sitting for fear that a witch will gain power over them through the indentations (116).

2. Gathering up food remnants: a group of Saa in Melanesia discovered that their enemies were near and so escaped, but in their haste they left behind some areca nuts that their chief had fingered—he had taken some along to chew on the journey. One of the chief's younger brothers volunteered to return for the nuts, lest they fall into the enemy's hands and endanger the chief's life (117).

3. Hiding your double or "life" up in a tree: the Cherokee would hide their "lives" in a treetop before battle to protect themselves against harm, but once in a battle against the Shawano, who knew this magic, the enemy chief told his men to shoot their arrows into the branches above the

Cherokee chief; they did, and the chief fell over dead (134–35).

4. Keeping your shadow or reflection out of the reach of ghosts: in Melanesia, for example, ghosts lived in a *vunuba* or sacred pool, and people were careful not to pass the pool when the sun could cast their shadows into it for fear that the ghosts would seize the shadows and draw them into the pool to drown (136). The same would happen if a person were to look into the pool and see her or his reflection—the reflection or "double" would then "fall into the water" and be grabbed by the ghosts (136).

Here we might want to draw on O'Keefe's suggestion that the wizard or witch is an unconscious or unwitting representative of the society, the collective, which through the wizard or witch is attempting to assimilate the individual back into the faceless mass; magic is the individual's only defense against this attempt. This suggestion offers a way of translating the attempt to protect a double against witchcraft into an allegory of translation: we can read the witch or wizard who would "eat" the individual's double as the assimilative culture that would subsume a foreign text utterly into its own language, leaving no traces of its "otherness"; the shaman who magically protects the individual against this assimilation then becomes the foreignizing postromantic translator who marks the translation-as-double with some magical trace of its original, rendering it resistant to assimilation. This is, believe it or not, the main thing I wanted to deal with in this chapter: foreignizing translation. I haven't yet discussed it directly—so far I have just mentioned it in passing—but I'm getting there, just now, in the very next paragraph. Schleiermacher's going doubled like a ghost was to be my inroad into the subject, and it ended up generating all this other interesting material first.

The significant effect this particular allegory of translation has on the ethos of foreignism is that it suggests its basis in fear—something that I've never seen romantic or postromantic translation theorists actually mention. There is a tonal tightness to arguments for foreignism that hints at fear or some other powerful but repressed emotion, a sense that foreignism *really matters* (we're not just saying this for our health!). The defense-against-witchcraft allegory is one way of undoing these repressions and uncovering what may (or may not) lie beneath. It's not just that foreignizing translations are good and reductive domesticating translations are bad, as Schleiermacher, the Schlegel brothers, Humboldt, Benjamin, Heidegger, Berman, Venuti, and others rather dogmatically and doggedly insist; it's that the foreign text is somehow inexpressibly valuable, valuable not in the abstract but to me personally. In fact it *is* me, not just some piece of writing but a piece of my own soul, consanguinous with *me*, my double. And the assimilative target-cultural forces that would quite callously reduce it to just another piece of the same old slime, the same brown faceless depersonalized sludge that passes as "literature" or "culture" in every segment of this debased society, are a threat to my integrity as an individual. That the self is expansive is essential to romanticism: "I am large, I contain multitudes," as Walt Whitman (who also called himself a "kosmos") wrote. For the romantic *every piece of true or authentic expression is me*, part of the cosmic visionary me, which is currently scattered all over the world due to fragmentation brought on by scientific atomism, but truly and authentically me nonetheless, and in dire need not only of being incorporated, eventually, back into my visionary body, but also and more immediately of being protected against assimilation into the collective sludge, the faceless mass. (This personal/collective identification with national or nationalist texts is particularly poignant in a postcolonial context, and judging from Niranjana's *Siting Translation*, Homi Bhabha's *The Location of Culture*, and other similar works, romantic foreignism is far more popular in the West's former colonies as a form of resistance to the lingering effects of colonialism than it is in the West, where it often takes the peripheral academic form of elitist contempt for "complacent" or lower-class readers.)

But foreignism remains vague in these formulations: is there just one way to employ it in translation, or one motivation behind it, or one fear that it defends against? These are issues that none of the foreignists ever seems to address. Note, therefore, what happens when we image foreignism through the stories of protected doubles in the Lévy-Bruhl material:

1. By sweeping or brushing out the physical traces of your presence, you *eliminate* your double—or perhaps you only eliminate the visible or public aspect of the double, the part that is vulnerable to attack. In translation this might be thought of as doing a translation but not publishing it: for example, had I gone ahead and done a translation of the Rex Lee Jim poem but then not included it in this book; or had I taken a class in Navajo and done a translation to help me understand the poem but not sent it off to magazines. As we'll see in a moment, Walter Benjamin says explicitly that art is never for the audience, and only bad translations are written to help readers understand what they can't read in the original; repressed beneath this statement may be a fear that readers are witches or wizards who will do harm to the translation-as-double. The "purest" romantic translator may, therefore, translate only for his or her own pleasure, not for public consumption: the translator may translate a favorite poem, say, as literally as possible so as to *feel* the wonderful contours of the original in as powerfully visceral a way as possible but then destroy the translation. The main thing was doing the translation, not showing it around; why keep it? It might later fall into the wrong hands.

2. By gathering up the remnants of a meal and carrying them with you, you keep the double *close* to you, where you can physically protect it against attack. The translator who translates a poem for his or her own pleasure, or as an act of worship, or perhaps only in recognition of his or her kinship with it—creating a double that is at once the poem's and the translator's, and thus a bond between them—might simply throw it in a desk drawer, keep it close at hand, take it out every now and then to read over, possibly show it to a good friend, someone who can be trusted with it, but not publish it.

3. By hiding your double in a tree, or tucking it away somewhere in the foundation of your house, or burying it in the ground, you keep it far from *you* and thus safe from any direct assault on your person. This scenario is hard to imagine in relatively stable political systems, where assaults on the person of a translator are rarely so direct as to be readily identifiable as assaults. Usually these "assaults" happen through your livelihood dwindling away, your clients or translation agencies or editors calling less and less, you finding it harder and harder to earn money translating. Assaults on translators might be more common in a state of political unrest, where a radical or revolutionary translator translating incendiary materials designed to stoke the fires of revolution might want to publish a translation anonymously, in *samizdat* or broadsheet form. Doing so would serve to protect both the translator from the state power and the "double" or translation itself from prejudicial readings from that segment of the public that has not yet joined the revolution and might dismiss unread any piece of writing signed by a known dissident.

4. By avoiding the places where the ghosts and witches live, you keep your double far from *danger*. A book-length translation published with a major trade press is just asking for trouble, as is walking too close to the ghost pool at sunset, the time of day when the ghosts can reach out and grab your shadow. Avoiding the ghosts might require publishing your book with a peripheral small press, a press with a tiny marketing budget, so that only those people who really want to read your translation (and hopefully for all the right reasons) will go to the trouble to seek it out. Poems published in the newsletter of some society you belong to, some group of right-minded people, people who love (even worship) great literature, may bring you less glory, but they will be safer than if you published them in *The New Yorker*.

Walter Benjamin and the Afterlife

I originally planned to devote this chapter to a series of readings of major romantic and postromantic statements—by Herder, the Schlegel brothers, Wilhelm von Humboldt, Walter Benjamin, Heidegger, Antoine Berman, and Lawrence Venuti—in terms of the fascinating interweavings of foreignism, magical doubles, and fear. I wanted, after all, to devote this last chapter to a portrait of an entire school of thought about translation, indeed a major sociocultural movement that is still very much alive today; and so far I have only begun to lay the groundwork for such a portrait, which in even a sketchy form would almost certainly have required a chapter as long as chapter 2. In the name of brevity, however, I have reluctantly decided to pare that list of names down to one: Walter Benjamin's famous 1923 esssay "Die Aufgabe des Übersetzers," "The Task of the Translator," a notoriously difficult piece that has been explicated at great length by some of the finest minds in the business, Jacques Derrida, Paul de Man, Tejaswini Niranjana, Andrew Benjamin, and many others. What I want to suggest here is that the essay's difficulty stems from a certain romantic vagueness in it that seems to me largely a way of *not* talking about magical doubles. There are numerous buried subtexts in Benjamin's essay, and magical doubles are unquestionably only one of them; but I do think the "Task" makes more sense if we explore the ways in which originals, translations, and languages for Benjamin *all* go doubled like ghosts.

I would suggest, in fact, that Benjamin's title is deceptive: part of the trouble I always have reading his argument is that I keep expecting him to talk about the task of the *translator*, what a human being in the act of translating should be trying to do, and while he does address that issue once or twice in passing, the major thrust of the essay concerns the task of *translation*. The focal agents in his argument are not people at all, but texts and languages, the source text and the target text, the source language and the target language (it's more complicated than that, but grant me that much to start with); hence, I think, the importance of beginning his argument by denying the relevance of readers, or generally of reception, to art: "Nirgends erweist sich einem Kunstwerk oder einer Kunstform gengenüber die Rücksicht auf den Aufnehmenden für deren Erkenntnis fruchtbar" (156), or, in the kind of literal arcade Benjamin calls for, "Nowhere proves itself in relation to an art work or an artform the backlook onto the receptor for its appreciation fruitful." "Denn kein Gedicht gilt dem Leser," he says at the end of that paragraph, "kein Bild dem Beschauer, keine Symphonie der Hörerschaft" (156): "For no poem concerns or is aimed at or is meant/intended for the reader, no picture for the beholder, no symphony for the audience."

And the corollary of that bald assertion in the context of Benjamin's essay as a whole, it strikes me, is that no poem is made by the poet, no painting by the painter, no symphony by the composer (or even, possibly, the orchestra), no translation by the translator. We're somewhere in the vicinity of Heidegger's assertion, which will come several decades after Benjamin but is steeped in the same romantic philosophy of language, that language speaks us, and we speak only insofar as we let ourselves be spoken by language, let it speak through us. The overriding assumption throughout Benjamin's essay seems to be that what *people* do is secondary to what their textual or linguistic doubles do—that the real action is performed not by translators or authors or painters or composers or audiences but by their doubles.

The dramatic action in Benjamin's essay in a nutshell is that the source language has taken pure language prisoner, put her under a spell (and this is where we start exploring the gender politics in all this aggressive magic), and only the translation, with the help of the intentions in both the source and the target languages, can free her. The dramatis personae in this action are, as I say, texts and languages, and in fact most of them—reading them through the literal arcade that Benjamin requires of truly "free" translation, the kind of translation that is capable of freeing pure language from prison, releasing her from her spell—are (grammatically) women: *die Übersetzung* "the translation" (which is, Benjamin tells us, *eine Form* [157], which Harry

Zohn translates "mode" [70] and Andrew Benjamin "model" [89]), which might be translated more loosely as "a way of proceeding," but more tightly—and thus according to Benjamin more "freely"—as "a feminine form"), *die Sprache* "language" and *die reine Sprache* "pure language," and *die Intention* "the intention." All are grammatically coded as feminine—a fact that the people Benjamin calls "bad" translators ignore but that must be taken seriously in the kind of rigorously literal translation he demands.

But more of that in a moment. Let me start a little further back; let me try to tease out of Benjamin's text the magical drama that I believe informs it. I'll start with the famous passage on the "afterlife" of a text:

> So wie die Äußerungen des Lebens innigst mit dem Lebendigen zusammenhängen, ohne ihm etwas zu bedeuten, geht die Übersetzung aus dem Original hervor. Zwar nicht aus seinem Leben so sehr denn aus seinem "Überleben". Ist doch die Übersetzung später als das Original, und bezeichnet sie doch bei den bedeutenden Werken, die da ihre erwählten Übersetzer niemals im Zeitalter ihrer Entstehung finden, das Stadium ihres Fortlebens. In völlig unmetaphorischer Sachlichkeit ist der Gedanke vom Leben und Fortleben der Kunstwerke zu erfassen. Daß man nicht der organischen Leiblichkeit allein Leben zusprechen dürfe, ist selbst in Zeiten des befangensten Denkens vermutet worden. Aber nicht darum kann es sich handeln, unter dem schwachen Szepter der Seele dessen Herrschaft auszudehnen.... (158)

> So as the expressions of the life most intimately with the living hang together, without signifying much to it, goes the translation out of the original forth. To be sure not out of its living so much as out of its "overliving." Is after all the translation later than the original, and marks she after all by the significant works, which there their chosen translators never in the era of their origin find, the stage of her forthliving. In fully unmetaphorical thinginess is the notion of the living and forthliving of the art work to be grasped. That one not as the organic bodiliness alone life address should [that you shouldn't think of life purely as organic corporeality], has itself in times of the most prejudiced thought been guessed. But not about that can it itself handle [but it can't be a matter of] under the frail scepter of the soul its mastery out to stretch....

This is, clearly enough, even through the arcade of my literal rendition, a paean to life and living—but what kind of paean? Benjamin has three different kinds of *Leben* "life, living," one plain *Leben* and two *Leben*-compounds, and *das Lebendiges* "the living, that which is alive," all of which I've tried to keep distinct in my translation. But in the first mention of *das Leben* I hear "life" as an abstract noun, in the second (where he contrasts it with *Überleben* "over-" or "outliving") I hear it as a nominalized verb, which of course it is, hence as "living"—partly, probably, to parallel "outliving"—which then rather confusingly overlaps with "the living," which renders *das Lebendiges*, a nominalized adjective. The key words in this passage, though, are the compounded "lives," *Überleben* and *Fortleben*, which I rendered above with radical literalism as "overliving" and "forthliving" (a delaying tactic—I didn't want to prejudice my discussion below); these Benjamin uses almost synonymously (but not quite), more or less under the broadest possible semantic umbrella of "survival." Harry Zohn gives for *Überleben* "afterlife," for *Fortleben* first "continued life," then "afterlife" (71)—an uneasy compromise that works, sort of, though only in the metaphorical sense that Benjamin renounces, since of the two only *Fortleben* can be used to mean "afterlife, life after death."

Both *Überleben* and *Fortleben* mean living beyond some temporal boundary, a living that goes on beyond a transitional event; the difference between them is that *Überleben* goes on past the death of a loved one, while *Fortleben* goes on past the actual or expected death of the self. You outlive or survive *(überlebt)* a spouse or a friend or a parent or a child, someone who should have gone on living with you (or apart from you) but died; you live on or survive *(fortlebt)* when you should have died (in a car crash, say, or past your statistical life expectancy) but didn't, or when you did die but somehow kept on living. It's only in this last sense that *Fortleben* means "afterlife, life after death"; but Benjamin does seem to be thinking about life after death, given his care to dissociate his objectively unmetaphorical *Fortleben* from both the body (and thus life *before* death) and the soul (and thus conventional Christian conceptions of the afterlife). He sounds, actually, a bit like Lévy-Bruhl in his attempt to sail between the Scylla and Charybdis of Christian eschatological dualism while naming a living-forward beyond the boundary of death.

Since Benjamin insists that we not forget the connotations of words, I should also note that both words resonate in other directions as well. *Überleben* has *über* "over" in it, and resonates with size, especially largeness, and more figuratively with superiority: the "overlife" or "superlife" of an original might be connected connotatively with *der Übermensch* "Superman, the overman," or with the imperialist anthem *Deutschland, Deutschland über alles* "Germany, Germany over everything." *Überlebensgross* also means "larger than lifesize," literally "overlifelarge." *Fort* is an adverb signalling both removal in space ("away," "gone," "off") and continuation in time; and while the conventional semantic field of *Fortleben* restricts *fort* there to the latter (temporal) extension, a literal arcade achieves its openness by embracing all resonances. It might be useful, therefore, to explore a *Fortleben/Daleben* pair along the lines of *Fortsein/Dasein*, living or being away versus living or being (t)here, especially drawing on Freud's *fort/da* game from *Beyond the Pleasure Principle*. *Ist der Walter da? Nee, der ist fort.* The spatial configuration of living in English, living in a certain place, is handled by a different verb in German, *wohnen*, so you wouldn't use *leben* in a parallel sentence like "Does Walter live there? No, he lives elsewhere, he lives away from here"; but where *do* you live after you die? Here? Da? Or fort?

One of the problems in the passage I quoted, of course, is that it's hard to say exactly when an original or source text "dies": the vehicle of Benjamin's (anti)metaphor is a little fuzzy. It's only after the death of the original, during the time of its outliving or living on, that the translation goes forth from it; but at what point does it stop living and start outliving or onliving? If we take the original as the double (say, the *kra*) of the original author, then perhaps its afterlife begins when the author dies? Or perhaps when the author is through writing (or rewriting) it, when it is sent off to be published and distributed to a wider readership? The *kra*, you will recall, continues its former owner's life after that owner's death—although *where* that life is continued the Tshi-speakers couldn't say, except that it is somewhere "away" *(fort)*, where the dead go. And like whatever it is that outlives (the author or his/her work) or onlives in or as the original, the *kra* is not the soul, nor exactly what we'd call a body; it's a double that is like a body and like a soul but is actually neither. It leaves the body in sleep, sneezes, and yawns; its adventures outside the body are played out in its owner's imagination as dreams, a common enough metaphor for (and imaginative source of) artistic creations as well; but it's also a body in itself. And whether we imagine an original artwork-as-*kra* as the afterlife of an act of creation or of the life of its creator, the *kra* story helps explain the language-speaks-us bias of romantic thought: the *kra* is an active personalized force that creates or perpetuates itself through the agency of its human "creator." It also helps explain the fact, and the relative unimportance, of reception: if the *kra* is a literary work, its next host is a reader, whose life is transformed by the experience of living with and as the work. Still, the active force, the agent, is the *kra;* the human owner or vehicle of the *kra* shares its experiences, feels them as his or her own, but they issue from the *kra*. Hence it is never fruitful to look back at the *kra*'s human vehicle, author *or* reader.

Benjamin's myth of the origin of translation, that it "goes forth" from the original *(geht aus dem Original hervor)* during its afterlife, fits this retelling as well, though problematically. If the *kra* inhabits first the original author and then a reader who experiences it in a different language (i.e., "translates" it), the translation-as-*kra* "goes forth" or issues from the original in the sense of succeeding it, of being the next "expression of life" in an ongoing series of such expressions. This retelling tends to undermine Benjamin's insistence on the once-and-for-all originality of the original and the dead end marked by the translation: the *kra* just goes from life to life, experiencing and expressing, carrying the experiences from one life on into the next, without a clear beginning or definite end. Like Jacques Derrida and most of Benjamin's other poststructuralist readers, I prefer the deferred *kra* version to Benjamin's; the notion that an original is truly original, that it marks the beginning of something totally new, is a rather dubious idealization, and the notion that translations are untranslatable, that the infinite process of formulating and reformulating texts somehow stops dead in a translation, is a bizarre invention. For that matter, Benjamin's claim that only certain originals are translatable is equally dubious, though somewhat less conventional than the claim that originals are original and somewhat less idiosyncratic than the claim that translations are untranslatable. The interesting thing to note about these latter distinctions (translatable/untranslatable, beginning/end) is that, retold as part of a *kra* story, they seem secondary and superficial, nervous tics important more as class indicators than as integral parts of the plot. Benjamin's elitist project requires that he be able to distinguish the "good" stuff (the books he and his friends like) from the "bad" stuff (the books that the masses like); but his argument doesn't depend on the relative persuasiveness of his elitism.

What does matter is why the translation comes into being, what its purpose or entelechy is (Benjamin doesn't use the Aristotelian word, but implies it, with words like *Zweckmäßigkeit*, literally "end-measuredness" [159]), or, dramatistically, what its role is in the drama being enacted. (In fact, "Der Zweck des Übersetzens" or "Die Rolle des Übersetzens" might have been a better title for the piece; Benjamin really couldn't care less about the translator's task.) "So ist die Übersetzung zuletzt zweckmäßig," he writes, "für den Ausdruck des innersten Verhältnisses der Sprachen zueinander" (159): "So is the translation last of all end-measured for the expression of the innermost relationality of languages to each other." That's the "end" or the "role" of translation: to express (and, as we'll see, to further) languages' interrelatedness. And it does this not by rendering words and phrases accurately from one language to another but by sounding out the mystical "intentions" of the source and target languages. This is a strange concept that nobody quite knows how to talk about:

> Worin kann die Verwandtschaft zweier Sprachen, abgesehen von einer historischen, gesucht werden? In der Ähnlichkeit von Dichtungen jedenfalls ebensowenig wie in derjenigen ihrer Worte. Vielmehr beruht alle überhistorische Verwandtschaft der Sprachen darin, daß in ihrer jeden als ganzer jeweils eines, und zwar dasselbe gemeint ist, das dennoch keiner einzelnen von ihnen, sondern nur der Allheit ihrer einander ergänzenden Intentionen erreichbar ist: die reine Sprache. Während nämlich alle einzelnen Elemente, die Wörter, Sätze, Zusammenhänge von fremden Sprachen sich ausschließen, ergänzen diese Sprachen sich in ihren Intentionen selbst. (161)

> Wherein can the relatedness of two languages, disregarding a[ny] historical [one], be sought? In the similarity of poems in any case even as little as in that of their words. Much more rests all suprahistorical relatedness of the languages therein, that in each of them as a whole at times one [thing], and indeed the same is meant, which nevertheless through no single one of them, rather only through the allness of their one-another [mutually] supplemented intentions reachable is: the pure language. While namely all single elements, the words, phrases, together-hangs [contexts] from foreign languages each other shut out [are mutually exclusive], supplement these languages each other in their intentions themselves.

Whew! For an arcade, that's hard labor (I thought arcades were supposed to be fun). Here's the gist, the fun part that Benjamin eschews (sorry, but I have a hard time sticking to his literalist ascesis). Sure, languages are historically related, but aside from that, how are they really *related* mystically—I guess he means "suprahistorically." The relationship between languages is not in the fact that you can take two literary works and show that they are overall alike or that they have similar words. Mystically their kinship arises out of the fact that they all strive for the same thing, pure language, but can do so only through the mutual supplementation of their intentions: no one language can do it alone (or rather the intention of no one language can *reach* pure language alone). Individual elements in different languages shun each other, as my lame attempts at literal translations of Benjamin show—the words and phrases are different, they are contextualized differently, as every translator knows—but (and here's the kicker) languages supplement each other (and thus push toward the achievement of pure language) "in" their intentions.

Did that clear things up?

Well, languages are agents too, like texts: they are dramatis personae in Benjamin's play. They have bodies, and they also have intentions, which could be thematized as their "spirits," perhaps even their "souls," though we have seen that Benjamin would rather not take his (anti)metaphor in that particular direction. They sound, though I know this is starting to get repetitive, like *kras*, the collectivized doubles of individual languages, which need each other to feel complete, need the supplementation they get from other *kra*-intentions. The languages themselves are the boring sign systems that philologists and linguists study, just as psychologists and sociologists study "humans themselves"; the *kra*-intention is the active double (the double agent) that magicians and mystical philosophers employ. Languages, like humans, are active, of course, in their own blind, stupid way; the thing is, like most humans they have no idea what they're doing. It's the intention in each of them, the *kra*, that knows what the language needs and goes after it:

> Wenn aber dieser [Kern der reinen Sprache], ob verborgen und fragmentarisch, dennoch gegenwärtig im Leben als das Symbolisierte selbst ist, so wohnt er nur symbolisiert in den Gebilden. Ist jene letzte Wesenheit, die da die reine Sprache selbst ist, in den Sprachen nur an Sprachliches und dessen Wandlungen gebunden, so ist sie in den Gebilden behaften mit dem schweren und fremden Sinn. Von diesem sie zu entbinden, das Symbolisierende zum Symbolisierten selbst zu machen, die reine Sprache gestaltet in der Sprachbewegung zurückzugewinnen, ist das gewaltige und einzige Vermögen der Übersetzung. In dieser reine Sprache, die nichts mehr meint und nichts mehr ausdrückt, sondern als ausdrucksloses und schöpferisches Wort das in allen Sprachen Gemeinte ist, trifft endlich alle Mitteilung, aller Sinn und alle Intention auf eine Schicht, in der sie zu erlöschen bestimmt sind. Und eben aus ihr bestätigt sich die Freiheit der Übersetzung zu einem neuen und höheren Rechte. Nicht aus dem Sinn der Mitteilung, von welchem zu emanzipieren gerade die Aufgabe der Treue ist, hat sie ihren Bestand. Freiheit vielmehr bewährt sich um der reinen Sprache willen an der eigenen. Jene reine Sprache, die in fremde gebannt ist, in der eigenen zu erlösen, die im Werk gefangene in der Umdichtung zu befreien, ist die Aufgabe des Übersetzers. (166–67)

> If but this [kernel of pure language], if hidden (in a mountain) and fragmentary, nevertheless present in the life as the symbolized itself is, so lives he [that kernel] only symbolized in the creations. Is that last essentiality, which there the pure language itself is, in the languages only to the linguistic and its wanderings bound, so is she [pure language] in the creations burdened with the heavy and foreign meaning. From this her to unbind, the symbolizing into the symbolized itself to make, the pure language formed in the language motion back to win, is the mighty and sole capacity of the translation. In this pure language, which nothing more means and nothing more expresses, but rather as expressionless and creative word which in all languages meant is, meets finally all communication, all meaning and all intention on a layer in which they to die out are destined. And even out of her [that layer], entitles itself the freedom of the translation to a new and higher right. Not out of the meaning of the communication, from which to emancipate precisely the task of the fidelity is, has she [fidelity] her permanence. Freedom much more tests itself around the pure language's will [for pure language's sake] on its own. That pure language, which in foreign bewitched is, in the own to let loose, the in the work imprisoned in the reworking to free, is the task of the translator.

This, it seems to me, is the climax of Benjamin's drama; a dénouement follows, rising to another rush of purple oratory in the last few lines of the piece, two pages away, but the action peaks in this daring magical jailbreak in which pure language is released from the spell that traps it in a single work in a single foreign language. This countermagic, traditionally the work of the shaman, is assigned provisionally to the translator in that last line in and through the act of reworking a source text in a target language; but by this point in the essay it's pretty hard to imagine the poor *translator* taking on a supernatural task like this one. The translator's magical double, maybe, or the translation itself could take on this task; or it could be done by what might be imagined as the translation's double, *die Treue*, fidelity, whose task Benjamin makes this "emancipation" a few lines above; or, better yet, by the two languages' doubles, the intentions, working together, supplementing each other. The translator (*der Übersetzer*, a man) translates—blindly, stupidly, without really knowing what he's doing. The translator's double, the translation, *die Übersetzung*, a woman (or perhaps, since German doesn't often make this distinction, not *the* translation but plain old "translation," translation as a generalized activity), does the first important work, which is to stir up the intentions (or doubles) of two different languages, to bring them into forcible confrontation, to commingle them. The intentions (*die Intentionen*, more women) do the rest and die gloriously in the process along with those inferior linguistic doubles, communication and meaning, which have been dragging their feet and making things harder for the intentions all along—actually, they may even be the witch (*die Mitteilung*, a woman) and wizard (*der Sinn*, a man) that cast the spell on pure language (*die reine Sprache*, a woman, the maiden in distress) in the first place and trapped it in a single source language.

And so we move from a dystopian scene, translators plugging away at meanings, trying to convey information to readers, blinded and stupefied by millennia of disinformation about translation, the intentions in each language languishing in sterile isolation, pure language under a spell, buried under tons of alien meaning, longing for release . . . to the exciting climax of the hero myth, the shaman summoned by the concerted efforts of the *kra*-intentions and uttering the words that break the spell, the prison dropping away like the air out of which it was made, the spellbinders and imprisoners and rescuers alike vanishing in a puff of blue smoke, and pure language finally emerging triumphant. The action is all magical, performed in the filmy realms of the occult, the supernatural, the thaumaturgical, where ordinary humans like the translator dare not tread.

And yet, in the end, Benjamin returns to the translator, saying in essence, okay, now you know what to do, go and do it. Who, me? *I* know what to do? Panic! Most translators, as if in confirmation of Benjamin's harsh judgment of their abilities, don't even read him; he's too difficult. He doesn't make sense! Others, having heard theorists speak highly of it, struggle through his essay, struggle to make sense of it, and get mainly the few remarks that Benjamin addresses to them (especially in Harry Zohn's translation, which I'll give this time):

> Eben darum muß sie [die Übersetzung] von der Absicht, etwas mitzuteilen, vom Sinn in sehr hohem Maße absehen, und das Original ist ihr in diesem nur insofern wesentlich, als es der Mühe und Ordnung des Mitzuteilenden den Übersetzer und sein Werk schon enthoben hat. (165–66)

> For this very reason translation must in large measure refrain from wanting to communicate something, from rendering the sense, and in this the original is important only insofar as it has already relieved the translator and his translation of the effort of assembling and expressing what is to be conveyed. (78)

> Die wahre Übersetzung ist durchscheinend, sie verdeckt nicht das Original, steht ihm nicht im Licht, sondern läßt die reine Sprache, wie verstärkt durch ihr eigenes Medium, nur um so voller aufs Original fallen. Das vermag vor allem Wörtlichkeit in der Übertragung der Syntax, und gerade sie erweist das Wort, nicht den Satz als das Urelement des Übersetzers. Denn der Satz ist die Mauer vor der Sprache des Originals, Wörtlichkeit die Arkade. (166)

> A real translation is transparent; it does not cover the original, does not block its light, but allows the pure language, as though reinforced by its own medium, to shine upon the original all the more fully. This may be achieved, above all, by a literal rendering of the syntax which proves words rather than sentences to be the primary element of the translator. For if the sentence is the wall before the language of the original, literalness is the arcade. (79)

Reading this, and understanding it, the translator says "this guy must be nuts." Willis Barnstone, for example, in *The Poetics of Translation*, argues that Benjamin can't possibly mean what he's saying (251). Foreignizing translators and translation theorists like Antoine Berman, Tejaswini Niranjana, and

Larry Venuti read Benjamin's radical mystical literalism more tamely as a call not for absolute word-for-word impossibility but for a more perspicacious foreignism, the willingness to leave some trace of the source text's foreignness in the translation. Postromantic theorists like George Steiner, Jacques Derrida, Paul de Man, Andrew Benjamin, and Doug Robinson, drawn to Benjamin's Kabbalistic mysticism and dense-pack imagery, deconstruct him, push and nudge him until he comes to sound as if he were supporting (or at least exemplifying) their own theories.

And all because, ultimately, Benjamin is assigning the translator a task that is (or seems) not only impossible but virtually unimaginable, a superhuman hero task that requires real magic, magic in the strong sense, the magic of dreams (and nightmares), the kind of magic that we see only in the movies and read about in the ancient myths. Even in Benjamin's own terms, when he is still of a mind to be fair about it, the translator is only the unwitting trigger or catalyst that sets the whole mystical Rube Goldberg contraption in motion, clickety-clack, toward the ultimate fulfillment of mystical dreams. So is it the "task" of the translator to be this trigger, to be flipped (by some mystical double, the true agent in the drama) like a switch? No, by the end of the essay the translator's task is to free the damsel in distress from magical powers and principalities and save the world. Maybe I'm just too cozy with the Other-as-reason, but I'll take a rain check. Find somebody else, Walter; I'm too busy translating chain saw manuals.

Blendlinge

Where do we go from here? How do we live, how do we translate? My take on both the metempsychotic theories of chapter 2 and the magical theories of chapter 3 has been largely negative, even pugilistic; is there any hope, any middle ground between or beyond the two?

In a trenchant reading of Schleiermacher's "Methods," Anthony Pym begins to point the way out of some of the worst dead ends into which both metempsychotic and romantic theories have led us precisely by showing how the dead ends are conditioned by the rationalist *non distributio medii* (the hidden form of all dualistic thought) and how the middles excluded by the polarized extremes—sense-for-sense and word-for-word, author-to-reader and reader-to-author, domestication and foreignism—always have to do with the ongoingness of real human life. His "underlying hypothesis," Pym writes, "is that Schleiermacher's two opposed methods suppress a hidden middle term, the living translator, and that the whole of Schleiermacher's text is designed to silence that middle term" (5). Here is the key passage in Schleiermacher:

> Aber der eigentliche Uebersezer, der diese beiden ganz getrennten Personnen, seinen Schriftsteller und seinen Leser, wirklich einander zuführen, und dem lezten, ohne ihn jedoch aus dem Kreise seiner Muttersprache heraus zu nöthigen, zu einem möglichst richtigen und vollständigen Verständniß und Genuß

> des ersten verhelfen will, was für Wege kann er hiezu einschlagen? Meines Erachtens giebt es deren nur zwei. Entweder der Ueberstzer läßt den Schriftsteller möglichst in Ruhe, und bewegt den Leser ihm entgegen; oder er läßt den Leser möglichst in Ruhe und bewegt den Schriftsteller ihm entgegen. Beide sind so gänzlich von einander verschieden, daß durchaus einer von beiden so streng als möglich muß verfolgt werden, aus jeder Vermischung aber ein höchst unzuverlässiges Resultat nothwendig hervorgeht, und zu besorgen ist daß Schriftsteller und Leser sich gänzlich verfehlen. (47)

> But what paths are open to the true translator, one who would bring those two utterly unconnected people together, the author and the reader—and would aid the latter, without banishing him or her from the sphere of the mother tongue, in attaining as accurate and thorough an understanding and enjoyment of the former? I believe there are only two. The translator either disturbs the writer as little as possible and moves the reader in his direction, or disturbs the reader as little as possible and moves the writer in his direction. The two approaches are so absolutely different that no mixture of the two is to be trusted, as that would increase the likelihood that the writer and reader would miss each other entirely; it is important, therefore, that one or the other be followed as closely as possible.

"No mixture of the two is to be trusted"—this is the hallmark of the anxious dualist. Schleiermacher's attempt to justify this excluded middle is pathetic: "that would increase the likelihood that the writer and reader would miss each other entirely." Sure. You can't have the source author and target reader meet halfway—say, at the border between Germany and France where Walter Benjamin committed suicide—because, well, why? Because they might miss each other. And is following "one or the other . . . as closely as possible" proof against such a "missing"? No, but . . . look, just do as I say. Stop bugging me with awkward questions.

This is where Pym picks up the argument, which he first situates in its historical context:

> This nationalistic opposition was made all the stronger by the Napoleonic invasion, which Schleiermacher certainly opposed. The matter was quite immediate. On 24 June 1813, as the lecture was being delivered in Berlin, the future of Europe hung in the balance. Napoleon had gained considerable successes at the battles of Lützen and Bautzen the previous month; on 4 June he had signed the Pleswitz armistice; the Prague congress was to open on 5 July. The question in Berlin was what kind of peace should be sought with the French. We know—Schleiermacher probably did not know as he spoke—that Napoleon was using the armistice to build up his army; we know the French were to have new victories at Dresden in late August and at Leipzig in October. But for Schleiermacher and his audience, in Berlin on 24 June 1813, the fighting might well have been over. Theirs was a moment to debate about what kind of nation or state they wanted a humiliated Prussia to be. And Schleiermacher, to tell all, was not looking for compromises. He had little contextual reason to look kindly upon a French translation method. (6)

Of course, there is more to Schleiermacher's binarism than this, and Pym goes on to sketch out some of the directions a full sociological reading of Schleiermacher's lecture might take, then dives into the specific problem of the excluded middle, arguing first that Schleiermacher muddles his metaphors by insisting that we have to belong to one place, one country, one culture, one language or another—or else hang disoriented in the unsettling gap between. That unsettling gap is the real-world haven, disorienting and truly unsettling but a haven nonetheless (especially in the face of rigid dualistic idealizations and reifications that leave us *no* place to live), toward which Pym is guiding us: it is our goal. Schleiermacher is "confusing physical with moral reality," Pym writes. "As a physical person I can't be in two places at once, but as a translating subjectivity I can dance all over many places, simultaneously backwards and forwards, untethered to any auctorial 'I-here-now'" (10). But then comes Schleiermacher's fulcral passage, the discussion of *Blendlinge:*

> Das Unternehmen erscheint als der wunderbarste Stand der Erniedrigung, in den sich ein nicht schlechter Schriftsteller versezen kann. Wer möchte nicht seine Muttersprache überall in der volksgemäßesten Schönheit auftreten lassen, deren jede Gattung nur fähig ist? Wer möchte nicht lieber Kinder erzeugen, die das väterliche Geschlecht rein darstellen, als Blendlinge? Wer wird sich gern auflegen, in minder leichten und anmuthigen Bewegungen sich zu zeigen als er woll könnte, und bisweilen wenigstens schroff und steif zu erscheinen, um dem Leser so anstößig zu werden als nöthig ist damit er das Bewußtsein der Sache nicht verliere? (55)

> In fact, there can hardly be a more astonishing form of self-abasement to which a not half-bad writer will knowingly submit. Who would not want his mother tongue to appear in the resplendence most characteristic of his people and of each individual genre? Who would willingly breed mongrels when he could instead sire loving children in the pure image of their father? Who would publicly cripple his own verbal facility and grace in order to appear, at least at times, churlish and clumsy, and as offensive as is necessary to keep the reader aware of what is going on?

This is in essence Pym's text, and the rest of his essay is a kaleidoscope of warm, personal, carnivalistic, blunt, global riffs on it. André Lefevere, for example, translates the *Blendlinge,* which I render "mongrels," as "bastards," and Pym finds informal affection in the way people say to each other, "You lucky bastard," then launches into the etymology of bastard in the medieval Latin *bastum* "packsaddle": a bastard was a "child conceived while travelling and not in the marriage bed" (15). The message, Pym says, is clear: "A movement away from the marriage bed—the marriage of mother tongue and fatherland, of balanced and similar likeness—risks producing bastards, and these might be 'Blendlinge'" (15). And it turns out that his maternal grandmother was conceived at sea, en route to Australia; his own daughter was conceived and born abroad, away from home, and of mixed blood no less, Australian father, French mother. "When Schleiermacher asks his rhetorical question about who would want to produce any 'Blendlinge,' when a certain implied receiver should step out from 1813 and disclaim any desire to created mixed children, bastards, acrobats, things stiff and stuck out a long way from home, how should I answer the question? Should I seek repentance for having produced a 'Blendling'?" (16). "'Blendlinge'," he goes on, "are most interestingly associated with a rather exotic kind of commerce, perhaps originally of fancy dogs but also of the kind carried out by people who are vagrant, idle, adventurous, deceptive, sly, cunning, and showy, living off deviant skills, no doubt like travelling acrobats who make children perform all sorts of strange tricks, perhaps like translators. The register is decidedly suspect" (17).

But note, Pym says, what Schleiermacher is doing: he is turning his own purity fetish on its head, rhetorically praising purity, patrilineage, a stable family life, mommy-daddy-junior-sis, three-bedroom ranch-style house in the suburbs with a patio and a curved drive, but only doing so in order to underscore the difficulties and the renunciations faced by his ideal translator, who is precisely the kind of person who is willing to sire *Blendlinge*, bastards, mongrels, half-breeds, the monstrous births by which a foreignizing translator, or *any* translator, reproduces or doubles himself or herself. This is, you'll recall, the man who inveigled against "hanging disoriented in the unsettling gap between"—now he urges us to throw all caution to the winds, renounce the security of home, and blend with life, blend with foreign cultures and languages and people, become mixed up with them, lived mixed-up lives with them, learn their languages and speak one language with one group of people, another with another, some oddball combination of the two with yet a third (or some members of each group in certain moods, certain circumstances).

(I speak English with my children, Finnish with my in-laws, English and Finnish with my wife, who speaks Finnish with our kids; at certain ages, around five, six, seven, eight, our kids tended to speak the language of the country we were living in back to both of us, my older two daughters speaking Finnish to me because at the time we were living in Finland, my youngest speaking English to my wife because now we're living in the United States. Visitors to our house wonder how we can possibly function this way; we don't even notice that there might be a problem. And how many translators live this way? I'd wager that it's a significant number.)

What is Schleiermacher doing, then? Pym situates his answer once again in German history: at the time Schleiermacher writes, the German fatherland and German mother tongue are not yet real parents—the one is still divided into tiny little states and in any case occupied by a foreign power, the other is not yet developed and is thus only a "partial" mother tongue that requires supplementation by Latin, and the child—well, who knew what the child might yet become? How then could Schleiermacher simply assert the importance of the stable nuclear family, living in one place, speaking one language, helping maintain one culture? The only path to that ideal is through non-translation, which is no solution because it is only through translation that the sociopolitical parents, mother language and fatherland, can grow strong. The happy nuclear family (writ large, on the screen of history) is Schleiermacher's ideal, but he can only imagine growth toward that ideal through the half-measures of *Blendlinge*—not a nice position for a dualist like Schleiermacher to find himself in. "This is why," Pym suggests, "Schleiermacher poses the question of human *Blendlinge* but fails to recruit them into any programme of action" (9). He can't bear to. He recognizes that the cultural logic of his time and place requires *Blendlinge*, mixtures, in-betweens, crossovers of all stripes; but it's too much for him to stomach. He can only bring himself to raise the possibility of *Blendlinge* in a series of convoluted negative rhetorical questions that leave an escape route open back into a comfortable exclusionary dualism.

Part of Schleiermacher's dilemma, too, is that he sees clearly how assimilative French translation has already staked out the rigid dualistic position he would like to occupy: seize the foreign and domesticate it without mercy, leave purely Greek and German and other foreign texts to simmer and seethe abroad, bring some of them home but only in radically altered form, utterly frenchified, with shots and language training and a crisp new French passport. Choose one language—or another. Don't get caught in that unsettling gap between. But this is the *French* position, so that any way he turns, he is already caught in the gap. To support the French in their neoclassical rage for order, for tidy boundaries between languages and cultures, and thus to buttress his own nervous need for dualistic categories would not only be to support the other, the enemy, French culture in lieu of German culture; it would be to support the foreign ruler of his state, the alien power that is already within the gates, the other that has occupied the self. Support for French translation is thus only superficially an attack on *Blendlinge;* more realistically it is support for the political blending of French and German cultures in Napoleon's radical modernization of Germany, his unification of German states, precisely what German nationalists desired but opposed because it came from "without," a without that was also, confusingly, within. To take the opposite side in that debate, to support German nationalism against the French, is to side with uncouth translators who make a virtue of blending this culture with that, leaving impure traces of foreignness in their German texts, because they are not as "civilized" as the French and proud of it; also because they believe that German will only grow strong if all sorts of foreign elements are blended into it and left swimming around in the stew like sweaty little carrots and potatoes. The German side of the argument is German, not French, domestic, not foreign, local, not global, this, not that—but the Germanity that it celebrates and seeks to consolidate is by necessity a *Blendling* that rejects everything French *in order to* accept everything foreign. Work that one out! Schleiermacher obviously couldn't; so he didn't.

Fortunately for us, he left the traces of his uncertainty all over his lecture.

Pym's finest moment comes toward the end of his piece, when he suddenly and with an enormous effort turns Schleiermacher on his head and celebrates the in-betweenness that Schleiermacher fights—the muddledness, even, or the middledness, that rationalist thought has always repressed. I can't resist quoting Pym at length, one last time:

> It would be foolhardy to say that all translators are *Blendlinge*, as if we knew everything about all of them. Yet the complex semantics of the German term can be used as a field for producing hypotheses about translators. The many practical reasons for pursuing such hypotheses are based on the idea that the translator's knowledge of foreign languages and cultures requires a certain subjective and social displacement towards a middle ground. But the immediate interest of the hypotheses lies in the fact that binary translation theory so effectively prohibits their formulation by excluding the middle ground. In historical terms, the exclusion suppresses most of the intercultural peoples that have produced great translators. It gets rid of the *Zwischenstaaten* [in-between states] that have long mediated—and translated—between France and Germany, and are all too easily forgotten as the gristle of the European Union. It also suppresses virtually all the conceptual tools I use to think about translation. Schleiermacher is concerned with works of the mind rather than with objects; I argue that texts are objects that only move because of materiality. He says negotiation is only for commerce; I see it as a frame for all intercultural relationships. He excludes multilingualism as a viable alternative to translation; I believe it is often a better alternative. He says middle grounds are unhappy and insubstantial; I try to find their principles, their virtues and even their joys. He establishes a metaphorical link between translation and the movement of people; I think moving people make translation happen. He ties the translator to the receiving community; I ask if translators belong to intercultural communities of traders, negotiators, diplomats, acrobats, adventurers, idlers, and bastards.
>
> The tremendous ambiguity of Translation Studies is that if one follows Schleiermacher's focus on textual inputs and outputs, if one sees *Blendlinge* as no more than textual simulacra [doubles!], subject positions, points for linguistics and its forerunners and its heirs, the fact of translation can only reinforce the cultural nationalisms of separate languages, societies, cultures, systems, or minds. That is why I am suspicious of models where interculturality is merely textual, embedded in translations within one language or culture, thus presupposing the limits of languages and cultures. . . . Even when deployed in literary isolation, such approaches tend to help those who are increasingly intolerant of the less prestigious brands of *Blendlinge*. In this light, one might ask why contemporary translation research in Europe's larger, more chauvinist countries is still marked by rigorous separation of literary and non-literary translation, separating the higher works of national identity from the base exchanges of intercultural commerce, in true Schleiermacherian spirit. One might also ask why the same countries (notably France and Germany), even within the commercial sphere, invest considerable academic resources in the training of high-level conference interpreters but very little in community interpreting. The social function of literary translation and conference interpreting is im-

> plicitly to defend and strengthen national target languages rather than help those displaced persons caught up in the less pretty sides of interculturality. There is as much bad as good in this kind of Translation Studies.
>
> On the other hand, if one focuses on *Blendlinge* as substantial people, as the intercultural communities to which translators could belong, Translation Studies might promote mediation rather than separation. Translation history could help give such communities a substantial past; translation ethics should help develop their regimes; and the training of translators could openly contribute to their ranks. Hence the importance of *Blendlinge* in Translation Studies. Hence the need at least to ask if translators really belong to one side or the other. (23–24)

It is good to have someone else state this hope for the future so strongly; as I have said before, this book is the dark double of *The Translator's Turn*, steeped in the negativity that it attacks and tries to fend off, and as I move toward an ending I am finding it hard, surprisingly hard for a utopian romantic thinker like myself, to summon the energy needed to radiate hope. I feel, to put it in the rather melodramatic terms I've used throughout, that I've been doing battle with dark forces from the underworld, forces of repression and constraint, stifling protection against the deadly contagions of mana and taboo—which are also, if we can learn to channel those energies rather than letting them kill us outright, vast resources of vitality and strength—and have been depleted by my struggles.

But, not to make too big of a whine fest out of this ending, good things are happening—things like the theoretical work of Anthony Pym, which rips the covers off taboos like the sacred distinction between literary and nonliterary translation. Or like the work done by postcolonial scholars of translation like Samia Mehrez, which explores the blending or bleeding together of languages and cultures and people across the rationalist boundaries between source and target languages, original and translation. Or like translators of all kinds who claim a public voice as translators, even as theorists, including not only literary and scitech and commercial and other professional translators but the second- and third-generation children of immigrants, too, who translate their ancestors' letters and obituaries; and poor bilinguals who help monolingual neighbors deal with the landlord and the police and the social worker and the tax man; and children like mine who have been translators all their lives.

Translation studies remains spiky with taboos that turn our eyes away from such people, stop up our ears when they speak, spark our laughter when they claim to be translators like us, theorists like us; our hope lies in the steady dismantling of these taboos, work that is already going on all around us in surprising places and ways. All we need to join in the effort is a little strength, a little energy, a little courage, a willingness to work through our fears and gradually overcome them. To that willingness, that hesitant anecdotal openness to the muddles and the middles of new experience, I dedicate this book.

BIBLIOGRAPHY

Abrams, M. H. *Natural Supernaturalism: Tradition and Revolution in Romantic Literature*. 1971. Reprint, New York: Norton, 1973.

Aelfric. "Preface to Genesis." In Albert S. Cook, ed., *Biblical Quotations in Old English Prose*, lxx–lxxi. London: Macmillan, 1898.

Althusser, Louis. "Ideology and Ideological State Apparatuses (Notes Toward an Investigation)." Translated by Ben Brewster. In *Lenin and Philosophy and Other Essays*, 121–73. London: New Left Books, 1971.

Aristeas. *Aristeas to Philocrates (Letter of Aristeas)*. Edited and translated by Moses Hadas. New York: Ktav Publishing, 1973.

Augustine. *On Christian Doctrine*. Translated by D. W. Robertson, Jr. 1958. Reprint, Indianapolis: Bobbs-Merrill, 1979.

———. *The City of God*. Translated by George Wilson and J. J. Smith. New York: Modern Library, 1950.

Bakhtin, Mikhail. "Discourse in the Novel." Translated by Caryl Emerson and Michael Holquist. In Holquist, ed., *The Dialogic Imagination: Four Essays*, 259–422. Austin: University of Texas Press, 1981.

Barnes, Jonathan, ed. and trans. *Early Greek Philosophy*. Harmondsworth: Penguin Books, 1987.

Barnstone, Willis. *The Poetics of Translation: History, Theory, Practice*. New Haven: Yale University Press, 1993.

Bateson, Gregory. *Steps to an Ecology of Mind*. 1972. Reprint, New York: Ballantine Books, 1985.

Benjamin, Andrew. *Translation and the Nature of Philosophy*. London: Routledge, 1989.

Benjamin, Walter. "Die Aufgabe des Übersetzers." In Störig, ed., *Das Problem des Übersetzens*, 156–69.

———. *Origin of German Tragic Drama*. Translated by John Osborne. London: New Left Books, 1977.

———. "The Task of the Translator." Translated by Harry Zohn. In Hannah Arendt, ed., *Illuminations*, 69–82. 1955. Reprint, Glasgow: Fontana/Collins, 1982.

Berman, Antoine. *L'Épreuve de l'étranger: Culture et traduction dans l'Allemagne romantique*. Paris: Gallimard, 1984. Translated by S. Heyvaert as *The Experience of the Foreign: Culture and Translation in Romantic Germany*. Albany: SUNY Press, 1992.

———. "La traduction et la lettre, ou l'auberge du lointain." In *Les Tours de Babel: Essais sur la traduction*, 35–150. Mauvezin: Trans-Europ-Repress, 1985.

Bhabha, Homi K. *The Location of Culture*. London: Routledge, 1994.

Bloom, Harold. *A Map of Misreading*. New York: Oxford University Press, 1975.

The Book of the Dead: According to the Theban Recension. In W. A. Wallis Budge, trans., *Egyptian Literature: Comprising Egyptian Tales, Hymns, Litanies, Invocations, The Book of the Dead, and Cuneiform Writings*, 1–131. New York and London: The Co-operative Publication Society, 1901.

Boyd, Brian. *Vladimir Nabokov: The American Years*. Princeton: Princeton University Press, 1991.

Bradford, William. *Of Plymouth Plantation, 1620–1647*. Edited by Samuel Eliot Morison. New York: Knopf, 1952.

Burke, Kenneth. *The Rhetoric of Religion: Studies in Logology*. 1961. Reprint, Berkeley: University of California Press, 1970.

Burkert, Walter. *Ancient Mystery Cults*. Cambridge: Harvard University Press, 1987.

Campbell, Joseph, ed. *The Mysteries: Papers from the Eranos Yearbooks*. Translated by Ralph Manheim and R. F. C. Hull. New York: Pantheon Books, 1955.

Cheyfitz, Eric. *The Poetics of Interpretation: Translation and Colonization from "The Tempest" to "Tarzan."* New York: Oxford University Press, 1991.

Copeland, Rita. *Rhetoric, Hermeneutics, and Translation in the Middle Ages: Academic Traditions and Vernacular Texts*. Cambridge: Cambridge University Press, 1991.

Dan, Joseph. "Midrash and the Dawn of Kabbalah." In Geoffrey H. Hartmann and Sanford Budick, eds., *Midrash and Literature*, 127–39. New Haven: Yale University Press, 1986.

Deleuze, Gilles, and Félix Guattari. *Anti-Oedipus*. Translated by Robert Hurley, Mark Seem, and Helen R. Lane. Vol. 1 of *Capitalism and Schizophrenia*. Minneapolis: University of Minnesota Press, 1983.

———. *A Thousand Plateaus*. Translated by Brian Massumi. Vol. 2 of *Capitalism and Schizophrenia*. Minneapolis: University of Minnesota Press, 1987.

de Man, Paul. "'Conclusions': Walter Benjamin's 'The Task of the Translator.'" *Yale French Studies* 69 (1985): 25–46.

Derrida, Jacques. "Des Tours de Babel." In Joseph F. Graham, ed. and trans., *Difference in Translation*, 165–207. Ithaca: Cornell University Press, 1985.

Díaz-Diocaretz, Myriam. *Translating Poetic Discourse: Questions on Feminist Strategies in Adrienne Rich*. Amsterdam: John Benjamins, 1985.

Dinełtsoi, Mazii. *Ahí ní nikisheegizh*. Princeton: Princeton Collections of Western Americana, 1989.

Douglas, Mary. *Purity and Danger: An Analysis of Concepts of Pollution and Taboo*. 1966. Reprint, Harmondsworth: Penguin Books, 1970.

Eagleton, Terry. *Walter Benjamin: Or Toward a Revolutionary Criticism*. London: Verso, 1981.

Ellwood, Robert S., Jr. *Mysticism and Religion*. Englewood Cliffs, N.J.: Prentice-Hall, 1980.

Even-Zohar, Itamar. "Polysystem Theory." *Poetics Today* 1.1–2 (1979): 283–305.

———. "Translation Theory Today: A Call For Transfer Theory." *Poetics Today* 2.4 (1981): 1–7.

Florio, John. "Epistle Dedicatory." In Florio, trans., *The Essayes of Michael, Lord of Montaigne*, 1–4. 1603. Reprint, New York: E. P. Dutton, 1928.

Foucault, Michel. "What Is an Author?" In Josué V. Harari, ed., *Textual Strategies: Perspectives in Post-Structuralist Criticism*, 141–60. Ithaca: Cornell University Press, 1979.

Freire, Paulo. *The Pedagogy of the Oppressed*. Translated by Myra Bergman Ramos. New York: Continuum, 1992.

Freud, Sigmund. *Beyond the Pleasure Principle*. Translated by James Strachey. New York: Bantam Books, 1967.
———. *Totem and Taboo: Some Points of Agreement Between the Mental Lives of Savages and Neurotics*. Translated by James Strachey. New York: Norton, 1950.
Gentzler, Edwin. *Contemporary Translation Theories*. London and New York: Routledge, 1993.
Grant, Frederick C., ed. *Hellenistic Religions: The Age of Syncretism*. Indianapolis: Bobbs-Merrill, 1953.
Graves, Robert, trans. *The Transformations of Lucius, Otherwise Known as The Golden Ass*, by Apuleius of Madaura. 1951. Reprint, New York: Noonday Press, 1967.
Griffiths, J. Gwyn, ed. and trans. *The Isis-Book (Metamorphoses, Book XI)*, by Apuleius of Madauros. Leiden: E. J. Brill, 1975.
Haight, Elizabeth Hazelton. *Apuleius and His Influence*. New York: Cooper Square Publishers, 1963.
Harpham, Geoffrey Galt. *The Ascetic Imperative in Culture and Criticism*. Chicago: University of Chicago Press, 1987.
Havelock, Eric A. *The Muse Learns to Write: Reflections on Orality and Literacy from Antiquity to the Present*. New Haven: Yale University Press, 1986.
Herder, Johann Gottfried. *Über die neuere Deutsche Litteratur. Eine Beilage zu den Briefen, die neueste Litteratur betreffend. Fragmente*. Second collection. In vol. 1 of Bernhard Suphan, ed., *Herders Sämmtliche Werke*, 131–531. Berlin: Weidmannsche Buchhandlung, 1877.
Herodotus. *The Histories*. Rev. ed. Translated by Aubrey de Selincourt. Harmondsworth: Penguin Books, 1972.
Holz-Mänttäri, Justa. *Translatorisches Handeln*. Helsinki: Finnish Academy of Science, 1984.
Hurt, James. *Aelfric*. New York: Twayne, 1972.
Jacquemond, Richard. "Translation and Cultural Hegemony: The Case of French-Arabic Translation." In Venuti, ed., *Rethinking Translation*, 139–58.
Jameson, Fredric. *The Political Unconscious: Narrative as a Socially Symbolic Act*. Ithaca: Cornell University Press, 1981.
Jaynes, Julian. *The Origin of Consciousness in the Breakdown of the Bicameral Mind*. 1976. Reprint, Boston: Houghton-Mifflin, 1990.
Jerome (Eusebius Hieronymus). "On the Art of Translation." Translated by Paul Carroll. In *The Satirical Letters of St. Jerome*, 132–51. Chicago: Gateway, 1958.
Johnston, John. "Translation as Simulacrum." In Venuti, ed., *Rethinking Translation*, 42–56.
Katz, Steven T. "The 'Conservative' Character of Mystical Experience." In Katz, ed., *Mysticism and Religious Traditions*, 3–60. New York: Oxford University Press, 1983.
Kerényi, C. "The Mysteries of the Kabeiroi." Translated by Ralph Manheim. In Joseph Campbell, ed., *The Mysteries*, 32–63.
Lacan, Jacques. "The Mirror Stage as Formative of the Function of the I." Translated by Alan Sheridan. In Lacan, *Écrits: A Selection*. New York: Norton, 1977.
———. *Speech and Language in Psychoanalysis*. Translated by Anthony Wilden. Rev. ed. Baltimore: Johns Hopkins University Press, 1981.
Laing, R. D. *The Divided Self*. 1960. Reprint, New York: Pantheon Books, 1969.
Lecercle, Jean Jacques. "Louis Wolfson and the Philosophy of Translation." *The Oxford Literary Review* 11.1–2 (1989): 103–20.
———. *The Violence of Language*. New York: Routledge, 1990.

Lévy-Bruhl, Lucien. *The "Soul" of the Primitive.* Translated by Lilian A. Clare. 1928. Reprint, New York: Praeger, 1966.

Lewis, I. M. *Ecstatic Religion: An Anthropological Study of Spirit Possession and Shamanism.* Harmondsworth: Penguin Books, 1971.

Lindsay, Jack, trans. *The Golden Ass,* by Apuleius. 1932. Reprint, Bloomington: Indiana University Press, 1962.

Luther, Martin. "Sendbrief vom Dolmetschen." In Störig, ed., *Das Problem des Übersetzens,* 14–32.

May, Gerald. *Addiction and Grace: Love and Spirituality in the Healing of Addictions.* San Francisco: HarperCollins, 1988.

Mehrez, Samia. "Translation and the Postcolonial Experience." In Venuti, ed., *Rethinking Translation,* 120–38.

Montaigne, Michel de. "On Cannibals." Translated by J. M. Cohen. In Montaigne, *Essays,* Book One, 105–19. Harmondsworth: Penguin, 1958.

More, Thomas. *The Confutation of Tyndale's Answer.* Vol. 8 (in three parts) of *The Complete Works of St. Thomas More.* Edited by Louis A. Schuster, Richard C. Marius, James P. Lusardi, and Richard J. Schoeck. New Haven: Yale University Press, 1973.

———. *A Dialogue Concerning Heresies.* Vol. 6 of *The Complete Works of St. Thomas More.* Edited by Thomas M. C. Lawler, Germain Marc'hadour, and Richard C. Marius. New Haven: Yale University Press, 1981.

Narayana Rao, Velcheru, trans. *Siva's Warriors: The "Basava Purana" of Palkuriki Somanatha.* Princeton: Princeton University Press, 1990.

Niranjana, Tejaswini. *Siting Translation: History, Post-Structuralism, and the Colonial Context.* Berkeley: University of California Press, 1992.

O'Keefe, Daniel Lawrence. *Stolen Lightning: The Social Theory of Magic.* New York: Continuum, 1982.

Plato. *The Collected Dialogues of Plato, Including the Letters.* Edited by Edith Hamilton and Huntington Cairns. 1961. Reprint, Princeton: Princeton University Press, 1980.

Pym, Anthony. "Schleiermacher and the Problem of *Blendlinge.*" *Translation and Literature* 4.1 (1995): 5–29.

Rafael, Vicente L. *Contracting Colonialism: Translation and Christian Conversion in Tagalog Society Under Early Spanish Rule.* 1988. Reprint, Durham: Duke University Press, 1993.

Rahner, Hugo, S. J. *Greek Myths and Christian Mystery.* Translated by Brian Battershaw. 1957. Reprint, New York: Harper & Row, 1963.

Reardon, B. P. "The Greek Novel." *Phoenix* (1969): 291–309.

———. "Aspects of the Greek Novel." *Greece and Rome* 23 (1976): 118–31.

Reiß, Katharina, and Hans J. Vermeer. *Grundlegung einer allgemeinen Translationstheorie.* Tübingen: Niemeyer, 1984.

Robinson, Douglas. "Imitation." In Mona Baker, ed., *Encyclopedia of Translation Studies.* London: Routledge, forthcoming.

———. "Paraphrase." In Mona Baker, ed., *Encyclopedia of Translation Studies.* London: Routledge, forthcoming.

———. *Ring Lardner and the Other.* New York: Oxford University Press, 1992.

———. "Theorising Translation in a Woman's Voice: Subversions of the Rhetoric of Patronage, Courtly Love, and Morality by Early Modern Women Translators." *The Translator* 1.2 (November 1995): 153–75.

———. *The Translator's Turn.* Baltimore: Johns Hopkins University Press, 1991.

Roscommon, Earl of (Thomas Wentworth). "An Essay on Translated Verse." In T. R. Steiner, ed., *English Translation Theory, 1650–1800*, 75–85. Assen/Amsterdam: Van Gorcum, 1975.

Rose, Marilyn Gaddis. "Foreignizing or Domesticating: Debating Norms Goes With the Territory." In Edith F. Losa, ed., *Keystones of Communication: Proceedings of the 34th Annual Conference of the American Translators Association*, 265–71. Medford, N.J.: Learned Information, 1993.

Schleiermacher, Friedrich. "Ueber die verschiedenen Methoden des Uebersezens." Lecture 3 of *Abhandlungen gelesen in der Königlichen Akademie der Wissenschaften*, 207–45. In vol. 2 (1838) of *Zur Philosophie*. Berlin: G. Reimer, 1835–1846. Part 3 of *Friedrich Schleiermacher's sämmtliche Werke*. Reprinted in Störig, ed., *Das Problem des Übersetzens*, 38–70.

Simon, Sherry. "The Language of Cultural Difference: Figures of Alterity in Canadian Translation." In Venuti, ed., *Rethinking Translation*, 159–76.

Stannard, David. *American Holocaust: Columbus and the Conquest of the New World*. New York: Oxford University Press, 1992.

Steiner, Franz. *Taboo*. London: Cohen & West, 1956.

Steiner, George. *After Babel: Aspects of Language and Translation*. New York and London: Oxford University Press, 1975.

Störig, Hans Joachim, ed. *Das Problem des Übersetzens*. Darmstadt: Wissenschaftlicher Buchgesellschaft, 1963.

Swann, Brian, ed. *On the Translation of Native American Literatures*. Washington, D.C.: Smithsonian Institution Press, 1992.

Tatum, James. *Apuleius and "The Golden Ass."* Ithaca: Cornell University Press, 1979.

Toury, Gideon. "Contrastive Linguistics and Translation Studies: Towards a Tripartite Model." In Wolfgang Kühwein, Gisela Thorne, and Wolfram Wilss, eds., *Kontrastive Linguistik und Übersetzungswissenschaft: Akten des Internationalen Kolloquiums Trier/Saarbrücken 25.-30.9.1978*, 251–61. Munich: Wilhelm Fink, 1981.

———. *In Search of a Theory of Translation*. Tel Aviv: The Porter Institute for Poetics and Semiotics, 1980.

———. "Translated Literature: System, Norm, Performance: Toward a TT-Oriented Approach to Literary Translation." *Poetics Today* 2.4 (Summer-Autumn 1981): 9–27.

Venuti, Lawrence. "Genealogies of Translation Theory: Schleiermacher." *TTR—Traduction, Terminologie, Rédaction: Études sur le texte et ses transformations* 4.2 (1991): 125–50.

———. "The Translator's Invisibility." *Criticism* 28 (1986): 179–212.

———. *The Translator's Invisibility*. London and New York: Routledge, 1994.

———, ed. *Rethinking Translation: Discourse, Subjectivity, Ideology*. London and New York: Routledge, 1992.

Voloshinov, V. N. *Marxism and the Philosophy of Language*. Translated by Ladislav Mateyka and I. R. Titunik. New York: Seminar Press, 1973.

Wili, Walter. "The Orphic Mysteries and the Greek Spirit." Translated by Ralph Manheim. In Campbell, ed., *The Mysteries*, 64–92.

INDEX

www.ingramcontent.com/pod-product-compliance
Ingram Content Group UK Ltd.
Pitfield, Milton Keynes, MK11 3LW, UK
UKHW042140050325
455862UK00005B/399